TWELFTH NIGHT,

OR WHAT YOU WILL

BROADVIEW / INTERNET SHAKESPEARE EDITIONS

Broadview Editions Series Editor
L.W. Conolly
Internet Shakespeare Editions Coordinating Editor
Michael Best
Internet Shakespeare Editions Textual Editor
Eric Rasmussen

TWELFTH NIGHT,

OR WHAT YOU WILL

William Shakespeare

EDITED BY

David Carnegie & Mark Houlahan

BROADVIEW / INTERNET SHAKESPEARE EDITIONS

Library and Archives Canada Cataloguing in Publication

Shakespeare, William, 1564–1616
[Twelfth night]
Twelfth night, or, what you will / William Shakespeare ;
edited by David Carnegie and Mark Houlahan.

(Broadview / Internet Shakespeare Editions)
Includes bibliographical references.
ISBN 978-1-55481-094-9 (pbk.)

1. Shipwreck survival—Drama. 2. Brothers and sisters—Drama. 3. Mistaken identity—Drama. 4. Illyria—Drama. 5. Twins—Drama. 6. Comedies. I. Carnegie, David, 1943-, writer of introduction, editor II. Houlahan, Mark, 1960-, writer of introduction, editor III. Internet Shakespeare Editions IV. Title. V. Title: Twelfth night. VI. Title: What you will. VII. Series: Broadview / Internet Shakespeare Editions

PR2837.A2C37 2014   822.3'3   C2014-901359-0

Broadview Press is an independent, international publishing house, incorporated in 1985.

We welcome comments and suggestions regarding any aspect of our publications—please feel free to contact us at the addresses below or at broadview@broadviewpress.com.

North America
PO Box 1243
Peterborough, Ontario
K9J 7H5, Canada
555 Riverwalk Parkway
Tonawanda, NY 14150
USA
Tel: (705) 743-8990
Fax: (705) 743-8353
email: customerservice@
broadviewpress.com

UK, Europe, Central Asia,
Middle East, Africa, India,
and Southeast Asia
Eurospan Group
3 Henrietta St.
London WC2E 8LU
United Kingdom
Tel: 44 (0) 1767 604972
Fax: 44 (0) 1767 601640
email: eurospan@
turpin-distribution.com

Australia and New Zealand
NewSouth Books
c/o TL Distribution
15-23 Helles Ave.
Moorebank, NSW 2170
Australia
Tel: (02) 8778 9999
Fax: (02) 8778 9944
email: orders@
tldistribution.com.au

www.broadviewpress.com

Copy-edited by Denis Johnston
Book design by Michel Vrana
Typeset in MVB Verdigris Pro

PRINTED IN CANADA

CONTENTS

FOREWORD

The Internet Shakespeare Editions (http://internetshakespeare. uvic.ca) and Broadview Press are pleased to collaborate on a series of Shakespeare editions in book form, creating for each volume an "integrated text" designed to meet the needs of today's students. The texts, introductions, and other materials for these editions are drawn from those prepared by leading scholars for the Internet Shakespeare Editions, modified to suit the demands of publication in book form. The print editions are integrated with the fuller resources and research materials that are available electronically on the site of the Internet Shakespeare Editions. Consistent with other volumes in the Broadview Editions series, each of these Shakespeare editions includes a wide range of background materials, providing information on the the play's historical and intellectual context, in addition to the text itself, introduction, chronology, essays on Shakespeare's life and theater, and bibliography; all these will be found in more extensive form on the website.

The Internet Shakespeare Editions, a non-profit organization founded in 1996, creates and publishes works for the student, scholar, actor, and general reader in a form native to the medium of the Internet: scholarly, fully annotated texts of Shakespeare's plays, multimedia explorations of the context of Shakespeare's life and works, and records of his plays in performance. The Internet Shakespeare Editions is affiliated with the University of Victoria.

The Broadview Editions series was founded in 1992 under the title "Broadview Literary Texts." Under the guidance of executive editors Julia Gaunce and Marjorie Mather, of series editors Eugene Benson and Leonard Conolly, and of managing editors Barbara Conolly and Tara Lowes, it has grown to include several hundred volumes— lesser-known works of cultural significance as well as canonical texts. Designed with the needs of undergraduate students in mind, the series has also appealed widely to scholars—and to readers in general.

Michael Best, Coordinating Editor, University of Victoria
Eric Rasmussen, General Textual Editor, University of Nevada, Reno
Don LePan, Broadview Press

ACKNOWLEDGEMENTS

Our thanks for the dedication of Michael Best, Eric Rasmussen, and the whole ISE team, and to Broadview Press, especially Marjorie Mather, Leonard Conolly, and our indefatigable copy-editor Denis Johnston. The brief essays on Shakespeare's life and Shakespeare's theater are reprinted from the Broadview edition of *As You Like It*, courtesy of David Bevington. Quotations from Shakespeare's plays other than *Twelfth Night* are from the *Complete Works* edited by David Bevington, 6th edition (NewYork: Pearson Longman, 2009).

David Carnegie wishes to thank Victoria University of Wellington for research funding and leave, and St Catherine's College, Oxford, and the Folger Shakespeare Library for research grants and valuable support. Personal thanks are due to, among many others, John Golder, the late Richard Madeleine, John Bell, and members of the Bell Shakespeare Company's *Twelfth Night*, when the Bell Shakespeare edition was in prospect; to Murray Lynch and the cast and crew of *Twelfth Night* at Circa Theatre; to colleagues and students at Victoria University, especially the cast and crew of that *Twelfth Night*; to John Russell Brown, Robert Cross at VUW Image Services, David and Lorna Evans, Penny Gay, Alfio Leotta, David Norton, David O'Donnell, Mary Rubio, Elizabeth Schafer, Matthew Trundle, Marion Virgo, Matt Wagner, and Lawrence Wright for support of all sorts; to David Lawrence and Lori Leigh for research assistance, theatrical collaboration, and much more; to Gisella Carr for support and love; and to my co-editor for opening the door to me.

Mark Houlahan acknowledges the support in travel grants, research assistants, and periods of leave from the Faculty of Arts and Social Sciences (Te Kura Kete Aronui) at the University of Waikato (Te Whare Wananga o Waikato). For other support, when it really counted, thanks to Joseph Black, Alexander Brown, Brett Hirsch, Sarah Knox, Fiona Martin, Rowena McCoy, David McInnis, Kirstine Moffatt, Helen Ostovich, Catherine Silverstone, and Linda Stockham; and to my co-editor who rebooted the project.

"Thanks, / And thanks, and ever thanks" (3.3.14–15, TLN 1481–82).

INTRODUCTION

Twelfth Night is the last of the great romantic comedies Shakespeare wrote, following *A Midsummer Night's Dream*, *Much Ado About Nothing*, and *As You Like It*. The story of the twins Viola and Sebastian seeking each other in Illyria and finding, along the way, a husband and a wife, is by turns romantic, comedic, dramatic, and musical. In performance it can be hilarious and then touching and heartfelt. Modern audiences love it and it is very frequently performed. But how does the play work? How should we take its special combination of mirth and melancholy?

Twelfth Night was in the repertoire of the Lord Chamberlain's Men by 2 February 1602, when John Manningham saw a performance at Middle Temple Hall in London and recorded his reaction in his diary. The play is not mentioned in a list of Shakespeare's plays from 1598, and internal evidence suggests a later rather than earlier period of composition within the time frame 1598–1602, likely in 1601.

A persistent question about the play is why Shakespeare called it *Twelfth Night*. Twelfth Night is a feast of the Christian church celebrating Epiphany, the "manifestation" or showing forth of Christ's

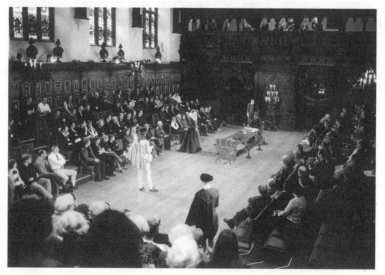

Middle Temple Hall, where the earliest documented performance of *Twelfth Night* took place in 1602. This 2002 production was by Shakespeare's Globe. (Photograph reproduced by permission of Shakespeare's Globe.)

divinity to the Gentiles in the persons of the Magi, the kings from afar (the French title for Twelfth Night—both the feast and the play—is "La Nuit des rois"—"The Night of the Kings"). But in neither English nor French does the title appear to have much to do with the play. Nor does English midwinter match references to season and climate in the dialogue: "sweet beds of flowers" (1.1.39, TLN 46), "let summer bear it out" (1.5.17, TLN 315), "midsummer madness" (3.4.50, TLN 1577), "more matter for a May morning" (3.4.127, TLN 1664). Spring and summer seem appropriate, too, for "roses, whose fair flower / Being once displayed, doth fall that very hour" (2.4.38–39, TLN 926–27).

Twelfth Night is, however, the end of the Christmas celebrations, the night when the Christmas tree comes down, the final night of twelve days of feasting and revels. In Shakespeare's time, a Lord of Misrule might be appointed to ensure that solemnity was banished and a topsy-turvy world allowed for a short while. *What You Will*, the subtitle of Shakespeare's play, is precisely what was allowed: whatever you wish. And although a specifically winter revel does not seem to fit with the romance plot, similar English festivities were held in the spring and summer, particularly around May Day (1 May) and Midsummer (sometimes called "Reveltide"). So similar were the revels of Christmas and summer that the author of the *Survey of Cornwall* in 1602 speaks of his partying neighbors at harvest time "spending a great part of the night in Christmas rule" (qtd Barber 25). Summer Lords and Summer Ladies served the same role as the Lord of Misrule at Christmas, and were equally disapproved of by Puritan extremists.[1] A good example of Christmas-time misbehavior is the report of the Warden of Corpus Christi College, Oxford, who "coming drunk from the Town sat in the hall amongst the scholars until 1 of the clock tottering with his legs, tippling with his mouth, and hearing bawdy songs with his ears."[2]

Thus, although it is difficult to be sure about the precise implications of Shakespeare's title, the thematic implications of a time of inversion of order, confusion, and festivity associated with winter revelry, and with its summer equivalent, seem well suited to this play. Twelfth Night marked the end of such revels, and this too suits the ending of the play.

---

1 I.e., radical Protestant sects committed to purging the Church of England and society of Catholic ceremony and any pleasure that was not godly; see Appendix G, p. 279.

2 See below, p. 273. For more accounts, see Appendix F, p. 273.

ROMANCE

The main plot of *Twelfth Night* is a love triangle that includes Orsino, Olivia, and a multifaceted third side comprised of Viola, her male counterpart Cesario, and her twin brother Sebastian. The play opens with Orsino pining for his love, but he is not solitary: he is surrounded by his court—a select and entirely male society to be sure, but a social context with its own expectations. Furthermore, his instructions and countermands to the musicians—"That strain again," then "Enough, no more" (1.1.4, 7; TLN 8, 11)—establish both a duke in control and a lover habitually changing his mind.

Orsino's elaborate rhetoric, full of imagery and convoluted syntax, dwells on change; like the music, what is valued one moment seems to be dismissed the next. Fancy is "full of shapes" (1.1.14, TLN 18), and Orsino cites Ovid's famous *Metamorphoses* when he speaks of his love for Olivia changing him from a hunter into a stag being hunted (see extended note, p. 78). While these images of changeableness are often taken as showing Orsino to be lightweight, we might view them rather as clues placed for the audience, who should be less surprised than Orsino when his love turns out to be "high fantastical" (1.1.15, TLN 19) and not at all what he expected. The entry of a messenger, less than 25 lines into the play, boosts the energy of the scene as Orsino eagerly questions him. Orsino exits to "sweet beds of flowers" to continue his "Love-thoughts" about Olivia (1.1.39–40, TLN 46–47). With music, rhetoric, and an urgent messenger, we have been offered a lover's dilemma full of potential for romance, comic misconstruction, or both.

Onto the empty stage enters a young woman, clearly shipwrecked, enquiring of her fellow survivors, "What country, friends, is this?" (1.2.1, TLN 51). The scene is constructed in two segments, the first about her sorrow for her brother Sebastian whom she believes to have drowned. As the Captain comforts Viola by telling her of seeing Sebastian "like Arion on the dolphin's back" (1.2.15, TLN 65) (another story from Ovid), Viola resolves to hope, gives the Captain money, and proceeds with new energy into the rest of the scene and the play.

The Captain explains that the local ruler is a duke named Orsino, a bachelor seeking the love of a countess named Olivia. Olivia, like Viola, has lost a brother, and she has gone into seclusion under the weight of that grief. Olivia has also recently lost her father, and is therefore in the rare situation for a Renaissance woman of having no immediate male family member to decide her future for her. Viola is similarly free of any family authority; more urgently, she is without protection or support.[1] Her decision to disguise herself and enter Orsino's service may in the first instance be simple self-preservation by a single woman alone in an unknown and potentially dangerous country, but it also parallels Olivia's withdrawal from the world of courtship and marriage expected of a young lady. Viola's desire to make her "occasion mellow" (1.2.43, TLN 94), to bide her time, hints that she will use this unexpected reprieve from the pressures of family and social expectation to observe and mature. This reflective quality marks her as a serious comic heroine, and one likely to share her self-awareness with the audience. And, unlike Olivia, Viola is not withdrawing from the world, but engaging with it. "What else may hap, to time I will commit" (1.2.61, TLN 112), she says, implying an openness to whatever may unfold. Given the events of these first two scenes—a duke in love with an inaccessible countess, a shipwrecked maiden donning a disguise to serve the duke—the audience can be in little doubt that the narrative will include love complications.

In 1.4 two sides of the triangle are linked as Viola has evidently passed muster in her disguise as a page to Orsino. His desire to talk to "Cesario" alone suggests an attraction to Viola, while his theatrical reference to "a woman's part" (1.4.33, TLN 285) will remind the audience of the pleasure of the comic artifice. Viola herself is usually well aware of both the danger of her disguise, and its irony. Dispatched to Olivia as Orsino's messenger of love, she confides to us what may be no great surprise, but will clearly complicate her life and the theatrical intrigue: "Whoe'er I woo, myself would be his wife" (1.4.41, TLN 294).

The anticipated complication follows in the next scene, when Olivia is introduced via her out-of-favor Clown, Feste. The depth of her grief for her dead brother, and therefore her reluctance to be wooed, varies in productions and in critical approaches, but the Clown succeeds, daringly, in suggesting to her that excessive grief is as unnatural as for young marriageable women (and men) to let their blossoms die unsavored. The stage is set for the arrival of a messenger who piques her interest by breaking conventions. Cesario insists on seeing her, alternates between elaborate courtly rhetoric ("Most radiant, exquisite

---

1 In Shakespeare's source, the heroine had only narrowly escaped rape at this point; see Appendix A1, p. 209.

and unmatchable beauty," 1.5.143, TLN 464–65) and casual deflation ("No, good swabber, I am to hull here a little longer," 1.5.169–70, TLN 497–98). Once alone with Olivia, Viola abandons her prepared speech to ask Olivia to reveal her face. Even as she admits Olivia's beauty, which makes her embassy more painful, Viola urges (as Shakespeare does in Sonnets 1–17) her conviction that marriage and reproduction should be both pleasure and duty ("you are the cruellest she alive / If you ... will leave the world no copy," 1.5.199–201, TLN 532–34).

This is a reiteration of a central theme for Viola and the play: "what is yours to bestow is not yours to reserve" (1.5.157–58, TLN 482–83). It is an article of faith for her that love, leading to marriage, mutual support, and children, is an obligation that is universal, natural, and joyous. Olivia should have the right to "bestow" herself, to decide where she loves and marries, but not to withhold entirely her natural and divine gifts of beauty, fertility, and aptness to complement a man—an essential element of the Renaissance view of marriage.

The love triangle is completed and complicated when Olivia conceives a sudden and overwhelming passion for Cesario. Henceforth Viola must increasingly respond to the comic and emotional complications arising out of the success of her disguise. In her final, central scene with Orsino before Act 5, plot takes a back seat to the exploration of situation and character. As Viola edges closer to declaring her love (2.4.26–28, TLN 911–15), Orsino seems as inconsistent as ever. While there is rich irony in the man who seems destined to become Viola's husband lecturing her that "no woman's heart [can] hold so much: they lack retention" (2.4.93–94, TLN 982–83), there is also pain. Viola's "Ay, but I know—" (2.4.101, TLN 991) breaks off the riddling love scene that has offered the actor playing Viola many options, including cheerful obscurity, melancholy for Sebastian, or such an intense emotional or even erotic engagement with Orsino that reassertion of her disguise role becomes essential. The half-line reveals to us her suffering for an apparently unattainable love: she breaks away from her riddling history of "all the daughters of my father's house, / And all the brothers too"— which includes the further pain of remembering Sebastian—with an oblique evasion: "yet I know not" (2.4.118–19, TLN 1009–10). Orsino's pain is more debatable: if he is presented satirically, then both his declarations and his suffering may appear of little worth; but if Viola and the audience take him seriously, then his deep love melancholy may both alarm Viola and reinforce her own anguish. At the same time, we never forget that the situation ultimately resides within a romantic comedy. Viola's further meetings with Olivia, as with Orsino in 2.4, are bittersweet. In 3.1 Olivia's worst fears are realized when her declaration is met by Viola's "I pity you" (3.1.113, TLN 1336). This attempt to evade Olivia's attentions is undermined by the intensity with which each of the young women feels the impossibility of the situation:

> VIOLA. ... you do think you are not what you are.
>
> OLIVIA. If I think so, I think the same of you.
>
> VIOLA. Then think you right: I am not what I am.
>
> (3.1.129–31, TLN 1354–56)

Olivia commits herself to a passionate declaration in which she swears "by the roses of the spring, / By maidhood, honor, truth, and everything" (3.1.139–40, TLN 1364–65), but Viola matches both her rhyming and her passion in her reply:

> By innocence I swear, and by my youth,
> I have one heart, one bosom, and one truth,
> And that no woman has; nor never none
> Shall mistress be of it, save I alone. (3.1.147–50, TLN 1372–75)

Neither the riddling nor the comedy can entirely hide their anguish. When they meet again, briefly, in the elaborations of 3.4, the stalemate seems complete.

For Viola's romance plot, nothing changes until the final scene. For Olivia's, however, things get worse: in 4.1, she mistakes Sebastian for Cesario, who is seemingly in danger from Sir Toby. Sebastian's entering the house seems to him a dream, and to her a blessed change of heart. His grief at the loss of his sister, and worry about the absence of Antonio, are put aside in the joy of a love and betrothal which, while sudden, are presented in solemn terms with a priest:

> I'll follow this good man, and go with you,
> And having sworn truth, ever will be true. (4.3.32–34, TLN 2147–48)

Audiences can relish Olivia's mistake even as they relax in the knowledge that a fitting match has been made.

The heading "Comedy" does not, of course, imply that the "Romance" characters and situations are not funny. But it is convenient to discuss the play in terms of main plot and subplot, romance and comedy; and the characters of the comic subplot do constitute a distinct society within the play.

The comic subplot is driven by Olivia's kinsman Sir Toby, her foppish suitor Sir Andrew, and her servant Maria, all of whom we meet in 1.3. The sheer energy with which the scene begins is a strong contrast to the courtliness of 1.1 and the uncertainty of 1.2, a contrast reinforced by the switch from verse to prose (Shakespeare's comic characters generally speak in prose). Sir Toby Belch, as his name implies, is a great drinker, but he is also a great talker. Maria's attempt to persuade Sir Toby to moderation may be simply out of duty to Olivia, or may be more personal: either to protect him from the danger of being thrown out, or to reform him as, ultimately, her husband.

Sir Toby and Sir Andrew can be seen as a classic comic pairing: fat and thin, witty and foolish, joker and straight man. Sir Toby appears to sweep Sir Andrew along with a torrent of verbiage, as when he encourages the thin knight to display his dancing abilities (see extended note, p. 90). Sir Toby cynically gulls Sir Andrew into giving him money ("I have been dear to him ... some two thousand strong, or so"; 3.2.45–46, TLN 1434–45) and into believing Sir Andrew may marry Olivia. Sir Toby's Falstaffian exuberance allows us to ignore or forgive everything; but it can also seem morally deplorable. How aware is Sir Toby of the morality of what he is doing? And how does self-awareness influence the tone of the play as a whole?

Morality and other higher matters do not concern Sir Andrew. Much of his character and humor depend on the low wattage of his brain. Part of his amiability, however, is his occasional dim awareness that he is not the sharpest knife in the drawer: "Nay, by my troth, I know not: but I know, to be up late, is to be up late" (2.3.3–4, TLN 703–04). Although Sir Toby is the driving energy of the subplot, and Maria the brains, Sir Andrew gets most of the laughs. Significantly, the Clown, the professional fool, does not join this group until Act 2.

When the Clown joins Sir Toby and Sir Andrew in 2.3, it is principally as a musician. His famous love song "O Mistress Mine" conveys the same traditional message he gave Olivia in 1.5: "Youth's a stuff will not endure" (2.3.48, TLN 752). The implication for the young, like Olivia (and possibly Sir Andrew), is to marry now and take advantage of their youth; but for others, particularly an older Sir Toby, it is a *memento mori*, a reminder of mortality. This mixture of love and melancholy repeats, in a different key, the pain of the Viola-Orsino relationship.

The scene's interruption by Malvolio, Olivia's puritanical steward, is vital to understanding both his character and the play's structure. How ridiculous should Malvolio appear? He has been played wearing his steward's chain of office even with his nightshirt, in hair curlers under a nightcap, with a teddy bear under his nightshirt, or secretly wearing yellow stockings. An ethical balance is key here: while Malvolio's plot function is to be a wet blanket, too much absurdity may undercut the seriousness of both the threat he poses and the character he cultivates (Wells 57). Is Malvolio right to try to close down an irresponsibly noisy late-night party, or is he just a humorless spoilsport irritated by anyone having even innocent fun? Whatever the view of Malvolio, the upshot is Maria's plan to dupe him by using his own weaknesses: that he is so conceited that he believes "that all that look on him love him" (2.3.134, TLN 843–44).

The gulling of Malvolio by means of a forged letter is the high point of the comic subplot. However, it is important to note that Malvolio has already been "yonder i'the sun practising behavior to his own shadow" (2.5.14–15, TLN 1032–33) before he appears, and that his fantasies—about being "Count Malvolio" (2.5.32, TLN 1050), sleeping with Olivia, and disciplining Sir Toby—all occur before he sees the faked letter. The reaction of the eavesdropping group builds the comedy as first one and then another is so outraged that he has to be restrained from bursting out of hiding. Considerable physical comedy may result from their changing their hiding places, pretending to be garden statues, or adopting other comic business of hiding or nearly being discovered. Nevertheless, it is essentially Malvolio's scene, and can be played as stand-up comedy to the audience, using audience laughter as part of an implicit dialogue with them (see extended note, p. 135).

The payoff comes in 3.4, when Malvolio greets Olivia dressed in a style totally inappropriate to his office or to a mourning household (see extended note, p. 155), and smiling in a manner so grotesque that it provokes her comment: "Smil'st thou? I sent for thee upon a sad occasion" (3.4.18, TLN 1540). Thinking himself Olivia's new lover,

Malvolio takes her suggestion that he go to bed as an invitation, with of course potential for physical comedy if he pursues her around the stage. He assumes he is sharing a secret understanding with her as he quotes the letter, but she is totally baffled by indecorum so gross that madness is the only explanation. His extravagant arrogance arises from both his character and the plot, allowing Sir Toby, Maria, and Fabian to carry out their elaborate charade of treating his "madness" as demonic possession. Nothing could more infuriate a respectable Puritan such as Malvolio, and every self-righteous exclamation provides more ammunition for his tormentors. After he leaves, they determine that they will carry the prank further by confining him "in a dark room" (3.4.121, TLN 1657), the standard treatment at the time for lunatics.

A key element in the gulling of Malvolio here and in the "dark house" scene (4.2) is not so much the comedy, which is readily apparent, but the seriousness of what lies behind it. If, as Charles Lamb argued in the nineteenth century, Malvolio is "neither buffoon nor contemptible," but "brave, honorable, accomplished," then his baiting by more trivial characters may evoke "a kind of tragic interest" (153–55; see below, p. 31). A number of twentieth-century critics have, however, perceived a structural morality underlying the play at a deeper level than that of Malvolio's character, a morality based on the ancient rituals of celebration, social cohesion, and rough justice associated with the great festivals of the pagan and subsequently Christian year, particularly Christmas, May Day, and Midsummer. The merriment that inverts the usual norms of respect and behavior (for a strictly limited time) is, at a deep level, a moral positive. Malvolio's tragedy is not that he is mistreated, but that he fails to perceive his own folly.

No sooner has Malvolio left than Sir Andrew arrives with his ludicrously inept challenge to Viola/Cesario. The development of the duel between a cowardly knight and a fearful and unqualified woman depends to a great extent on the preparation and anticipation of what will ensue. In plot terms, it is significant in joining the subplot to the main plot through the involvement of Viola. When Sebastian's friend Antonio interrupts the beginning of the duel in order to rescue Viola (whom he believes to be Sebastian), we move from farcical stage business to the potential seriousness of Antonio's arrest and demand for his money back from (as he thinks) Sebastian. This intermingling of the plots continues in 4.1 with the Clown's attempt to bring Sebastian to

Olivia, and with Sir Andrew's ill-advised decision to assault Sebastian (whom each believes to be Cesario). Olivia's intervention draws Sebastian into the main plot, and we can see, though the characters as yet cannot, how the resolution of the romance plot will be achieved. As if to tantalize us, however, the dénouement is delayed by the Clown's long scene with Malvolio in the dark house. Malvolio is "*within*" in the Folio stage direction, so the Clown holds center stage. By disguising himself as Sir Topaz the priest (a disguise he does not need, as Maria makes clear at 4.2.61–62 (TLN 2049–50), he may in the first instance be drawing our attention to the role of disguise in the play. Both the disguise and the theological language of the Clown's catechism imply a deliberate attack on Malvolio's Puritan tendencies. An Elizabethan theater audience would certainly share the Clown's antipathy to those who wanted to close down traditional festivals, morris dancing, bear baiting—and theaters. For the audience, Malvolio's darkness is not only the darkness of his ignorance about the comic intrigue against him, but also of his own delusions about Olivia and his place in the Illyrian world of romance. The play shifts at this point, preparing us for a more serious and critical view of the ending, removing our sympathy from Sir Toby and company, and even making us look more critically at the romantic resolution of the main plot.

ACT 5: WHAT YOU WILL

The romance plot and comedy subplot converge in Act 5. As it begins, Orsino's evocation of Antonio's exploits in battle may bring into the play "an experience much tougher than we have associated with him so far" (Warren 61), and in doing so may ensure that we do not view Orsino entirely in terms of love melancholy and blindness to Viola. While Antonio's proud defiance of Orsino, and Orsino's equally honorable acceptance of Antonio's "fame and honor" (5.1.52, TLN 2210), raise the stakes, they do not remove us from the realm of comedy. Indeed, the comedy is intensified by the incomprehension created by each of them knowing (correctly) that he has had Sebastian/Cesario with him since the shipwreck.

The emotional turning point for Orsino occurs as Olivia rudely ignores him to talk to his page Cesario. As he finally turns away from his commitment to Olivia, his full and frightening frustration is redirected against Cesario: "Come, boy, with me; my thoughts are ripe in mischief" (5.1.121, TLN 2285). This threat, however, is formulated in terms that will precipitate the romantic discovery, since Viola, whom, he says "I swear I tender dearly," is "the lamb that I do love" (5.1.119, 124; TLN 2282, 2286). Viola's response that she will follow him willingly because she loves him "More, by all mores, than e'er I shall love wife," (5.1.129, TLN 2293) seems the ultimate betrayal to Olivia, who believes she has just been betrothed to Cesario. She commands Cesario to stay and brings in the Priest to confirm her (mistaken) reality.

Orsino's threatened departure, which could usher in tragedy, is deflected by the eruption of the comic subplot onto the stage. Since Sir Andrew and Sir Toby have been beaten, though not very seriously, we know Sebastian must be in the offing. Before he arrives, however, Sir Andrew is rejected by Sir Toby: "Will you help? An ass-head, and a coxcomb, and a knave? A thin-faced knave, a gull!" (5.1.196–97, TLN 2369–70). We have known all along that Sir Toby is gulling Sir Andrew, both financially and for his amusement value with the duel. Is this revelation serious and cruel? Or is it a minor element of reality showing itself as we near the end of the play, sufficient to complicate our view of the meaning of the play, but not enough to divert the main flow away from its anticipated comic closure?

Sebastian's long-delayed appearance creates on stage the "natural perspective, that is, and is not" (5.1.207, TLN 2381). This moment is a kind of magic in which each twin sees his and her impossible, hoped-for, reflection. "Most wonderful!" (5.1.215, TLN 2390) says Olivia; and a sense of wonder does indeed surround the rightness of the reunion. Viola has kept her brother alive not only in her hopes, but also in her impersonation of him, despite the increasing danger. The coming together of the twins resembles the final chords of a piece of music, or the closing steps of a dance that seemed confusion and is now revealed to have a perfect shape. Choreography is necessary in the theater anyway, since Sebastian must not see Viola until after he has spoken to Antonio, thus allowing everyone else on stage to register the marvel of the apparition. But choreography in modern productions often goes further than this in order to emphasize the "natural perspective," the apparent optical illusion of Cesario/Sebastian "cleft in two" (5.1.213, TLN 2388). The twins frequently circle each other, suggesting dance, interchangeability, and a cautious approach to what may be a spirit. The dialogue, too, holds the moment in suspension, as each tentatively seeks confirmation of what seems too good to be true; and if not true, too cruel to be borne. When Peggy Ashcroft played Viola in 1950, the British critic J.C. Trewin described the moment in this way:

> At the end, as Sebastian faces his sister, he cries: "What countryman? What name? What parentage?" There is a long pause now before Viola, in almost a whisper (but one of infinite rapture and astonishment) answers: "Of Messaline." Practically for the first time in my experience a Viola has forced me to believe in her past.... (qtd Brown 210)

The next two stages of reconciliation fall into place with the inevitability and satisfaction of placing the final pieces of a jigsaw puzzle. Sebastian and Olivia, total strangers who are now effectively married, have no complaint with how "nature to her bias drew," like the weighted curve of a ball in bowls (see extended note, p. 196). Everything that attracted Olivia to Viola is fulfilled in Sebastian, plus at least one thing that was missing. Orsino, having gone through a similar yet steeper learning curve (confined in his case only to the final scene), realizes his folly and then claims his unexpected reward.

In traditional terms this ending to the romance plot is complete and satisfying. The difficulties with which the play and the characters started have, after a period of further confusion (including both comedy and danger), been resolved. The conventions of comedy as a genre lead to marriage and feasting, to "cakes and ale" (2.3.104, TLN 811). The formal artifice of the ending, like the diminishing number of pages at the end of a novel, tell us that the resolution is come.

Yet unfinished business intrudes, in the person of Malvolio. Unless we are excessively hostile to "cakes and ale," and sympathetic to Malvolio's humorlessness, we are unlikely to relish the prospect of his sitting in judgment over Maria, Sir Toby, and the others. Fabian's intervention seems in the spirit of the traditional comic ending, in which the happiness of Viola and the other lovers "spreads to the other characters on the stage, creating an emotional solvent in which their problems are resolved; and it spreads to the audience too" (Wells, 60). Fabian confesses, shields Maria from most of the blame, reveals the unexpected news of a further marriage, and submits that all that has passed should "rather pluck on laughter than revenge" (5.1.351, TLN 2537).

Malvolio's final line, "I'll be revenged on the whole pack of you" (5.1.362, TLN 2548), sounds a powerful discord in the harmony of the ending. He may or may not be entreated to a reconciliation later; what is certain is that he is not part of the completion of the play now. For some critics, Malvolio's refusal to be reconciled creates a darkness at the heart of the play, a human despair too deep for conventional romance endings to encompass. For others it is seen not in opposition to the romance ending, but more like a dark border of reality by contrast with which the wonder of the romance is that much more magical. Still others see it as a recognition that there will always be some who place themselves outside the reach of forgiveness and generosity (Barton, Ryan).

Orsino reiterates the golden promise of the double marriage to come, and the play is complete—except for the Clown's final song. Just as each stage in the ending has been qualified by what follows, so the epilogue in the form of a song seems to comment on the play as a whole, even as it gently removes us from the world of illusion and art to the world of "every day" (5.1.392, TLN 2579). The Clown sings of a sad, even cynical view of downward progress of a man through childhood, adult knavery, marriage, drunkenness, and death. If this reflects back on the play's presentation of aspirations, pain, love, and mortality, it does so in a minor key, repeating that "the rain it raineth every day" (5.1.379, TLN 2563). Nevertheless, it is a song, not a sermon. The final two lines change the focus to the theatrical event in which the audience has participated:

> But that's all one, our play is done,
> And we'll strive to please you every day. (5.1.391–92, TLN 2578–79)

LANGUAGE AND RHETORIC:
PROSE, VERSE, AND POETRY

While the language of *Twelfth Night* may be divided into prose (60%) and verse (40%) (Bate/Rasmussen 649), it may be more useful to consider it as prose, verse, and poetry. A section of 1.5 will illustrate a few of the significant strengths of Shakespeare's use of each form.[1]

Viola's second speech in 1.5 indicates the dangers of us trying to speak of prose, or any mode, as if it were a single form:

> Most radiant, exquisite, and unmatchable beauty—I pray you tell me
> if this be the lady of the house, for I never saw her. (1.5.144–45, TLN
> 464–66)

---

1   For a fourth category, song, see A Note on the Music and Songs, pp. 69–71.

The vocabulary and balance of the first phrase to Olivia are elaborate, highly wrought, and deliberately artificial: as Viola says, "'tis poetical" (1.5.162, TLN 488–89), and it is appropriate to Orsino's self-consciously artistic mode of loving. The second phrase is so prosaically functional as to provide a comic contrast. Then a third mode is displayed, as Olivia steers a middle course:

> I ... allowed your approach rather to wonder at you, than to hear you.
> If you be not mad, be gone; if you have reason, be brief.... (1.5.163–66,
> TLN 491–93)

Olivia combines straightforward vocabulary with a rhetorical series of oppositions (wonder/hear, mad/reason, be gone/be brief). As Viola becomes more "poetical," even starting to speak in verse at line 197 (TLN 530), Olivia seems to use prose in order to deflate the disturbing messenger, and to evade speaking about love. Finally, however, Viola's passion pushes Olivia into verse.

At first Olivia's verse is workaday iambic pentameter, the standard blank verse meter, sounding less "poetical" than Viola's prose greeting:

> Your lord does know my mind, I cannot love him.
> Yet I suppose him virtuous, know him noble,
> Of great estate, of fresh and stainless youth;
> In voices well divulged, free, learned, and valiant,
> And in dimension, and the shape of nature,
> A gracious person. But yet I cannot love him:
> He might have took his answer long ago. (1.5.214–20, TLN 549–55)

This verse is deliberately flat, unelevated in vocabulary, with no figurative images or rhetorical flourishes. Viola's reply is only slightly more poetic, but a key element of it is that Olivia completes the last line, having finally, in effect, come under the spell of Viola's passionate pressure:

> In your denial I would find no sense;
> I would not understand it.
> OLIVIA   Why, what would you?
> (1.5.223–25, TLN 558–60)

The Folio prints this short speech of Olivia's on a separate line, but we have "stepped" it in order to reproduce typographically what an Elizabethan actor would have done in performance: picked up the rhythm of the first three beats of the line from Viola, and then provided the two concluding beats. Just like musicians, Viola and Olivia are now cooperating at a technical level of the verse, which conveys to the audience an ever closer involvement with each other.

This is the point at which the scene shifts unmistakably into poetry.

> Make me a willow cabin at your gate,
> And call upon my soul within the house;
> Write loyal cantos of contemnèd love,
> And sing them loud even in the dead of night ...
> (1.5.225–28, TLN 561–64)

As her errand to woo Olivia collides both with her passionate conviction that a woman's purpose and fulfillment are love and marriage, and with her own apparently hopeless love for Orsino, Viola's deep emotion is supported by the full resources of poetic utterance. The first of the five verse feet is not an iamb (unstressed then stressed), but a trochee (stressed then unstressed); thus she seizes the initiative with the irregular contrapuntal stress at the start of the line:

Make me/ a **will**/ow **cab**/in at/ your **gate**

The vocabulary and images are heightened too. The willow tree was associated in England with lovers' melancholy: for Viola to propose building an actual cabin in which to maintain her vigil, and for the cabin to be of willow, is the kind of image that carries both romantic commitment and a hint of self-conscious exaggeration. She imagines Olivia as the soul separated from her (the hypothetical lover's) body, creating a metaphor of love as a destined union that would be sinful to impede. And having composed her sorrowing songs, she then startles us by saying she would sing them loud at the time when everyone is asleep. The entire speech builds to either (1) another shared line, or (2) a significant pause, either option eloquent in its brevity. Here is (1):

VIOLA.... you should not rest
Between the elements of air and earth,
But **you** should **pity me**.
OLIVIA.   You **might** do **much!**
What is your parentage?

Olivia's half-line response can be heard as an instant impulsive engagement with Viola; and the final half-line about parentage will leave a pause in which tension builds as Viola considers her reply. Option (2) works slightly differently:

[VIOLA.] But **you** should **pity me**.
OLIVIA. You **might** do **much!** What **is** your **parentage?**

If this acting choice is made, the significant pause comes after Viola's half-line, leaving time for Olivia to think, and deliver what will seem a more considered complete and regular iambic pentameter line. Either way, Viola's poetic speech has been successful beyond her intentions. And there are a number of points in the play at which choices about stepped half-lines invite similarly careful consideration by actors and readers.

Elizabethan actors were so accustomed to the musical beat of iambic pentameter that they would have pronounced or elided syllables that often break the rhythm of modern actors in unintended ways. For instance, Viola in her willow cabin speech would have elided the disyllabic "even" to a single syllable to provide an iambic pentameter (with an internal contrapuntal trochee following the mid-line caesura or pause) at:

And **sing** them **loud** || e'en in the **dead** of **night**....

The opposite situation demands addition of a syllable: after Olivia has dismissed Cesario/Viola she starts a long sentence with this line:

Methinks I **feel** this **youth's** perfections....

In modern English "perfections" is only three syllables, resulting in a broken-backed line with four regular iambic beats undercut (because we are expecting five beats) by only a final unstressed syllable; but an Elizabethan actor (and a few acute modern actors) would hear the break in rhythm, and supply the early modern English disyllabic "-ion" ending: "per**fec**tions." Thus language skills retain the rhythm that is as important as in modern rap poetry or in jazz.

Language also becomes the subject of a witty but serious discussion between Viola and the Clown in 3.1, with particular reference to how slippery and ambiguous a medium it is. Mistaking is very easy. Viola, like the Clown, has scenes with every other character in the play, and her ability to adapt to their language is a measure of her intelligence and sensitivity, and a reflection of their natures. She is a match for Maria, who as we know from her treatment of Sir Andrew in 1.3 is quick-witted and sharp-tongued, and who later displays her wit even further with the letter to Malvolio. Viola also encounters Malvolio briefly, and his tone to her is similar to his tone to the revelers in 2.3. Throughout the play, he tends toward a somewhat exaggerated vocabulary, and several of his words, such as "element" (3.4.112, TLN 1646) and "notorious" (5.1.314, TLN 2498) seem to be regarded by other characters as idiosyncratically affected.

The only characters whose language gives Viola problems are Sir Toby and Fabian. While she can easily slip back into prose, and respond to Sir Toby's "Taste your legs" with a pun on "understand" (3.1.70–71, TLN 1290–91), the plot requires that her fear and confusion rob her of any ability to penetrate the extravagance of his description of Sir Andrew's prowess as a fighter. Her generosity does not equip her to detect malice, and her own disguise compounds the confusion. She and Sir Andrew are utterly at cross-purposes during and after their duel, as much so as when she replies to his French at 3.1.73. As usual, Sir Andrew appears to confuse himself as much as everyone around him by his utterances. Viola's brief scene with Antonio, whom she has just encountered for the first time, continues the confusion, but Antonio's passionate language of devotion to Sebastian returns her to the realms of ideals and hopes. By the final act, Sebastian is the only significant character in the play that Viola has not yet seen, and their meeting is in a poetic verse that initially hesitates, pausing halfway through lines. Then the reunion is sealed in an irresistible flow of verse that requires of the actor great technical breath-control as much as it requires the deepest wells of emotional truth.

Viola's brief sequence in 3.1 with the Clown, mentioned above, may stand as a key to a significant strand of the play. The sequence has no plot function; its purpose is thematic and entertaining. One of its most striking elements, apart from their agreement that "words are very rascals," is the way in which Viola can match wits, and witticisms, with Feste. Her wit is as good as his, just as it is for Orsino's and Olivia's. More importantly, her skill is cooperative, not competitive. She extends the Clown's metaphors rather than trumping them, picking up his cues and throwing back responses. "Mutuality" is the key to both joking and loving, and Viola, far from being passive in either situation, proves the most responsive player of all.

TWELFTH NIGHT IN THE ELIZABETHAN THEATER

"If music be the food of love, play on" (1.1.1, TLN 5): the first sounds an audience hears in *Twelfth Night* are not words, but music already playing. At the first performance, the instruments and music for the first scene would not have been the trumpets, drums, and other loud music required for history plays and tragedies with battle scenes, but gentler woodwinds and strings appropriate to a duke's court. The music itself, as Orsino makes clear, is melancholy, appropriate for an aristocratic lover. Thus the musicians have a vital role in establishing for us where the story starts. An audience at the Globe was used to responding to such clues, since the stage was a neutral platform with no scenery to convey visual information about locale (see Shakespeare's Theater, p. 58).

In the absence of any scenery, the music and actors alone must convey a sense of place, time, and situation. A duke would be costumed in the rich clothing reserved by law for the aristocracy: velvets, silks, brocades, cloth of gold perhaps, feathers in his hat (for all gentlemen wore hats indoors as well as out), or he may wear a coronet. His tone with his courtiers is informal, but their deference to him makes his authority clear enough. These lords would also be richly dressed, and wear fashionable rapiers. Although the stage direction does not specify anyone else, two or more of the company's "hired men" would be present as attendants and guards. Their clothing would contrast sharply with that of the duke and lords, being principally of wool and leather, and the guards' pikes would further establish the power of Orsino's court.

As the duke and his courtiers leave the stage, the audience could not say what country the play is set in, nor Orsino's name, nor even where or at what time of day the scene took place, but they would know they had seen a ruler in a tranquil and orderly court, exiting to a spring or summer garden. There is no dramatic need to know more.

The stage has been neutralized by the exit, and is available to be any place or time the actors create. Thunder may now be created by drums or the "rolled bullet" (a cannonball rolled on a sheet of metal, or down a wooden trough). With the change in weather enter several actors who may be wet, as they are in *The Tempest*, to indicate that they have been shipwrecked. We know that mariners had distinctive apparel, so the Captain and Sailors will be instantly identifiable (see extended note, p. 170).

Viola's costume would indicate her social standing: a gentlewoman, a member of the aristocracy. Her dress too would be of rich material. Moreover, Viola has money and valuables with her. When she says to the Captain "there's gold," the property money or jewelry not only rewards the Captain but also confirms a hierarchy. The other crucial aspect of Viola's costume is that it is women's clothing. The boy actor playing Viola would be a specialist in playing women's roles, and would be familiar with the clothes, wigs, and possibly makeup required. The next time the audience sees Viola, this boy actor will appear playing a girl disguised as a boy (now minus the long hair), so it is vital that Viola be established in this scene as female. Again, place has been established on the bare stage by actors, costume, and props; what more we need to know is supplied by the dialogue.

Since the space of the stage is unlocalized, the question of where characters enter from and leave to has a different significance from what we take for granted in realist plays and films. If a character goes offstage in a play or film, we almost unthinkingly provide (or in film, have provided for us) an offstage continuation of realistic time and place. When characters enter, we expect realistic logic. Elizabethan staging, however, is not realist.

An example from 2.2 indicates the pitfalls of modern realism being applied to Shakespearean dramaturgy. Malvolio, who has been sent after Viola, meets her and gives her Olivia's ring. The Folio stage direction reads "*Enter Viola and Malvolio, at several doors.*" "Several" means "separate, different," but the spatial logic would seem to dictate that

Viola would enter from the direction of Olivia's house and exit by the other door in the direction of Orsino's. Indeed, editors from the mid-eighteenth century until the twentieth century have changed the direction to read "*Enter VIOLA, MALVOLIO following.*" Recently, editors have returned to the original direction because we now understand that Malvolio *meeting* Viola rather than *overtaking* her is not bad logic, but different logic. Shakespeare is concerned not with realist geography, but with metaphorical geography: a *confrontation* between Malvolio and Viola. To be concerned with whether Malvolio might have taken a shortcut in order to get ahead of her is to miss the (emblematic) point.

CRITICAL RECEPTION OF *TWELFTH NIGHT*

1. Renaissance to Edwardian (1602–1912)
Seventeenth-century critics commented sporadically on performances of the play (see below, pp. 38–39); then in 1709 Nicholas Rowe published the first serious edition of Shakespeare's plays, and was the first editor to write a detailed interpretation of it. He highlighted Malvolio: "something singularly Ridiculous and Pleasant in the fantastical Steward" (Smith 1949, 28). A year later Charles Gildon dismissed "that Episode of the Steward," praising rather the "under-Plot of Sir Toby's bubbling Sir *Andrew.*" Gildon drew attention also to the poetry of the play, praising the "captain's description of *Sebastian's* coming ashore"; and "*Olivia's* declaration of Love to *Viola*" (Vickers 2: 333). In his 1765 edition Samuel Johnson described the play as "in some of the lighter scenes exquisitely humorous," praising also the poetry as "in the graver part elegant and easy" (Vickers 2: 448). This did not however make up for the lack of moral fiber, for the "marriage of *Olivia* ... wants credibility, and fails to produce the proper instruction required ... as it exhibits no just picture of life" (Vickers 2: 448).

Not all of Johnson's peers were so censorious, although Richard Farmer in his 1767 *Essay on the Learning of Shakespeare* thought the play did "not exhibit a just censure of life," finding Olivia's marriage to Sebastian "not altogether consistent with a woman in her exalted situation," but thought highly of the play anyway as a "Piece full of exquisite entertainment" (Vickers 5: 439). George Steevens endorsed Farmer's praise of one "of the most entertaining Plays in any Language," returning attention to Malvolio as "that most consummate Coxcomb...."

In the nineteenth century, appreciation of the play grew, both as a delightfully poetic text and as a vehicle for performance. William Hazlitt described the play in 1817 as

> perhaps too good-natured for comedy. It has little satire, and no spleen.... It makes us laugh at the follies of mankind, not despise them. (Hazlitt 1)

August Schlegel in 1815 praised likewise its combination of "the richest fund of comic characters and situations, and the beauteous colours of an ethereal poetry" (Furness 378). Both critics represent the trend, since the 1760s, of educating a wider public about Shakespeare; they also show nineteenth-century critics moving away from the moralizing demands of critics such as Johnson, and appreciating the play as an entertainment. That trend is epitomized in Charles Lamb's famous description of the play in "On Some of the Old Actors" (1823). This was strong performance criticism, "based more on nostalgic reminiscence than on fresh observation" (Barnet 183). Lamb marks the plangent notes struck by Mrs. Jordan as Viola, "thought springing up after thought ... as they were watered by her tears" (Lamb 151); this was matched by Mrs. Powell's incarnation of the "the imperious fantastic humour" of Olivia (Lamb 152).

Lamb crucially directed attention back to the character of Malvolio as performed by Richard Bensley. Malvolio, Lamb insisted, was not to be taken as the "eternal, low steward of comedy," but merited quasi-tragic status: "Even in his abused state of chains and darkness, a sort of greatness seems never to desert him" (Lamb 154). Lamb emphasized the comic pathos of Malvolio, comparing him to Cervantes's Don Quixote: "He was starch, spruce, opinionated ... you would have thought ... the hero of La Mancha stood before you" (Lamb 154). Lamb's empathy for Malvolio anticipated a strong trend in modern criticism, and in modern productions, that depict the "baiting" of Malvolio as tiresome and cruel: "[Lamb] shifts the object of value from Illyria to Malvolio, and thus brings us into the tragic realm" (Barnet 187).

Lamb anticipated the character analysis that marked Victorian criticism, with the play understood as a novel. In her 1833 *Characteristics of Shakespeare's Women*, Anna Brownell Jameson praised the "exquisite refinement of Viola," which "triumphs over her masculine attire";

"she is deep-learned in the lore of love" (Furness 392). Her description of Viola is matched by the Olivia evoked in Mary Cowden Clarke's *Girlhood of Shakespeare's Heroines* (1850–52). She devised backstories for Olivia and Viola, showing how their growth to adulthood led to the events described in the play, emphasizing the devotion of both to their respective brothers. Olivia becomes the kind of wealthy, beleaguered heroine found in so many Victorian novels.

Empathy marked also nineteenth-century discussions of Viola. Sir Edward Russell wrote in 1884 of Ellen Terry's Viola: "She feels the pathos of the story. Her frame quivers as she tells it" (Furness 393). Mingling grace with zest is something Joseph Knight emphasized also in his 1893 notes:

> [Viola] enjoys thoroughly the confusion her assumption of manly dress creates, and her delight when she finds herself taken for a man by Olivia is infectious. Not less happy is she in the more serious passages, the grace and delicacy of the play being ... fully preserved.
> (Furness 394)

Was there then "a philosophy in this poetic masquerade?" asked T. Kenny in his appreciation of the *Life and Genius of Shakespeare*, published in 1916 for the tercentenary of Shakespeare's death. "Ay, there is ... we are all, in varying degrees, insane; for we are all the slaves of our defects, which are genuine chronic follies" (Furness 384). This approach hinted at a Feste-centric *Twelfth Night*, evident also in the comments of A.C. Bradley, the most celebrated Shakespeare critic from before World War I. Bradley confesses that he loves Feste more than all of Shakespeare's fools, except that of *King Lear*. He praises the clown's singing, in particular the melancholy of the final "old rude song about the stages of man's life ... at once cheerful and rueful, stoical and humorous" (Gollancz 168).

2. Modern to Post-Modern: 1912–2012

In the last century, discussion of the play has drastically changed, traversing a bewildering range of topics. Yet these build on ones that have gone before (if only to refute them). Many still govern twenty-first-century interpretation and performance.

When Virginia Woolf saw *Twelfth Night* early in the 1930s, what struck her most was its language: "From the echo of one word is born another word.... the play seems ... to tremble perpetually on the brink of music" (1981, 34). To her the play was a triumph of Shakespearean style. What mattered was the way all its words related to each other, an internal whole. This approach (still called "New Criticism") was taken up by many in the middle of the twentieth century. Caroline Spurgeon, in *Shakespeare's Imagery and What It Tells Us* (1935), noted only fourteen images in the play "which can be called poetical," but praised its "peculiar mixture of tones ... music, romance, sadness and beauty interwoven with wit, broad comedy, and quick-moving snapping dialogue" (268). The suggestibility of the play's language was praised also by William Empson in *Seven Types of Ambiguity* (1929), in which he rates Orsino's speeches at 2.4.78 (TLN 965) "a fair case for ambiguity" of his second type "when two or more meanings are resolved into one." (98, 48). Woolf also was struck by this, wondering at "queer [odd] jingles such as 'that *live* in *her*; when *liver*, brain, and heart'" (34) (emphasis added).[1] This feeling for the resonance of the play's language remains common, as in Frank Kermode's account of *Shakespeare's Language* (2000): "the play is a splendid example of how serious language games can be played without slowing down dramatic progress" (66). Kermode continues a line of thought well displayed in Alexander Leggatt's enduringly useful *Shakespeare's Comedy of Love* (1974):

> For all these characters, language is not a means of escaping from the private self, and making contact with others; it is rather a means of defining the self and confirming its privateness—one more barrier erected against the realities of the world outside. (229)

It was not just that the play was "poetical" like Viola/Cesario's speech in Olivia's praise (1.5.225, TLN 561, ff.), but that the whole play was a poem in dramatic form. This is emblematized by D.J. Palmer's lush praise of the way "the play, art itself, contains and orders the ... mutability and confusion of nature" (1967, 212).

---

1 Woolf is recalling 1.1.36 (TLN 43).

The "queer jingles" Woolf delighted in continued to puzzle. If you could construct meanings—so went new thinking, in the late 1970s and 1980s—you could equally well deconstruct them, leaving readers and viewers unsure whether "meaning" had ever existed. Thus Geoffrey Hartman, in a widely anthologized 1985 essay, praised "Shakespeare's Poetical Character" as expressing the spirit of deconstruction: "We tumble through the doubling, reversing, mistaking, clowning, even cloning; we never get away from the tumult of the words themselves.... The text ... keeps turning" (47, 51). But how could such verbal puzzles still delight? Stephen Booth explored this issue at length in *Precious Nonsense* (1998), expanding from his 1985 essay "The Audience as Malvolio." Booth suggests that the play's opening speech by Orsino does not make sense, yet readers and audience members for over four hundred years have made sense of it. Combining sense and nonsense is crucial to the play's art.

Recent critics have read the play against its historical background of the Elizabethan era and Shakespeare's life, including James Shapiro's detailed and illuminating book *1599*, an account of Shakespeare's imaginative life that year. Historical study is an unfinished project begun by Victorian scholars. The playfulness of *Twelfth Night*'s language runs alongside its allusions to actual or imagined Renaissance events (see extended note, pp. 150–51). There remain minor mysteries: who was "The Lady of the Strachy" (see p. 131, note 1), and who was the yeoman who so presumptuously married her? Detailed glossing of the play continues, as in recent work by Parker (2008) and Stanivukovik (2002, 2004), showing how much Shakespeare might have known of Illyria. The Adriatic coast near the port of Ragusa had been known in Europe since classical times, with a brace of associations useful to the play: links, for example, to pirates and the exotic practices of the Turkish court (such as the castration of eunuchs).

What then occasioned the play? Perhaps a play named for a famous festival day was itself presented as a festival event. In 1954 Leslie Hotson made a case for a play performed at court on 6 January 1601; however, the panache with which Hotson evoked a royal performance is not sufficient to be persuasive, in the absence of any external evidence whatsoever. Anthony Arlidge, in 2000, presented an insider's guide to Middle Temple practice and the Candlemas revel during which Manningham saw the play in 1602. Despite Arlidge's very detailed presentation of Middle Temple customs, he has not convinced many that the play was devised for this specific occasion either. Many have mapped the play onto wider patterns in Renaissance culture. Most influentially, C.L. Barber depicted the play as the summit of *Shakespeare's Festive Comedy* (1959), using historical anthropology to trace festive customs Shakespeare knew. The battle between Sir Toby and Malvolio, the "excellent practice" that so amused Manningham, enacts the wider battle between Carnival and Lent. This approach underpins studies inspired by the Russian theorist Bakhtin, where favoring carnival means also favoring the world turned upside down. Manningham identified the play's comedy as turning on issues of status. That has made it available also for Marxist readings, such as those of Draper (1950) and Krieger (1979), in whose eyes the play reveals the ideological tensions of the Elizabethan state. The play, as Tennenhouse puts it, shows *Power on Display* (1986). Desire is subjected to the powers of the state. That is the theme also of Greenblatt's famous chapter "Fiction and Friction" in his *Shakespearean Negotiations* (1988), in which Renaissance concepts of "masculine" and "feminine" are seen to permeate the play. David Schalkwyk's *Shakespeare, Love and Service* (2008) seeks to move beyond a baldly Foucauldian position where power exercises total control. His nuanced readings show how tenderly the play yokes political power with service (out of duty and love) and how vital feminist approaches have been.

3. Performance Criticism

Since the 1960s, approaches to *Twelfth Night* have been strongly influenced by the rise of performance criticism as an academic discipline. To understand the play we need to grasp both how it might originally have been produced and how subsequent production styles and venues continuously reshape our perception of it. If interpretation is a kind of academic performance, then any performance stands also as an embodied interpretation. These assumptions have been integral in raising the status of Shakespeare's comedies, which have often in the past been treated as less worthy of serious critical attention than the tragedies. The most useful performance criticism on *Twelfth Night*, then, combines a detailed grasp of the specifics of important productions with a clear sense of the overall design of the play. While YouTube footage has recently proven very useful for allowing access to sections of performances one might otherwise never see, performance critics have often described productions for which the only available records are now in archives. John Russell Brown's *Shakespeare's Plays in Performance* initiated this mode in 1966; through his many publications he has continued to refine our sense of what playing *Twelfth Night* means. In the 1970s, J.L. Styan extended this approach with his historical survey of *The Shakespeare Revolution: Criticism and Performance in the Twentieth Century*. Laurie Osborne's *The Trick of Singularity*, despite its sometimes dizzying postmodern ingenuity, offers a detailed examination of nineteenth-century performance editions of the *Twelfth Night*, and their significance for acting as well as critical interpretations. She is particularly engaged by the gender politics of the play in both Victorian and modern productions (see below, p. 39). Among many other books on the play, Lois Potter's handbook on *Twelfth Night* in the "Text and Performance" series shows how useful thinking through performance can be. She analyzes character, plot, and language in detail, emphasizing the play as it unfolds for actors and audience members. The text is brought to life through details from iconic English productions, including John Barton's celebrated 1970 *Twelfth Night* with a young Judi Dench as Viola. Paul Edmondson's 2005 "Shakespeare Handbook" updates and extends Potter's approach, with a far more detailed account of key productions, including commentary on TV and film versions and an extensive scene-by-scene analysis of the play. Elizabeth Schafer's edition of *Twelfth Night* for the Cambridge "Shakespeare in Production" series (2009) goes even further: promptbooks, reviews, and visual archives are used to describe, line by line, production choices for the play. Schafer emphasizes British and North American productions, but she also shows that lively *Twelfth Night*s have been staged round the world. The depth of Schafer's analysis suggests also that performance criticism will continue to be central to discussions of the play.

4. Gender and Queer Sexualities

Twelfth Night has readily generated feminist and queer readings, for its central plot device of "[c]ross-dressing calls assigned gender roles into question, and allows the theater to become a place where ... gender identities might be put into play" (Waller 14). The categories of male and female, and the choice of sexual object (hetero- or homosexual), have been seen by recent critics (starting with Jan Kott's *Shakespeare Our Contemporary*, which influenced directors as well as critics in the 1960s) to be destabilized. The play has been celebrated for the complexity of its gender-bending manner, and Michael Shapiro's *Gender in Play on the Shakespearean Stage* is a balanced survey of this territory. And as Schafer (2009) shows, feminist theories of the play have directly affected recent performance.

Feminist readings have come in two overlapping waves. In the first, Olivia and Viola are seen as icons of womanhood, melancholy, poetical, amorous, yet proactive. In this model, Viola is paired with Rosalind from *As You Like It*: empowered by doublet and hose, yet essentially "female." Such readings are driven by 1960s and 1970s feminist thought. They have roots, too, in the performance traditions of the play dating back to the Victorian period, and the celebration of the charismatically feminine in the works of Cowden Clarke and Mrs. Jameson. The quest for a feminine "essence" aligns with modern acting, driven by the quest to reveal the inner life of characters. Olivia and Viola's troubles, from this perspective, are very real.

Yet though these parts have been played by women since 1662, they were originally written for boys and men. Much recent scholarship has investigated this paradox, combining post-structuralist, new historicist, and feminist approaches. Catherine Belsey (1985) places the play within the rebalancing of male and female roles within Renaissance dynasties. She sees the play exploring gender difference at a time when codes in the "real" world were perhaps beginning to harden. The cross-dressed female character is "neither Viola nor Cesario but a speaker who ... occupies a place which is not precisely masculine or feminine, where the notion of identity itself is disrupted" (Belsey 187). Illyria can be seen as a utopia of sexual difference. This perspective has governed "queer" writing on the play, in which the intensity of the relations between Antonio and Sebastian, Orsino and Cesario, suggests that the older man in each relationship might be gay; or that there might be a lesbian attraction between Olivia and Viola/Cesario. Renaissance discourses of sexuality and subjectivity showing the wide range of possibilities in Renaissance lives as well as their fictions have been influentially explored by, among others, Stephen Greenblatt, Stephen Orgel, Laura Levine, and Valerie Traub. These concepts, like those developed by feminist scholars, have had a strong effect on the development of modern stage and screen interpretations.

A more rueful, less utopian account of sexual difference has been offered by Marxist critics such as Jean Howard (2003). She reads the play against the demands of genre and audience expectation, both of which tend to be more conservative, perhaps, than many critics would like. The play seems to affirm, finally, the conventional values of marriage; and the female characters must submit to patriarchal control. Antonio is excluded from the sextet of happy couples, as are Malvolio and the Clown. In turn, the final song suggests that there is, new marriages aside, much sadness still in Illyria to be endured.

TWELFTH NIGHT IN PERFORMANCE

Twelfth Night's performance history began with John Manningham writing in 1602:

> At our feast we had a play called "Twelve Night, or What You Will"; much like the *comedy of errors*, or *Menechmi* in Plautus, but most like and near to that in Italian called *Inganni*.[1]
> A good practice in it to make the Steward believe his Lady widow was in Love with him, by counterfeiting a letter as from his Lady, in general terms, telling him what she liked best in him, and prescribing his gesture in smiling, his apparel &c., and then when he came to practise, making him believe they took him to be mad. (48)

The two elements he evidently thought most noteworthy were, first, other similar plays or potential sources, ranging from an earlier Shakespeare comedy and its classical Roman source to a modern Italian piece; and secondly, what he regards as the excellent intrigue of gulling Malvolio.

Renaissance audiences took the ridiculing of Malvolio as its comic highlight. This is shown by other early witnesses to the play, such as Leonard Digges who wrote in 1640 that "The Cockpit Galleries, Boxes, all are full / To hear *Malvolio* that crosse garter'd Gull"

---

1 Extracts from the play Manningham mentions can be found in Appendix A, pp. 223–27.

(Chambers 2: 233), or Charles I, who wrote "Malvolio" beside the title *Twelfth Night* in his own copy of Shakespeare's works.

London's theaters were closed in 1642, opening again after the English Civil Wars with the restoration of the monarchy in 1660. The play was revived in 1662, "got up on purpose," John Downes remarked, "to be acted on Twelfth Night" (Furness 378). The fashion for staging the play on 6 January, the feast of Epiphany or "Twelfth Night," continued until the end of the eighteenth century (Schafer 5) but, despite Viola/ Cesario being a classic "breeches" part for the newly engaged female actors, the play did not always meet with favor. Downes marked the 1662 performance as a "great success," but Samuel Pepys sneered: "but a silly play, and not related at all to the name or day" (Vickers 1: 30).

The play then dropped out of the repertoire until Charles Macklin's triumphant revival in 1741. His Malvolio was stern and dignified, and the tradition continued that the company's star would play Malvolio, epitomized by Richard Bensley's Malvolio so praised by Lamb (see above, p. 31). Later in the eighteenth century the comic business between Sir Toby and Sir Andrew expanded, but from the publication of the Bell edition of 1773 (in association with the presentations by David Garrick, the greatest English actor of the century), the Clown's songs "O Mistress Mine" and "Come Away Death" were generally cut.

Shakespeare production in the nineteenth century was characterized by realism and idealism. In 1811 John Philip Kemble, with a series of productions and publication of texts based on them, established lines of interpretation that were to last most of the century. Reordering of scenes, particularly the reversal of 1.1 and 1.2, so that the play starts with Viola's shipwreck before moving to Orsino's court, became common.[1]

In late-nineteenth-century theater, as stage scenery became heavier and more realistic, reversing the first two scenes had the practical advantage of allowing the seashore set to be struck completely after the opening scene to reveal a lavish court for Orsino. Starting with Viola tended to make it more her play, in keeping with the Victorian idealizing of the heroically suffering female. Other changes gave her "curtain lines" at the end of several scenes. The idealization of Viola as modest, passive, and patient was in contrast to nineteenth-century

---

1 The same storytelling device is used in many film and television versions; see below, p. 42 ff.

uneasiness about Olivia's self-assertive lack of decorum. The bolder elements of Olivia's courtship of Cesario, like some of Viola's word-play with Feste, were cut in performance, just as the impropriety of Viola's male disguise was reduced by the choice of the most modest costume possible. A mid-century Viola was the perfection of womanhood, expressing "Shakespeare's ideal of the patient idolatry and devoted, silent self-sacrifice of perfect love" (Winter, qtd Furness 394).

Malvolio continued to be the role for the leading male actor, and the conception of his character became ever more elaborate. Samuel Phelps at Sadler's Wells in 1848 "made Malvolio the embodiment of colossal conceit ... he walked with a heaviness that implied a consciousness of his own grandeur, and there was condescension in every gesture" (Allen 182). Although this led to a greater comedown when he was tricked, Malvolio's seriousness was undercut by ever-increasing comic business in the late-night drinking scene (2.3). So divergent became the conception of Malvolio set against the other characters of the comedy plot, that when Henry Irving played Malvolio in 1884 a number of critics thought his treatment in 4.2, in the dark house, tragic. This was partly because Irving's Malvolio reminded everyone of his grandly heroic Shylock, and partly because, throughout the century, greater scenic realism had led to a depiction of a prison grating through which Malvolio's hands or face could be seen, a clanking of chains, and eventually, to Irving's dungeon occupying half the stage. The scene had ceased to be a Clown's bravura comedy act with Malvolio "within," but rather a realistic depiction of Malvolio's psychological torment. A Malvolio who was pitiable (and not just laughable) has been seen too in many contemporary productions (Carnegie, "*Maluolio* within"). These can also provide discomforting allusions to the post-9/11 world of the "war on terror," such as Michael Bogdanov's production which featured a bound and hooded Malvolio.

The extreme level of nineteenth-century realism, so unlike the conventions of the Elizabethan stage, led to the new technology of controllable gas and electric lighting being used to give an effect of moonlight, thus justifying how Olivia can mistake Sebastian for Cesario. It also led to the triumphant *fin-de-siècle* productions when scenery revealed that "the art of landscape gardening, as pursued in Illyria three hundred years ago, appear[ed] to have reached a very high pitch of excellence" (qtd Odell II: 432). Herbert Beerbohm Tree, in 1900, presented, "the most extraordinary single setting ... the garden of Olivia, extending terrace by terrace to the extreme back of the stage, with very real grass, real fountains, paths and descending steps" (Odell II: 455). Such massive sets could not be quickly changed, however, so not only were scenes reordered, but some scenes took place in Olivia's garden that were never intended for it. While modern productions have avoided such obsessively realist detail, they have often evoked quite specific locales in the Mediterranean. Australasian productions have explored south sea variants on this, emphasizing Illyria's coastline, since the beach is central to Australian and New Zealand mythology (Schafer 2009; and Carnegie 2011).

In 1912 Harley Granville Barker in London (following experimental productions by William Poel on an open stage) initiated a countermove to the prevailing scenic and psychological realism. A simple and slightly stylized set (using suggestion rather than realism) allowed the action to flow freely, and Viola's passion and clarity banished Victorian dreaminess. Furthermore, the knights were restored to a more gentlemanly status than their now traditional low comedy roles had allowed them, and the Clown was cast as old and melancholic rather than as a youthful comic jester. Playing status on the modern stage has also allowed the humors of Sir Toby and Sir Andrew to delight, as in Cheek By Jowl's celebrated Russian *Twelfth Night* (2003) in which "Alexander Feklistov's Tony Belch [was] an exorbitantly mannered construct of funny walks and burblings" (Shore 19).

Over the past fifty years, the strongest trend has been to emphasize the erotic possibilities of the various gender roles and disguises adopted in the play, an aspect not mentioned by the play's earliest witnesses. This has been most evident in all-male productions, designed to simulate the working conditions of Shakespeare's theater. The Shakespeare's Globe male production was performed in the Middle Temple Hall in 2002 for the four-hundredth anniversary of the performance Manningham saw. This production was remounted to great acclaim in 2012, with the addition of Stephen Fry as Malvolio. Mark Rylance's complex impersonation of Olivia was widely praised, his characterization helped by meticulous recreation of late-sixteenth-century formal dress, heavily starched and restricting easy movements. Rylance's charisma emphasized Olivia's seriousness within the gender trickery of the play's main plot. This revival is now available on DVD, which is especially useful in showing frequent interaction between actors and spectators.

London's Unicorn Theatre presented a version for children in 2008–09 that worked the other extreme of zany high action. This took place in a dementedly crowded garden set complete with a sandpit and boardwalks (like those on construction sites). Five actors played all parts. The male actor who appeared first as Sebastian was persuaded, somewhat reluctantly, to change into women's clothing to play Viola; he then received an even greater shock (to the delight of the young audience) when, in a prologue shipwreck sequence, he found himself doused with a bucket of water. It was excellent to see a thoroughly wet Viola who so clearly had been shipwrecked. This was a *Twelfth Night* constantly in motion, the better to engage twenty-first-century viewers otherwise more inclined, perhaps, to seek out online or DVD versions of the play.

TWELFTH NIGHT ON FILM AND TELEVISION

While Shakespeare has been on screens since the earliest days of film-making in the 1890s, his theatricality and his reliance on heightened language have both proven difficult for a largely realist and visual medium.[1] A 12-minute silent Vitagraph film from the USA in 1910, directed by Charles Kent (who also played Malvolio), is readily accessible in the *Silent Shakespeare* compilation. This manages, amazingly, to include most of the major plot incidents of the play; and, typically for a film, it smooths the narrative by providing an initial shot of Viola and Sebastian embracing before cutting to Viola unpacking a well-stocked sea chest and Sebastian wading ashore through gently lapping waves onto Long Island.

The first feature-length film of *Twelfth Night* was a well-made Soviet color film of 1955; the Sovcolor (the Soviet version of Technicolor) process makes this the most visually lustrous of filmed *Twelfth Nights*. Like many nineteenth-century stage versions, it starts with 1.2, Viola's arrival from shipwreck, before revealing an enchanting landscape straight from a Renaissance or Claude Lorrain painting, filmed in the striking terrain that borders the Black Sea. Orsino is found sitting under a

---

1 Extracts from many of the versions discussed here can be seen online via YouTube.

tree listening to a shepherd playing ("like the old age," 2.4.48, TLN 938), while the rest of the court has gone hunting. Both Olivia and Orsino live in grand palaces and travel with entourages much larger than is common in stage productions, and larger too than in the more domestically focused English-language films. At the beginning of Act 5, for example, Orsino rides up to Olivia's house with five horsemen in train.

In the Soviet film, Viola, at her first glimpse of Orsino, plays her mandolin, serenading him into interest in "Cesario." Sir Toby, Maria, and the comic-plot characters are very merry in a traditional nineteenth-century mode, with a diverting range of non-textual comic business. Malvolio struts so outrageously that the question of sympathy for him never arises. He is grotesque, aging, fat, and heavily rouged. The similarity of the twins is emphasized by one actress playing both Viola and Sebastian: film editing, of course, makes it possible for them to meet in the final scene.

John Dexter's 1968 production for British television also doubled Viola and Sebastian, with Joan Plowright displaying her great versatility in both roles. As in the Soviet film, Dexter reverses 1.1 and 1.2, and rearranges some other scenes for narrative simplicity. Viola's love for Orsino is played for the deep pain it causes her (as, for instance, when she admits to her rival, Olivia, "you are fair" (1.5.208, TLN 542), and in the overflowing feeling with which she delivers the willow cabin speech. The pain of proximity to what, it seems, she may not have, is physicalized in 2.4, which is played as a levee around Orsino's bed. Viola has to avert her eyes from his nakedness, and is then required to sit between his naked thighs (facing away!) to put his slippers on. Sir Toby and Malvolio are played by two of Britain's outstanding actors of the period, Ralph Richardson and Alec Guinness. Despite being a studio-bound television version, the production generally gives a good representation of the best stage acting of the era.

There are eight more recent film and video productions that are readily available. The BBC-TV *Twelfth Night* (1980) was one of the plays presented under the conservative eye of producer Cedric Messina. He required so-called "straight" Shakespeare, more or less in period costume, avoiding strong directorial interpretation. The result, in *Twelfth Night*, is an understated, almost conversational piece with passion indicated only by tone of voice. The setting is the dark interiors and sunny leafy courtyard of a Jacobean manor house, with Cavalier costumes (apart from the Puritan garb of Malvolio). The house appears well run, and the carousing in 2.3 that incites Malvolio's ire is so restrained as to suggest he is a very light sleeper. However, apart from an ill-conceived prison setting for 4.2 (which is neither dark nor able to conceal the Clown, Sir Toby, or Maria from Malvolio's view), the production is, in its understated way, coherent and moving. With the boisterous comedy contained, and the Clown a gentle, pleasant fellow, the weight of interest falls on the romance plot, and particularly on Viola and Olivia. Both are generous in spirit and ready to be pleased, and Viola seems always to be secretly smiling at the irony of her position. Illyria in this production is spring-like, charming, and without tension or pain.

In his 1988 film, based on his Renaissance Theatre stage production, Kenneth Branagh made much more radical choices. The studio in which the film was shot is deliberately stage-like. Where the BBC production shows spring, Branagh's *Twelfth Night* is set in winter. The opening credits appear over a stormy sky and ominous music, and Viola drags herself in from a shipwreck that has left her exhausted, soaking wet, and with her clothes so torn that she could not conceivably be mistaken for a boy. This disconsolate opening is followed by Orsino sitting on a garden bench in the snow in his overcoat, in deep melancholy. Every scene at Orsino's court is sunk in painful gloom, and is leached of color by a pervading wintry blue light. When Orsino questions Viola, "But *died* thy sister of her love, my boy?" (2.4.117, TLN 1009), it is clear he fears he may die of his love for Olivia. He strikes a lugubrious note that sounds throughout.

Olivia's household, however, has some sun shining, in a pale wintry color, even though snow falls there too. A Christmas tree confirms that a northern hemisphere "Twelfth Night" (6 January) is the time of the play, and Sir Toby, Sir Andrew, and particularly Maria imbue the comedy scenes with great energy. Sir Andrew's entry wearing snowshoes is typical of the cheerful lunacy. Viola and Sir Andrew both shriek with terror at the mere sound of their swords touching. The Clown, however, has an ambiguous edge, sometimes seeming to have fits of dangerous and arbitrary aggression.

Neil Armfield's lesser-known Australian version from two years earlier was, like Branagh's, based on a recent stage success and filmed in what is clearly a studio, but the mood is summer festivity—perhaps Twelfth Night in Australia, where of course January is high summer. As in his Lighthouse Theatre production, Armfield draws attention to the artifice of the medium by having the blue sky behind the noisy introductory beach party revealed as no more than a cyclorama: a hidden door in it opens, and Orsino enters. In the dead silence that follows this breaking of illusion, he saunters onto the streamer-decorated terrace, glances at the Caribbean combo, and restarts the party with "If music be the food of love, play on" (1.1.1, TLN 5). This festive atmosphere, though always with a sardonic edge of theatrical self-awareness (particularly from the sexually ambiguous Clown), gives the film both great gusto and sharp poignancy.

Departing from Armfield's stage production, the actress playing Viola here also plays Sebastian, though the filmic cross-cutting between them suggests a low budget more than a thematic intermingling. In the comic scenes, however, the energy, timing, and of Sir Toby and Sir Andrew's broad parody of Australian boorishness in particular ensure that the performance is borne on with gusts of laughter. Music supports the performance, with the small combo available at a moment's notice to play for the Clown, provide martial drumbeats for Sir Andrew's arrival at the mock duel, or create the mood for a change of scene. Close-ups bring the viewer into intimate consideration of individual psychology, so the love and uncertainty of Orsino, Olivia, and Viola are immediate. By the same token, the deeply wary observation of the Clown, a sad Buster Keaton persona apparently adopted by a middle-aged torch singer in drag (the actor is female), is brought to our attention most forcefully. In the final scene, as she sings "The Rain It Raineth Every Day," the moon on the night sky slips down to be revealed as a theater follow-spot, thus mirroring the self-reflexive artifice of the opening sequence.

Trevor Nunn's 1996 film could hardly be a greater contrast to Branagh's and Armfield's. Filmed on location during a late English fall, its comedy plot at Olivia's house is full of the sadness and bitterness of unfulfilled lives. Youth and happiness seem transient at best. Maria is getting on in years, and losing hope of reforming the drunken, brutal Sir Toby, who is himself full of self-disgust. Nunn has re-allocated some characters' lines to reinforce this tension. Malvolio's humiliation is such that he leaves the household at the end, as do the rejected Antonio, the dejected Sir Andrew, and even the practical Maria with Sir Toby, accepting second-best, since it is all she can get. The Clown, too, sets off on a road overlooking the restless sea, singing directly to the cinema audience about the entire tale he has told, which we must now leave behind. Throughout the film the Clown has been played with elegiac world-weariness by Ben Kingsley. He is frequently seen observing the action, a device used often in modern stage productions where the Clown watches scenes in which, in the script, he does not appear, a commentator on the action as much as a participant in it, "one of life's privileged spies into the mystery of things" (Greif 61).

The romance side of the tale in Nunn's film is delightful. In the opening shots of a small passenger ship at sea in a storm, we see Viola and Sebastian performing at an evening concert for other passengers, first both disguised as women behind Muslim veils, then both revealed, apparently, as men with moustaches, then Viola having her moustache playfully torn off. Before she can retaliate, the ship founders and the play starts (as so often in film and TV versions) with 1.2. Nunn has upped the stakes, however, by introducing lines that indicate Messaline and Illyria are at war, and Viola and the sailors therefore in danger of their lives. This not only gives urgency to their disguises (and Antonio's later capture), but also puts great pressure on Viola (wearing her brother's little blond moustache) to succeed in her impersonation of a military cadet. The Clown, too, is a danger, since he seems to see through her disguise, and is rough and unfriendly.

The romantic love is emphasized by drastic intercutting of scenes, particularly 2.3 and 2.4. The Clown's singing of "O Mistress Mine" in the kitchen of Olivia's house is steeped in sadness, particularly the isolation of Maria from Sir Toby. The same music is heard by Orsino and Viola, each desperately enveloped in the loneliness of love. Even Olivia, asleep in bed, hears it drifting through her dreams. Other scenes between Orsino and Viola take place on cliff-tops above a grey, surging sea, with a fully romantic, windswept tempest of emotions. With a boisterous, very young-seeming Olivia (and a young Orsino), the final unification of happy lovers leads to a brilliantly costumed nineteenth-century fairy-tale ball, which seems infinitely removed from the rainy reality of all those who have already left to face "every day." What lingers in the memory, however, is the spirit of Viola's luminous generosity.

Tim Supple's 2003 TV version preserves the charming fantasy of *Twelfth Night*, while eclectically blending multicultural casting and modern politics. The opening sequence intercuts the sad and handsome Orsino, played by Chiwetel Ejiofor, listening to mournful piano music, with the backstory of Viola and Sebastian, played respectively by Parminder Nagra and Rhonny Jhutti. We see their father fall victim in a coup, with their homeland "Messaline," presumably, being somewhere on the Indian subcontinent. The two children then become refugees, buying passage in the gloomy hold of a rusting modern ship.

The Illyria they arrive in is reminiscent of modern London. When Antonio and Sebastian walk the town, they wander through a market in the East End; in the crowd the duke's men can easily spy on Antonio. Soon after leaving the market Antonio happens by the gates of Olivia's mansion, apparently an expensive house on the Thames. Both Olivia and Orsino live in lavish, streamlined modern houses marbled and pedimented like those in upmarket design magazines. Both have large terraces, looking out on a flat, pretty sea, which would not literally be possible from the Thames, but which is excellent for the colorful backdrop of gorgeous sunsets.

Where Orsino here is of black British descent, and the twins clearly come from India (and speak in Hindi on occasion), Olivia's household is white and English. Here manners and restraint are the keynotes, which makes Olivia's pursuit of Cesario/Sebastian seem even more determined. Her family is Catholic: in their private chapel, she mourns in Latin. Sir Toby and Sir Andrew (David Troughton and Richard Bremme) are mad old rockers left over from the 1960s. First they play LP records really loud, and then they "make the welkin dance indeed" (2.3.53, TLN 757) by playing their guitars as loudly as they can. They look like backup guitarists for the Rolling Stones. This production is full of other elegant touches. Both Maria and Malvolio are Scottish servants in an English household. Later Malvolio throws off his business suit, donning a kilt to show off his yellow stockings. Belch and Aguecheek carouse in Olivia's wine cellar, which then serves as a convenient (and ironic) dark room in which to lock Malvolio. To the last, Olivia remains grief-stricken while being in love: in most productions her dead brother is forgotten after Act 1, but here we see her weeping over photos of him in Act 5, then being consoled by Orsino. Orsino is not just a lovesick fool, but also a lover who projects an eloquently commanding presence. The sensuality of his relationship with Cesario/Viola is obliquely registered (perhaps as a gesture toward the physical restraint common in Bollywood romance films), but in the end Orsino and Viola make a convincing couple.

Barry Avrich's 2012 film records Des McAnuff's popular stage production of *Twelfth Night* at the 2011 season of Canada's Stratford Festival. Like the recent DVD of the Shakespeare's Globe 2012 production (see above, p. 41), Avrich gives viewers a lively sense of performance on a thrust stage, with the audience heard (and occasionally seen) relishing the production throughout. This is an eclectically modern-dress production, as opposed to the historically accurate costuming the Globe uses. Illyria seems like a lavishly appointed country house from the 1920s, but with some characters—notably Feste—dressed as aging rock stars from the 1960s. All the songs are played live by a rock band supported by highly choreographed backup singers. They start the show with a song based on "If music be the food of love, play on" (1.1.1, TLN 5). They continue playing as the play proper starts, becoming Orsino's courtiers, and they reprise the sentimental "play on, play on" refrain at various points during the play as a thematic signpost, notably when Antonio decides to follow Sebastian at the end of 2.1. By also closing the play (they join with Feste in "The Rain It Raineth Every Day," as eventually does the entire cast, including Viola now in a silk dress), and playing throughout the elaborate curtain call, the musicians effectively bookend the production.

Finally, the *Animated Tales Twelfth Night* (1992) opts for complete fantasy. It sets stop-go animation characters who look like well-dressed puppets into a storybook land, showing what Illyria would look like if re-imagined as a fantasy for children under ten, "a green and pleasant land" the narration tells us, "where beating seas give way to beating hearts." This is a dreamy, Renaissance Illyria, with bright pastel colors, and sparkly touches to many of the costumes, which look like the kind of Renaissance clothes a clever child might fashion from scraps of cloth. While the play is very heavily cut down to a 23-minute running time, scriptwriter Leon Garfield skillfully condenses the play so that as much dialogue as possible comes from the play, and is eloquently spoken by seasoned English actors. For those coming to *Twelfth Night* for the first time, it would serve as an excellent visual prologue to studying the whole play.

SHAKESPEARE'S LIFE

BY DAVID BEVINGTON

The website of the Internet Shakespeare Editions (http://internetshakespeare. uvic.ca), in the section "Life & Times," has further information on many topics mentioned here: Shakespeare's education, his religion, the lives and work of his contemporaries, and the rival acting companies in London.

William Shakespeare was baptized on 26 April 1564, in Holy Trinity Church, Stratford-upon-Avon. He is traditionally assumed to have been born three days earlier, on 23 April, the feast day of St. George, England's patron saint. His father, John Shakespeare, prospering for years as a tanner, glover, and dealer in commodities such as wool and grain, rose to become city chamberlain or treasurer, alderman, and high bailiff, the town's highest municipal position. Beginning in 1577, John Shakespeare encountered financial difficulties, with the result that he was obliged to mortgage his wife's property and miss council meetings. Although some scholars argue that he was secretly a Catholic, absenting himself also from Anglican church services for that reason, the greater likelihood is that he stayed at home for fear of being processed for debt. His wife, Mary, did come from a family with ongoing Catholic connections, but most of the evidence suggests that Shakespeare's parents were respected members of the Established Church. John's civic duties involved him in carrying out practices of the Protestant Reformation. John and Mary baptized all their children at the Anglican Holy Trinity Church, and were buried there.

As civic official, John must have sent his son William to the King Edward VI grammar school close by their house on Henley Street. Student records from the period have perished, but information about the program of education is plentifully available. William would have studied Latin grammar and authors, including Ovid, Virgil, Plautus, Seneca, and others that left an indelible print on the plays he wrote in his early years.

Shakespeare did not, however, go to university. The reasons are presumably two: his father's financial difficulties, and, perhaps even more crucially, Shakespeare's own marriage at the age of eighteen to Anne Hathaway. Neither Oxford or Cambridge would ordinarily admit married students. Anne was eight years older than William. She was also three months pregnant when they were married in November 1582. A special license had to be obtained from the Bishop of Worcester to allow them to marry quickly, without the customary readings on three successive Sundays in church of the banns, or announcements of intent to marry. The couple's first child, Susanna, was born in late May 1583. Twins, named Hamnet and Judith, the last of their children, followed in February 1585. Thereafter, evidence is scarce as to Shakespeare's whereabouts or occupation for about seven years. Perhaps he taught school, or was apprenticed to his father, or joined some company of traveling actors. At any event, he turns up in London in 1592. In that year, he was subjected to a vitriolic printed attack by a fellow dramatist, Robert Greene, who seems to have been driven by professional envy to accuse Shakespeare of being an "upstart crow" who had beautified himself with the feathers of other writers for the stage, including Christopher Marlowe, George Peele, Thomas Nashe, and Greene himself.

Shakespeare was indeed well established as a playwright in London by the time of this incident in 1592. In that same year Thomas Nashe paid tribute to the huge success of the tragic death of Lord Talbot in a play, and the only play we know that includes Talbot is Shakespeare's *1 Henry VI*. We do not know for what acting company or companies Shakespeare wrote in the years before 1594, or just how he got started, but he seems to have been an actor as well as dramatist. Two other plays about the reign of Henry VI also belong to those early years, along with his triumphantly successful *Richard III*. These four English history plays, forming his first historical tetralogy, were instrumental in defining the genre of the English history play. Following shortly after the great defeat of the Spanish Armada in 1588, these plays celebrated England's ascent from a century of devastating civil wars to the accession in 1485 of the Tudor Henry VII, grandfather of Queen Elizabeth I. Shakespeare's early work also includes some fine ventures into comedy, including *A Comedy of Errors*, *The Two Gentlemen of Verona*, *Love's Labor's Lost*, and *The Taming of the Shrew*. He wrote only one tragedy at this time, *Titus Andronicus*, a revenge tragedy based on fictional early Roman history. Shakespeare also turned his hand to narrative poetry in these early years. *Venus and Adonis* in 1593 and *The Rape of Lucrece* in 1594, dedicated to the Earl of Southampton, seem to show Shakespeare's interest in becoming a published poet, though ultimately he chose drama as more fulfilling and lucrative. He probably wrote some of his sonnets in these years, perhaps to the Earl of Southampton, though they were not published until 1609 and then without Shakespeare's authorization.

Shakespeare joined the newly-formed Lord Chamberlain's Men, as an actor-sharer and playwright, in 1594, along with Richard Burbage, his leading man. This group quickly became the premier acting company in London, in stiff competition with Edward Alleyn and the Lord Admiral's Men. For the Lord Chamberlain's group, Shakespeare wrote his second and more artistically mature four-play series of English histories, including *Richard II*, the two *Henry IV* plays centered on the Prince who then becomes the monarch and victor at Agincourt in *Henry V* (1599). He also wrote another history play, *King John*, in these years. Concurrently Shakespeare achieved great success in romantic comedy, with *A Midsummer Night's Dream*, *The Merchant of Venice*, and *The Merry Wives of Windsor*. He hit the top of his form in romantic comedy in three plays of 1598–1600 with similar throw-away titles: *Much Ado About Nothing*, *As You Like It*, and *Twelfth Night, or What You Will*. Having fulfilled that amazing task, he set comedy aside until years later.

During these years Shakespeare lived in London, apart from his family in Stratford. He saw to it that they were handsomely housed and provided for; he bought New Place, one of the two finest houses in town. Presumably he went home to Stratford when he could. He was comfortably well off, owning as he did one share among ten in an acting company that enjoyed remarkable success artistically and financially. He suffered a terrible tragedy in 1596 when his only son and heir, Hamnet, died at the age of eleven. In that year, Shakespeare applied successfully for a coat of arms for his father, so that John, and William too, could each style himself as gentleman. John died in 1601, Shakespeare's mother in 1608.

Having set aside romantic comedy and the patriotic English history at the end of the 1590s, Shakespeare turned instead to problematic plays such as *All's Well That Ends Well*, *Measure for Measure*, and *Troilus and Cressida*, the last of which is ambivalently a tragedy (with the death of Hector), a history play about the Trojan War, and a bleak existential drama about a failed love relationship. He also took up writing tragedies in earnest. *Romeo and Juliet*, in 1594–96, is a justly famous play, but in its early acts it is more a comedy than a tragedy, and its central figures are not tragic protagonists of the stature of those he created in

1599 and afterwards: *Julius Caesar, Hamlet, Othello, King Lear, Macbeth, Timon of Athens, Antony and Cleopatra,* and *Coriolanus,* this last play written in about 1608. Whether Shakespeare was moved to write these great tragedies by sad personal experiences, or by a shifting of the national mood in 1603 with the death of Queen Elizabeth and the accession to the throne of James VI of Scotland to become James I of England (when the Lord Chamberlain's Men became the King's Men), or by a growing skepticism and philosophical pessimism on his part, is impossible to say; perhaps he felt invigorated artistically by the challenge of excelling in the relatively new (for him) genre of tragedy.

Equally hard to answer with any certainty is the question of why he then turned, in his late years as a dramatist, to a form of comedy usually called romance, or tragicomedy. The genre was made popular by his contemporaries Beaumont and Fletcher, and it is worth noting that the long indigenous tradition of English drama, comprising the cycles of mystery plays and the morality plays, was essentially tragicomic in form. The plays of this phase, from *Pericles* (c. 1606–08) to *Cymbeline, The Winter's Tale,* and *The Tempest* in about 1608–11, would seem to overlap somewhat the late tragedies in dates of composition. These romances are like the early romantic comedies in many ways: young heroines in disguise, plots of adventure and separation leading to tearfully joyful reunions, comic high-jinks, and so on. Yet these late romances are also as tinged with the tragic vision that the dramatist had portrayed so vividly: death threatens or actually occurs in these plays, the emotional struggles of the male protagonists are nearly tragic in their psychic dimensions, and the restored happiness of the endings is apt to seem miraculous.

Shakespeare seems to have retired from London to Stratford-upon-Avon some time around 1611; *The Tempest* may have been designed as his farewell to the theater and his career as dramatist, after which he appears to have collaborated with John Fletcher, his successor at the King's Men, in *Henry VIII* and *The Two Noble Kinsmen* (1613–14). His elder daughter, Susanna, had married the successful physician John Hall in 1607. In his last will and testament Shakespeare left various bequests to friends and colleagues, but to Anne, his wife, nothing other than his "second-best bed." Whether this betokens any estrangement between him and the wife, whom he had married under the necessity of her pregnancy and from whom he then lived apart during the two decades or so when he resided and worked in London, is a matter of hot debate. Divorce was impossible, whether contemplated or not. He did take good care of her and his family, and he did retire to Stratford. Anne lived on with Susanna and John Hall until she died in 1623. Shakespeare was buried on 25 April 1616, having died perhaps on 23 April, fifty-two years to the day after his birth if we accept the tradition that he was born on the Feast of St. George. He lies buried under the altar of Holy Trinity, next to his wife and other family members. A memorial bust, erected some time before 1623, is mounted on the chancel wall.

SHAKESPEARE'S THEATER

BY DAVID BEVINGTON

The website of the Internet Shakespeare Editions (http://internetshakespeare. uvic.ca) includes an extensive discussion of the theaters of Shakespeare's time, and the audiences that attended them: click on "Life & Times" and choose the menu item "Stage."

Where Shakespeare's plays of the early 1590s were performed we do not know. When he joined the newly-formed Lord Chamberlain's Men in 1594, with Richard Burbage as his leading man, most public performances of Shakespeare's plays would have been put on in a building called The Theatre, since, when it was erected in 1576 by Richard· Burbage's father James Burbage, it was the only structure in London designed specifically for the performance of plays, and indeed the first such building in the history of English theater. Earlier, plays were staged by itinerant companies in inns and innyards, great houses, churchyards, public squares, and any other place that could be commandeered for dramatic presentation. In Shakespeare's time the professional companies still toured, but to a lesser extent, and several of them also derived part of their income from private performances at court.

The Theatre had been erected in Shoreditch (also called Moorfields), a short walking distance north of London's walls, in order to evade the too-often censorious regulations of the city's governing council. There, spectators might have chosen to see *Romeo and Juliet, A Midsummer Night's Dream, The Merchant of Venice, King John*, or *Richard II*. They would also have seen some earlier Shakespeare plays that he had brought with him (perhaps as the price needed to pay for a share in the company) when he joined the Lord Chamberlain's Men: plays such as *Richard III* and *The Taming of the Shrew*. When in the late 1590s the Puritan-leaning owner of the land on which the building stood, Giles Allen, refused to renew their lease because he wished "to pull down the same, and to convert the wood and timber thereof to some better use," the Lord Chamberlain's Men performed for a while in the nearby Curtain Theatre. Eventually, in 1599, they solved their problem with the landlord by moving lock, stock, and barrel across the River Thames to the shore opposite from London, just to the west of London Bridge, where audiences could reach the new theater—the Globe—by bridge or by water taxi, and where the players were still outside the authority of the city of London. At the time of this move, the River Thames was frozen over solid in an especially harsh winter, so that possibly they slid the timbers of their theater across on the ice.

At any event, the Globe Theatre that they erected in Southwark, not far from the location of today's reconstructed Globe, was in the main the same building they had acted in before. Because timbers were all hand-hewn and fitted, the best plan was to reassemble them as much as was feasible. No doubt the company decided on some modifications, especially in the acting area, based on their theatrical experience, but the house remained essentially as before.

No pictures exist today of the interiors of the Theatre, the Curtain, or the Globe. We do have Visscher's View of London (1616) and other representations showing the exteriors of some theatrical buildings, but for the important matter of the interior design we have only a drawing of the Swan Theatre, copied by a Dutchman, Arend van Buchell, from a lost original by the Dutch Johannes de Witt when he visited London in about 1596–98. In many respects, the Swan seems to have been typical of such buildings. As seen in the accompanying illustration, the building appears to be circular or polygonal, with a thatched roof (called *tectum* in the illustration's labels) over the galleries containing seats and another roof over the stage, but leaving the space for standing spectators open to the heavens. (In the modern Globe, similarly constructed, spectators intending to stand in the yard for a performance can purchase a plastic rain poncho to ward off England's frequent rain showers.) From other kinds of information about Elizabethan playhouses, we can estimate a diameter of about 70 feet for the interior space. A large rectangular stage labeled the *proscaenium* (literally, "that which stands before the scene"), approximately 43 feet wide and 27 feet deep, juts out from one portion of the wall into the yard or *planities siue arena* ("the plain place or arena"). The stage stands about 5½ feet above the surface of the yard. Two pillars support the roof over the stage, which in turn is surmounted by a hut. A flag is flying at the top, while a trumpeter at a door in the hut is presumably announcing the performance of a play. The spectators' seats are arrayed in three tiers of galleries. Stairway entrances (*ingressus*) are provided for spectators to gain access from the yard to the seats, labeled *orchestra* on the first level and nearest the stage, and *porticus* above.

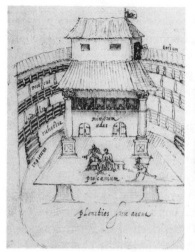 

ABOVE, LEFT: This sketch of the Swan is the most complete we have of any theater of the time. The Swan was built in 1596; Shakespeare's company, The Chamberlain's Men, played there in the same year. RIGHT: This view of the first Globe by the Dutch engraver J.C. Visscher was printed in 1625, but must be taken from an earlier drawing, since the first Globe was burnt to the ground in 1613 at the first performance of Shakespeare's *Henry VIII*. There is substantial evidence that Visscher simplified the appearance of the theater by portraying it as octagonal: most scholars now believe that it had twenty sides, thus making it seem more circular than in this engraving.

The stage area is of greatest concern, and here the Swan drawing evidently does not show everything needed for performance in a theater such as the Globe. No trapdoor is provided, though one is needed in a number of Renaissance plays for appearances by ghostly or diabolical visitations from the infernal regions imagined to lie beneath the earth. The underside of the stage roof is not visible in this drawing, but from the plays themselves and other sources of information we gather that this underside above the actors' heads, known as the "heavens," displayed representations of the sun, moon, planets, and stars (as in today's London Globe). The back wall of the stage in the drawing, labeled *mimorum ades* or "housing for the actors," provides a visual barrier between the stage itself and what was commonly known as the "tiring house" or place where the actors could attire themselves and be ready for their entrances. The two doors shown in this wall confirm an arrangement evidently found in other theaters like the Globe, but the absence of any other means of access to the tiring house raises important questions. Many plays, by Shakespeare and others, seem to require some kind of "discovery space," located perhaps between the two doors, to accommodate a London shop, or a place where in *The Tempest* Prospero can pull back a curtain to "discover" Miranda and Ferdinand playing chess, or a place to which Falstaff, in the great tavern scene of *1 Henry IV*, can retire to avoid the Sheriff's visit and then be heard snoring offstage before he exits at scene's end into the tiring house. The modern Globe has such a discovery space.

Above the stage in the Swan drawing is what appears to be a gallery of six bays in which we can see seated figures watching the actors on the main stage, thereby surrounding those actors with spectators on all sides. But did theaters like the Swan or the Globe regularly seat spectators above the stage like this? Were such seats reserved for dignitaries and persons of wealth? Other documents refer to a "lords' room" in such theaters. The problem is complicated by the fact that many Elizabethan plays require some upper acting area for the play itself, as when Juliet, in Act II of *Romeo and Juliet*, appears "*above*" at her "*window*" to be heard by Romeo and then converses with him, or later, when Romeo and Juliet are seen together "*aloft*" at her "window" before Romeo descends, presumably by means of a rope ladder in full view of the audience, to go to banishment (3.5). Richard II appears "*on the walls*" of Flint Castle when he is surrounded by his enemies and is obliged to descend (behind the scenes) and then enter on the main stage to Bolingbroke (*Richard II*, 3.3). Instances are numerous. The gallery above the stage, shown in the Swan drawing, must have provided the necessary acting area "*above*." On those many occasions when the space was needed for action of this sort, seemingly the acting company would not seat spectators there. It is unclear how spectators sitting above would have seen action in the "discovery space" since it may have been beneath them.

On stage, in the drawing, a well-dressed lady, seated on a bench and accompanied perhaps by her lady-in-waiting, receives the addresses of a courtier or soldier with a long-handled weapon or staff of office. Even though the sketch is rough and imperfect, it does suggest the extent to which the plays of Shakespeare and his contemporaries were acted on this broad, open stage with a minimum of scenic effects. The actors would identify their fictional roles and their location by their dialogue, their costumes, and their gestures. On other occasions, when, for example, a throne was needed for a throne scene, extras could bring on such large objects and then remove them when they were no longer needed. Beds, as in the final scene of *Othello*, were apparently thrust on stage from the tiring house. The building itself was handsomely decorated and picturesque, so that the stage picture was by no means unimpressive, yet the visual effects were not designed to inform the audience about setting or time of the action. The play texts and the actors took care of that.

We have a verbal description of the Globe Theatre by Thomas Platter, a visitor to London in 1599, on the occasion of a performance of *Julius Caesar*. The description unfortunately says little about the stage, but it is otherwise very informative about the London playhouses:

> The playhouses are so constructed that they play on a raised platform, so that everyone has a good view. There are different galleries and places, however, where the seating is better and more comfortable and therefore more expensive. For whoever cares to stand below pays only one English penny, but if he wishes to sit, he enters by another door and pays another penny, while if he desires to sit in the most comfortable seats, which are cushioned, where he not only sees everything well but can also be seen, then he pays yet another English penny at another door. And during the performance food and drink are carried around the audience, so that for what one cares to pay one may also have refreshment.

Shakespeare's company may have included ten or so actor/sharers, who owned the company jointly and distributed important roles among themselves. Richard Burbage was Shakespeare's leading man from 1594 until Shakespeare's retirement from the theater. Other actor/sharers, such as John Heminges and Henry Condell, who would edit the First Folio collection of Shakespeare's plays in 1623, were his longtime professional associates. The quality of performance appears to have been high. Hired men generally took minor roles of messengers, soldiers, and servants. The women's parts were played by boys, who were trained by the major actors in a kind of apprenticeship and remained as actors of women's parts until their voices changed. Many went on in later years to be adult actors.

WILLIAM SHAKESPEARE:
A BRIEF CHRONOLOGY

(Some dates are approximate, especially those of the plays.)

1509–47	Reign of Henry VIII.
1534	Act of Supremacy, declaring Henry VIII head of the Church of England.
1547–53	Reign of Edward VI.
1553–58	Reign of Mary I; England returns to Catholicism.
1558–1603	Reign of Elizabeth I.
1563	Adoption of the Thirty-Nine Articles, establishing Anglicanism as a middle path between Roman Catholicism and more fundamentalist Protestantism.
1564	William Shakespeare baptized, 26 April; birthdate unknown, but traditionally celebrated on St George's Day, 23 April.
1569	Suppression of Northern Rebellion of Catholic earls.
1576	James Burbage builds The Theatre.
1581	Barnabe Riche, *Riche His Farewell to Militarie Profession*.
1582	Shakespeare's marriage to Anne Hathaway, late November.
1583	Birth of their daughter Susanna, 26 May.
1583–84	Plots against Elizabeth on behalf of Mary Queen of Scots.
1584	John Lyly, *Galatea*.
1585	Births of Shakespeare's twins, Hamnet and Judith, 2 February. Earl of Leicester sent to aid the Dutch against the Spanish.
1587	Execution of Mary Queen of Scots, 8 February.
1588	At some point Shakespeare moves to London; family remains in Stratford. War with Spain; the Spanish Armada destroyed in July.
1588–94	Shakespeare writes his early comedies and histories, and his early tragedy *Titus Andronicus*.
1590	Philip Sidney, *Arcadia*; Spenser, *Faerie Queene*, Books 1–3.

1592	Shakespeare attacked in print by Robert Greene in *Greene's Groatsworth of Wit.*
1593	*Venus and Adonis.*
1593–1603	*The Sonnets.* Mostly composed late 1580s–early 1600s; published 1609.
1594	Shakespeare joins the Lord Chamberlain's Men; *The Rape of Lucrece.*
1594	*Comedy of Errors* performed at Grays Inn, 28 December.
1595	William Warner's translation of Plutarch's *Menaechmi* published.
1594–95	*A Midsummer Night's Dream, Richard II, Romeo and Juliet.*
1596–98	*The Merchant of Venice, Henry IV Parts 1 and 2.*
1597	Earl of Essex sent to Ireland to put down a rebellion led by the Earl of Tyrone. George Chapman, *An Humorous Day's Mirth.*
1598	Ben Jonson, *Every Man in His Humor.*
1598–99	*Much Ado About Nothing, The Merry Wives of Windsor.*
1599	Shakespeare's company moves to the Globe; *As You Like It, Henry V, Julius Caesar.* Robert Armin replaces Will Kempe as the company's clown.
1600–02	*Twelfth Night, Troilus and Cressida, Hamlet, All's Well That Ends Well.*
1601	Shakespeare's father dies. Essex's abortive rebellion and subsequent execution.
1602	First recorded performance of *Twelfth Night*, Middle Temple Hall, 2 February.
1603	Death of Elizabeth I; coronation of James I, 24 March. Shakespeare's company renamed the King's Men.
1603–04	*Measure for Measure, Othello.*
1604	James's confrontation of the Puritans at the Hampton Court Conference. Peace with Spain.
1605	The Gunpowder Plot foiled, 5 November.
1605–06	*King Lear.*
1606–07	*Macbeth, Timon of Athens, Antony and Cleopatra, Pericles.*
1608–10	Beaumont and Fletcher, *Philaster.*
1608	*Coriolanus.*
1609–11	*Cymbeline, The Winter's Tale, The Tempest.*

1613–14	(with Fletcher) *Henry VIII*, *The Two Noble Kinsmen*, *Cardenio*; Globe burns down, soon rebuilt; Shakespeare in retirement, living in Stratford.
1616	Death of Shakespeare, 23 April.
1618	*Twelfth Night* performed at Court, Easter Monday, 6 April.
1623	*Twelfth Night* performed at Court, Candlemas, 2 February; First Folio published, containing first extant text of *Twelfth Night*.

A NOTE ON THE TEXT

Twelfth Night was never printed during Shakespeare's lifetime. It was first published in 1623 in the First Folio (F1), which is the only text with authority: all subsequent editions, including this Broadview edition, are based on it. The very first readers of *Twelfth Night*, however, would have been Shakespeare's fellow actors, likely some time in 1601, for whom their parts (their own speeches, plus the last couple of words of the preceding speech as a cue) would have been copied out onto individual scrolls by a theater scribe. The only complete official version of the play would also have been handwritten, the manuscript "Book" of the play licensed by the Master of the Revels. This was retained by the "bookholder" at the theater for use as the prompt copy; the theater company, not the author, owned the play.

The Folio's printers do not appear to have set the play from the "Book." The Folio text has loose ends that would have had to be tidied up in the playhouse, in particular inadequate stage directions, especially entrances, which are at points insufficient to guide a performance. It does, however, reflect some of the characteristics of a text prepared by a professional scribe. In the stage directions and speech prefixes, Orsino is consistently called "Duke," yet the characters alternate between calling him Duke and Count. It is likely that if the copy for the Folio text had come from the "Book" of the play used in the playhouse, then these titles would have been more consistent (unless Duke implies a ruler, Count a lover). The play begins with noting the beginning of each new scene and act in Latin. If you look, for example, at page 255 of F1 on the Internet Shakespeare Editions (ISE) website (<http://internetshakespeare.uvic.ca>), you will see the terms *Actus Primus*, *Scaena Prima*, and *Scena Secunda* (Act One, Scene One, Scene Two). The Folio then marks each scene in Latin, and notes the end of each Act (except Act Three) with *Finis* (the end). This is a clear characteristic of a text prepared to be read, as it reflects the desire to make English texts resemble Renaissance editions of Latin and Greek playtexts.

We know from Charlton Hinman's groundbreaking work that a delay in preparing the First Folio took place when most of the comedies had been printed, and that the press jumped ahead from *All's Well That Ends Well* to print the first two histories—*King John* and *Richard II*—before coming back to finish the comedies (Hinman, II: 480–86). *All's Well*, which precedes *Twelfth Night* in the Folio, was likely set from a manuscript in Shakespeare's hand, though this manuscript has not survived (Wells and Taylor 1987, 492). This would probably be a rough draft containing errors and inconsistencies, and evidence shows the compositors had some difficulty reading it. The subsequent delay may well have resulted from the printer demanding that the two comedies remaining to be printed be first recopied professionally. We know that *The Winter's Tale* was set from a transcript prepared by a scribe called Ralph Crane; it seems likely that *Twelfth Night* was also a transcript of Shakespeare's manuscript in a good ("fair") copy, though probably not by Crane (Howard Hill 128).

Thus our earliest printed copy of the play has been through the hands of compositors and proofreaders in the printing house, themselves working from a scribal transcript, itself a copy of another manuscript that may or may not have been in Shakespeare's hand, and that was almost certainly not identical to the company's promptbook. At each stage of transmission we can be sure that minor errors, alterations, and attempted corrections or even improvements were added. And at no stage was consistency of spelling a matter of concern. Nevertheless, *Twelfth Night* is, by Renaissance standards, a clean text with relatively few significant misprints or obvious misreadings.

Several aspects of the play suggest the possibility of revision, as if the manuscript showed Shakespeare changing his mind as he wrote the play. In 1.2, Viola's first plan is to dress as a eunuch who can sing. Instead, when we next see her, she has been accepted at Orsino's court as a boy courtier who never sings. Instead it is the Clown who sings for the Duke in 2.5 ("Come away, come away Death"); of all Shakespeare's clowns, he is the one most identified as being a professional entertainer, who sings, plays music and makes jokes for money. Though our edition tidies some of the typos in the Folio and amends terms that seem clearly mistaken, we assume that, on the whole, the Folio text is the closest we can come to the play Shakespeare actually devised.

The fair copy of the play delivered to the theater would have been adapted to the requirements of the company in details of casting, props, and other practical elements. On stage, the actors provided the punctuation, deciding for themselves where to pause as they spoke, and their "parts" would contain either very light or no punctuation (Palfrey and Stern, *Shakespeare in Parts*). For the printed edition, the scribe and compositors supplied most of the punctuation, producing a text intended for readers rather than actors. In neither case can we recover an authentic "Shakespearean" original, because a play (as so many modern studies have shown) is a cooperative, social enterprise, subject to negotiation and adaptation, whether in the theater or the printing house.

This Broadview edition enters into a similar collaboration in presenting a text with modernized spelling and punctuation, and speech prefixes and stage directions that provide consistency in order to allow the reader to visualize a performance and the actor to get on and off the stage at the right time. Our stage directions not only indicate what Shakespeare's company *almost certainly* did in performance, but also what they *probably* did. (Readers interested in viewing a separation of these two categories may consult the modern spelling *Twelfth Night* on the ISE website.) There is always a danger, however, that editorial choices, particularly in punctuation and stage directions, may close off genuine alternative interpretations. Editors, like Shakespearean actors, select options that appear best to serve the play. Others who come later may make other choices; and the curious reader should consult the digital copy of the Folio on the ISE website, which uses a modern typeface but preserves all the spelling, punctuation, and stage directions from the Folio.

In this edition, the names of characters have been regularized in speech prefixes and stage directions. Variations in spelling or presentation (e.g. Antonio/Anthonio, Andrew/Sir Andrew) are silently made consistent. Orsino and Olivia, except for the first entry of each, are referred to by name only, although the Folio always refers to Orsino as "Duke" (or its abbreviation) in speech prefixes and stage directions. Unlike many modern editions that employ the name Feste, this edition follows the Folio in referring to him throughout as Clown, thereby emphasizing his role in the structure of the play and in the company, rather than seeing him as a "character" with a novelistic "inner" life. The speech prefix "Clown," Keir Elam remarks, "looks today like a form of strategic distancing or alienation" (Elam 372). We agree with Elam, but draw a different conclusion, seeing the Clown's strategic distance as part of Shakespeare's scheme, allowing the Clown to stand both within and without the world of Illyria. The staging experiments at the new Shakespeare's Globe in London have shown how much direct contact the Clown might make with the audience in his eye-line and all around him.

Part lines of verse are "stepped" in our text to provide a visual assurance of a completed iambic pentameter line. Often one character completes a blank verse line started by another. Such completions are rich in implications about cooperation, harmony, urgency, interruption, quick or slow cuing, pauses, and other possibilities for actors (see Introduction, pp. 25–27). Since entry directions for characters have been silently moved where necessary to precede the first words spoken to them, an iambic pentameter line is often broken at these points.

When "and" means "if," the spelling "an" has been adopted. Prose has silently been restored in the early part of 3.4 for several speeches that the Folio mistakenly set as verse. Latin act and scene headings, and indication of the end of acts, as in the Folio, are not included.

Spelling and punctuation have been modernized in the appendices as well as the playtext.

A NOTE ON THE MUSIC AND SONGS

Music is heard in *Twelfth Night* before any dialogue is spoken, and the play ends with the Clown's ballad-like epilogue, "When That I Was." Shakespeare's comedies always feature music, but in *Twelfth Night* music is intrinsic to the design of the play, with a strong effect on its shifting moods; music here also assumes an unusual thematic importance.

Evidence from Henslowe's *Diary*, from Elizabethan playtexts, and from performers' wills readily shows the presence of musical instruments in playhouses such as the Globe. Lucy Munro lists the following as being available to players:

> treble and bass viols, violins, lutes, citterns (... wire-strung, but played with a plectrum); brass instruments such as trumpets and sackbuts (early trombones); wind instruments such as bagpipes, fifes, pipes, horns, and perhaps hautboys (... comparable with the modern oboe, albeit rougher and louder) ...; and percussion instruments such as drums and tambourines. (Munro 548)

While no scores have survived from the first performances of *Twelfth Night*, all the sounds called for in the Folio text could be comfortably generated with a selection of these instruments, played either by the theater's musicians or possibly by the actors, who "probably had considerable versatility, able ... to play a range of wind and stringed instruments" (Lindley 103). Boy actors were expected to be able to sing, and clowns were also noted for their musical skill. In his will Augustine Phillips, a long-term member of Shakespeare's company who specialized in comic parts, left instruments to a former and current apprentice. Robert Armin, for whom the part of *Twelfth Night*'s Clown was probably written, was noted as a singer.

In 1.2 Viola indicates she is going to sing at Orsino's court, but in 2.4 it is rather the Clown who sings. We do not know why Shakespeare changed his mind, and there is no proof for the theory that the boy actor's voice broke before the first performances and so he could no longer sing. In any case, the Clown has three set-piece songs: "Oh Mistress Mine," "Come Away Death," and "When That I Was." He "is a professional singer, the most developed representation of such a figure in the whole canon" (Lindley 201). Other characters comment on his skill at singing, and he self-consciously links payment and music. Like the Lord Chamberlain's Men, the Clown is in the entertainment business.

Elizabethans loved music, and listening now to acoustic "unplugged" music and song in the Middle Temple Hall (where John Manningham saw the play in 1602)[1] or in the largely wooden confines of the new Shakespeare's Globe in London can be extraordinarily moving. These are the spaces where we can approach closest the acoustic experience of the Renaissance. Music held a philosophical importance too. Earthly sounds were regarded as linked to the music of the nine crystal spheres that surrounded the earth, each one making a separate sound, a music so refined that, according to the tradition passed on by Plato and Pythagoras, "human ears cannot grasp it, just as you are unable to look directly into the Sun, because your sight and sense are overcome by its rays" (Cicero 6.18). Olivia alludes to this idea when she pleads to Cesario: "But would you undertake another suit, / I had rather hear you to solicit that / Than music from the spheres" (3.1.98–100, TLN 1320–22).

Music could stir up earthly passions, as it has Orsino's as the play begins, but it also could cause "mirth, joy and delight," and so, in terms of the theory of the humors that Elizabethans believed dominated the bloodstream and personality, music could have the power to "rectify the blood and spirits ... digest melancholy, and bring the body into a good temper" (Wright 160), and thus align, as the Renaissance Italian humanist Ficino claimed ideally one should, with the forces of the universe.[2] The Clown's last song functions as this kind of charm, showing the "good temper" to which Illyria has been brought by the outcomes of Act 5.

Shakespeare likely wrote lyrics specifically for the Clown's three set-piece songs (rather than borrowing words from existing songs, as was common practice); throughout, the play draws on a wide range of popular songs from the period, often alluded to in a single line. Duffin has traced all these, giving the full text of the songs from which they come, and scores from the period. These are all spoken or half-sung by the comic, reveling characters in the play: Sir Toby, Sir Andrew,

---

1 See Introduction, pp. 38–39.
2 See Appendix H1.

and the Clown. The pleasure-hating Malvolio places these sounds precisely: they belong more in "an ale-house" than "my lady's house" (2.3.79, TLN 787–88). These sounds are part of the misbehaving allowed on Twelfth Night (6 January) and on feast days such as Candlemas (2 February), when the play was staged at the Middle Temple Hall in 1602 (see Introduction, p. 38).

The ISE (<http://internetshakespeare.uvic.ca>) has further information, including audio excerpts and scores for music often used in performance.

ABBREVIATIONS

ARDEN 2   J.M. Lothian and T.W. Craik, eds. *Twelfth Night.*
The Arden Shakespeare: Second Series. London:
Methuen, 1975

ARDEN 3   Keir Elam, ed. *Twelfth Night.* The Arden
Shakespeare: Third Series. London: Cengage
Learning, 2008

DENT   R.W. Dent, *Shakespeare's Proverbial Language: An
Index.* Berkeley: U of California P, 1981

EEBO   *Early English Books Online* <http://eebo.chadwyck.
com>

FIRST FOLIO OR *Mr. William Shakespeares Comedies, Histories,*
FOLIO OR F1 *& Tragedies.* London, 1623

ISE   Internet Shakespeare Editions <http://internet-
shakespeare.uvic.ca>

OED   *The Oxford English Dictionary.* Second edition.
Oxford: Clarendon, 1989; online version March
2012

TILLEY   Morris Palmer Tilley, *A Dictionary of the Proverbs
in England in the Sixteenth and Seventeenth Centuries.*
Ann Arbor: U of Michigan P, 1950

TLN   Through line numbers, as provided by *The Norton
Facsimile: The First Folio of Shakespeare,* prepared by
Charlton Hinman. New York: Norton, 1968

TWELFTH NIGHT, OR WHAT YOU WILL

[CHARACTERS IN THE PLAY

ORSINO'S HOUSEHOLD

ORSINO, *Duke of Illyria (sometimes called Count Orsino)*[1]

CURIO[2]
VALENTINE[3] } *lords attending on Orsino*

Lords, attendants, musicians

OLIVIA'S HOUSEHOLD

OLIVIA, *a countess*

SIR TOBY BELCH,[4] *kinsman of Olivia*

MALVOLIO,[5] *Olivia's steward*

MARIA,[6] *waiting gentlewoman to Olivia*

FABIAN

CLOWN[7] *(Feste), Olivia's jester*

Servant

Priest

Gentlemen, ladies

OTHER ILLYRIANS

SIR ANDREW AGUECHEEK,[8] *a foolish knight courting Olivia*

---

1 Always "*Duke*" in stage directions and speech headings. See A Note on the Text, p. 65.

2 From Latin *curia*, court; hence a name for a courtier.

3 Possibly a reference to St. Valentine, since he carries love messages for Orsino.

4 Olivia refers to Sir Toby as cousin; he refers to her as both cousin and niece, so he is probably a generation older.

5 The name suggests "Ill-wisher" (Italian *mal* + *voglia*). A gentleman, he wears a gold chain of office.

6 The frequent stage pronunciation "Mah-rye-ah" is not Shakespearean, but Victorian.

7 The Clown's name is Feste (pronounced "Fest-ay"), though he is usually addressed as "fool." See extended notes, p. 97 and 114, and A Note on the Text, pp. 67–68.

8 An ague (pronounced "eh-gyew") is a fever, characterized by thin and even shaking cheeks; Sir Andrew's thinness and cowardice seem specified by his name. He is probably tall, with lank hair.

Sea captain[1]
Sailors
Officers

STRANGERS
VIOLA[2] (*later disguised as* CESARIO), *twin sister of Sebastian*
SEBASTIAN,[3] *twin brother of Viola*
ANTONIO, *a sea captain, devoted to Sebastian*]

[1.1]

[*Music.*] *Enter Orsino Duke of Illyria, Curio, and other Lords.*
ORSINO. If music be the food of love, play on,[4]
　　Give me excess of it, that surfeiting,
　　The appetite may sicken, and so die.
　　[*To the Musicians*] That strain again! It had a dying fall;[5]
5　　Oh, it came o'er my ear like the sweet sound[6]
　　That breathes upon a bank of violets,
　　Stealing, and giving odor. [*To the Musicians*] Enough, no more.[7]
　　'Tis not so sweet now as it was before.
　　O spirit of love, how quick and fresh° art thou,　　*lively and eager*
10　　That notwithstanding thy capacity
　　Receiveth° as the sea, nought enters there,　　*swallows*
　　Of what validity and pitch° soe'er,　　*value*
　　But falls into abatement and low price
　　Even in a minute. So full of shapes is fancy,

1　His profession will be evident from his clothing, as may Antonio's;
see extended note, p. 170.
2　Accent is on the first syllable.
3　The sexual ambiguity of the beautiful young St. Sebastian may have suggested
the name.
4　Possibly a command to the musicians. For staging possibilities,
see Introduction, p. 13.
5　A musical phrase dropping to its resolution or cadence.
6　I.e., of the gentle wind that distributes the scent of the violets.
7　Orsino seems to exemplify the comic capriciousness of lovers by first telling
the musicians to play a musical phrase again, then stopping them altogether.

That it alone is high fantastical.[1] 15
CURIO. Will you go hunt, my lord?
ORSINO.   What, Curio?
CURIO.   The hart.°   stag
ORSINO. Why so I do, the noblest[2] that I have.
　　O when mine eyes did see Olivia first,
　　Methought she purged the air of pestilence;°   plague, disease
　　That instant was I turned into a hart, 20
　　And my desires, like fell and cruel hounds,
　　E'er since pursue me.

Enter Valentine.[3]

　　　　　　　　　How now,[4] what news from her?
VALENTINE. So please my lord, I might not be admitted,
　　But from her handmaid do return this answer:
　　The element[5] itself, till seven years' heat,[6] 25
　　Shall not behold her face at ample° view;   full, complete
　　But like a cloistress[7] she will veilèd walk,
　　And water once a day her chamber round
　　With eye-offending brine°—all this to season[8]   stinging tears
　　A brother's dead love,[9] which she would keep fresh 30
　　And lasting in her sad remembrance.[10]
ORSINO. O she that hath a heart of that fine frame
　　To pay this debt of love but to a brother,

1　Love ("fancy") is, like the sea, so full of imagined forms ("shapes") that it is
supremely imaginative ("fantastical"). Both fancy and its root word, fantasy, can
imply deception or illusion.
2　I.e., noblest heart, punning on "hart"; see extended note, p. 78.
3　Probably wearing boots and spurs, indicating arrival from a journey: see
extended note, p. 84.
4　Abbreviation of "how is it now?"
5　Here, the air or sky, one of the "four elements" (2.3.8, TLN 709). The word
is apparently fashionable (or "overworn," 3.1.51, TLN 1270; see also 3.4.112,
TLN 1646).
6　Summer (i.e., the heat of the seven summers).
7　Nun (cloistered from the world and the sun).
8　Preserve (in "brine").
9　(1) The love her dead brother bore her, and/or (2) her love for her dead brother.
10　The meter requires the old pronunciation "rememberance."

1.1.20–22: ACTAEON AND METAMORPHOSIS
(TLN 26–28)

Orsino draws on Ovid's *Metamorphoses*, one of Shakespeare's favorite sources. Having said that he hunts a hart/heart (1.1.17, TLN 23), Orsino now imagines himself the quarry, like Actaeon, who was transformed to a stag (hart) by the goddess Diana (whom he spied bathing naked, and was enamored of) and torn apart by his own savage ("fell") hounds. Orsino is consciously using Actaeon as an allegory, but is unconscious of the irony that Olivia will indeed turn out to be an inappropriate object of his passion. Sixteenth-century paintings and woodcuts often depict Actaeon's metamorphosis in process: his human legs are visible, but his hunting hounds are attacking the upper half of his body, already a hart, as Diana and her nymphs look on.

Lucas Cranach the Elder, "Diana and Actaeon" (first third of 16th century) from the Wikimedia Commons, <http://www.commons.wikimedia.org>. A color version is available at TLN 26–28 on the ISE website (<http://internetshakespeare.uvic.ca>).

How will she love, when the rich golden shaft[1]
Hath killed the flock of all affections else°   *other feelings* 35
That live in her—when liver, brain, and heart,[2]
These sovereign thrones, are all supplied,° and filled *occupied*
Her sweet perfections,[3] with one self king!
Away before me, to sweet beds of flowers;
Love-thoughts lie rich, when canopied with bowers.[4]   40

           Exeunt.

[1.2]

Enter Viola, a Captain, and Sailors [as from a shipwreck].
VIOLA. What country, friends, is this?
CAPTAIN. This is Illyria, lady.
VIOLA. And what should I do in Illyria?
 My brother he is in Elysium.[5]
 Perchance[6] he is not drowned—what think you, sailors? 5
CAPTAIN. It is perchance that you yourself were saved.
VIOLA. Oh, my poor brother! And so perchance may he be.
CAPTAIN. True, madam, and to comfort you with chance,[7]
 Assure yourself, after our ship did split,
 When you, and those poor number saved with you, 10
 Hung on our driving boat,[8] I saw your brother,
 Most provident in peril, bind himself—
 Courage and hope both teaching him the practice—
 To a strong mast, that lived[9] upon the sea;

---

1 Cupid's arrow of love (in contrast to his lead-tipped arrow, which caused aversion).
2 Three governing organs (which also control attributes of love: desire, reason, and emotion).
3 Her perfections are made complete.
4 Orsino may well, as last on the stage, share the second line of the couplet with the audience rather than his courtiers.
5 The classical heaven. Similarity of sound to "Illyria" emphasizes Viola's sense of the contrast of places.
6 Perhaps; repetition in the next two lines plays on an alternative meaning "by chance."
7 Possibility.
8 The ship's boat, driven by the storm.
9 Remained afloat (a nautical term).

15 Where, like Arion[1] on the dolphin's back,
  I saw him hold acquaintance with the waves
  So long as I could see.
 VIOLA. [*Giving him gold*] For saying so, there's gold.[2]
  Mine own escape unfoldeth to my hope,
20 Whereto thy speech serves for authority,
  The like of him.[3] Know'st thou this country?[4]

---

1 A classical poet and musician reputed to have been rescued, after jumping
overboard to escape murder, by a dolphin charmed with his music.
2 A valuable coin, or possibly a piece of jewelry.
3 My escape opens the hope, supported by your account, that he too has escaped.
4 Both Viola and the audience need this information. Equally important, Viola
now puts aside her grief and faces the unknown with energy.

1.2.2:   ILLYRIA (TLN 52)

The Captain's information that they have been shipwrecked in Illyria
seems to leave Viola at a loss. Various suppositions have been made
about what images an Elizabethan audience in England might have had
of the land to the east of the Adriatic Sea, what we now call Dalmatia or
Croatia: a dangerous place renowned for pirates ("Notable pirate, thou
salt-water thief" is Orsino's abuse of Antonio at 5.1.62, TLN 2220); a
literary setting from romance tales or the *Metamorphoses* where those
thought drowned at sea may miraculously be saved; or simply a far-off
place of the imagination, like the sea-coast of Bohemia in *The Winter's
Tale*. What is important to Viola is that it is unknown, and that she has
here lost her brother.

 Historically, Illyricum (to use the Latin name) had been in use since
classical Greek times, and was well known to Renaissance readers and
cartographers (e.g., Mercator, 1578; Ortelius, 1588; and Girolamo Porro,
1598). It identified the Roman province covering most of the Balkans
north of Greece, and appearing in more recent maps to designate part
or all of the territories on the eastern coast and a good distance inland
of the Adriatic Sea from Macedonia almost to Venice, which controlled
the coastal region (hence the Italian names in the play, despite the very
English local color).

CAPTAIN. Ay,[1] madam, well, for I was bred and born
　Not three hours' travel from this very place.
VIOLA. Who governs here?
CAPTAIN. A noble duke,[2] in nature as in name.　　　　　　　25
VIOLA. What is his name?
CAPTAIN. Orsino.
VIOLA. Orsino! I have heard my father name him.
　He was a bachelor then.
CAPTAIN. And so is now, or was so very late;°　　　*recently*　30
　For but a month ago I went from hence,
　And then 'twas fresh in murmur° (as you know,　　*rumor*

1　Pronounced, as spelled in Folio, "I."
2　For Orsino's rank, see A Note on the Text, p. 65.

The map of "Illyrie" (the French spelling) identifies "ILLYRICUM" (the Latin spelling) east of the Adriatic Sea (here misspelled "Golfe Ariatique"), above Greece. (From Alain Mallet's book of maps entitled *Description de l'univers* [Paris, 1683], p. 111, in the Geography and Maps Division, Library of Congress; photograph by David Carnegie.)

    What great ones do, the less will prattle of)
    That he did seek the love of fair Olivia.

35 VIOLA. What's she?

    CAPTAIN. A virtuous maid, the daughter of a count
    That died some twelvemonth since, then leaving her
    In the protection of his son, her brother,
    Who shortly also died; for whose dear love,

40   They say, she hath abjured the sight
    And company of men.

    VIOLA. Oh, that I served that lady,
    And might not be delivered to the world
    Till I had made mine own occasion mellow,
    What my estate is![1]

45 CAPTAIN.   That were hard to compass,°   *accomplish*
    Because she will admit no kind of suit,°   *petition*
    No, not the duke's.

    VIOLA. There is a fair behavior in thee, Captain;
    And though that nature with a beauteous wall

50   Doth oft close in pollution,[2] yet of thee
    I will believe thou hast a mind that suits
    With this thy fair and outward character.°   *appearance*
    I prithee—and I'll pay thee bounteously—
    Conceal me what I am,[3] and be my aid

55   For such disguise as haply shall become
    The form of my intent.[4] I'll serve this duke.
    Thou shalt present me as an eunuch to him—
    It may be worth thy pains, for I can sing,[5]
    And speak to him in many sorts[6] of music,

---

1   The "occasion" (business) which is not yet mature ("mellow") includes a need to confirm her status ("estate") before she is, in effect, born ("delivered") into the public world.

2   Concern about a fair outside concealing a corrupted interior is a common Renaissance preoccupation. Cf. 3.4.334–35, TLN 1889–90; and 5.1.124, TLN 2287.

3   Conceal the fact that I am a woman.

4   As may chance to suit the shape of my plan.

5   Male singers were sometimes castrated before puberty to retain a soprano voice.

6   Possibly indicating instrumental music as well as songs.

That will allow me very worth[1] his service. 60
What else may hap,° to time I will commit, *happen, occur by chance*
Only shape thou thy silence to my wit.[2]
CAPTAIN. Be you his eunuch, and your mute[3] I'll be;
When my tongue blabs, then let mine eyes not see.
VIOLA. I thank thee. Lead me on. 65

Exeunt.

[1.3]

Enter Sir Toby [booted], and Maria [with a light].

SIR TOBY. What a plague[4] means my niece[5] to take the death of her
brother thus! I am sure care's an enemy to life.
MARIA. By my troth,[6] Sir Toby, you must come in earlier a-nights.[7]
Your cousin, my lady, takes great exceptions to your ill hours.
SIR TOBY. Why let her except, before excepted.[8] 5
MARIA. Ay, but you must confine yourself within the modest[9] limits
of order.
SIR TOBY. Confine? I'll confine myself no finer[10] than I am! These
clothes are good enough to drink in, and so be these boots too;
an[11] they be not, let them hang themselves in their own straps.[12] 10
MARIA. That quaffing and drinking will undo you. I heard my lady
talk of it yesterday—and of a foolish knight that you brought in
one night here, to be her wooer.
SIR TOBY. Who, Sir Andrew Aguecheek?

---

1 That will prove me worthy of.
2 (1) Stratagem, (2) intelligence, ingenuity.
3 (1) Dumb servant in a Turkish court, sometimes attending eunuchs, (2) a silent
extra in the theater.
4 I.e., what in the name of the plague (a mild oath).
5 Young kinswoman (Olivia). Cf. "cousin" in Maria's reply, and see note on Sir
Toby in List of Characters, p. 75.
6 By my faith (a very mild oath).
7 Of a night, at night.
8 Excepting those things previously named to be excepted.
9 Moderate.
10 Sir Toby slides from "confine" as "keeping within limits" to being confined by
"finer" clothing. "Fine" can mean both slender and elegant.
11 If.
12 Looped bands of leather or cloth attached to the top of boots to draw them on.

BOOTS AND SPURS (TLN 118)

"To enter booted is to imply a recently completed journey or one about to be undertaken and by extension to suggest weariness or haste" (Dessen and Thomson, under "booted"; see also "riding" and "spurs"). In 1.1, Valentine's function as a returning messenger would thus be reinforced if he entered in haste, booted and spurred, and perhaps wearing a riding cloak. So would a sense of both the geographical and emotional distance between the two households, far enough that it may be regarded as riding distance (although not incompatible with Viola apparently being on foot in 2.2). If Orsino were also wearing boots, dressed to "go hunt" (1.1.16, TLN 20), his failure to do so would reinforce a sense of love overwhelming his usual habits and determination; on the other hand, if he first wears boots and spurs only when he arrives at Olivia's in 5.1, the change would reinforce for the audience a metaphorical sense of movement and development in the character, and help prepare for the transfer of his affections from Olivia to Viola.

Here, Sir Toby's night-time return in riding boots not only indicates the distance he has traveled to join drinking companions, but also an emblematic sense of a man who is unwilling to allow anyone to "confine" him within "modest limits." Maria may help Sir Toby off with his boots, a task that can invite physical low comedy.

Illustration of boots and spurs on stage, detail from the 1625 title page of Thomas Middleton's play *A Game at Chess* (Folger Shakespeare Library, photograph by David Carnegie).

MARIA. Ay, he.   15

SIR TOBY. He's as tall[1] a man as any's in Illyria.

MARIA. What's that to th'purpose?

SIR TOBY. Why, he has three thousand ducats[2] a year.

MARIA. Ay, but he'll have but a year[3] in all these ducats. He's a very[4] fool, and a prodigal.   20

SIR TOBY. Fie that you'll say so! He plays o'th'viol-de-gamboys, and speaks three or four languages word for word without book,[5] and hath all the good gifts of nature.

MARIA. He hath indeed, all most natural.[6] For besides that he's a fool, he's a great quarreler; and but that he hath the gift[7] of a cow- 25 ard, to allay the gust[8] he hath in quarreling, 'tis thought among the prudent he would quickly have the gift of a grave.

SIR TOBY. By this hand, they are scoundrels and substractors[9] that say so of him. Who are they?

MARIA. They that add, moreover, he's drunk nightly in your company. 30

SIR TOBY. With drinking healths to my niece! I'll drink to her as long as there is a passage in my throat, and drink in Illyria. He's a coward and a coistrel[10] that will not drink to my niece till his brains turn o'th'toe, like a parish top.[11]

Enter Sir Andrew.[12]

---

1 Valiant. Maria deliberately takes the word in its other, more usual, sense of height.

2 Venetian currency, approximately four to the English pound. Thus Sir Andrew has about £750 annually, a rich income.

3 He'll squander his income (and sell all the land which produces it) within a year.

4 Real, true.

5 From memory.

6 Playing on Sir Toby's "all" as "almost" (so Folio) and "natural" (an idiot).

7 (1) Talent, (2) present, leading to pun in the next line.

8 Gusto, relish.

9 Sir Toby's drunken error for "detractors"; in her reply, Maria's "add" puns on "subtract."

10 Knave, base fellow.

11 Large version of a child's spinning top, for public use (sometimes "town top"), about which little is known.

12 The size of the Elizabethan stage made it possible for characters already on stage to comment on the approach of another character, as here.

The Viol da gamba is held between the legs (Italian *gamba*) like the modern cello, and therefore frequently, as here, with an obscene connotation. This instrument has more strings than a cello, and playing a melody on it was a minimum accomplishment expected of any gentleman. In the preceding scene Viola was confident that her evidently more advanced musical education, encompassing "many sorts of music" (1.2.59, TLN 110) would help admit her to Orsino's service.

Man playing a viol da gamba. Detail from an illustration in *Nieuwen Ieucht* (Netherlands, 1620), C4ʳ (p. 23), from the collection of the Folger Shakespeare Library; photograph by David Carnegie.

What, wench! *Castiliano vulgo*;[1] for here comes Sir Andrew 35
    Agueface.[2]

SIR ANDREW. Sir Toby Belch! How now, Sir Toby Belch!

SIR TOBY. Sweet Sir Andrew!

SIR ANDREW. Bless you, fair shrew.[3]

MARIA. And you too, sir. 40

SIR TOBY. Accost,[4] Sir Andrew, accost!

SIR ANDREW. What's that?

SIR TOBY. My niece's chambermaid.[5]

SIR ANDREW. Good Mistress Accost, I desire better acquaintance.

MARIA. My name is Mary, sir. 45

SIR ANDREW. Good Mistress Mary Accost—

SIR TOBY. [*To Sir Andrew*] You mistake, knight.[6] "Accost" is front[7]
    her, board[8] her, woo her, assail[9] her.

SIR ANDREW. [*To Sir Toby, indicating audience*] By my troth, I would
    not undertake[10] her in this company.[11] Is that the meaning of 50
    "accost"?

MARIA. Fare you well, gentlemen.

SIR TOBY. [*To Sir Andrew*] An thou let part so,[12] Sir Andrew, would
    thou might'st never draw sword[13] again.

---

1 Obscure. Perhaps, seeing Sir Andrew, "speak of the devil [and he will appear]";
or possibly a drinking cry with no meaning.

2 Presumably a rude play on the significance of Sir Andrew's name; see note in
List of Characters, p. 75.

3 Perhaps an inadvertent reference to (1) an ill-tempered woman, when he
intends (2) a shrew-mouse. This is the first of several references to Maria's small
stature.

4 Hail, go alongside (a nautical term, used figuratively here to mean "make up
to").

5 It is unclear whether Sir Toby deliberately misleads Sir Andrew into thinking
Maria a menial servant, or if the word at this time could mean "waiting gentlewoman," which she clearly is.

6 Sir Toby may here and in his next speech speak aside to Sir Andrew, thus leaving Maria to cope as best she can; but comedy can also derive from allowing her to
hear.

7 (1) Confront (military), (2) woo.

8 Come alongside (nautical).

9 (1) Assault (military), (2) attempt to seduce.

10 Enter into combat with (here with a sexual implication).

11 Sir Andrew jokingly acknowledges the presence of the theater audience.

12 If you allow her to leave "unaccosted."

13 Cease to be a gentleman (cf. "forswear to wear iron," 3.4.225, TLN 1770). Sir
Andrew's repetition in the next line, since it refers to her action rather than his, is
comically foolish.

55 SIR ANDREW. An you part so, mistress, I would I might never draw
    sword again! Fair lady, do you think you have fools in hand?[1]
MARIA. Sir, I have not you by th'hand.
SIR ANDREW. Marry,[2] but you shall have, and here's my hand.
MARIA. [*Taking his hand*] Now sir, thought is free.[3] I pray you, bring
60 your hand[4] to th' buttery bar, and let it drink.
SIR ANDREW. Wherefore,[5] sweetheart? What's your metaphor?
MARIA. It's dry,[6] sir.
SIR ANDREW. Why, I think so. I am not such an ass but I can keep
    my hand dry.[7] But what's your jest?
65 MARIA. A dry jest,[8] sir.
SIR ANDREW. Are you full of them?
MARIA. Ay, sir, I have them at my fingers' ends.[9] [*Letting go his hand*]
    Marry, now I let go your hand, I am barren.[10]

                                                    Exit Maria.

SIR TOBY. O knight, thou lack'st[11] a cup of canary. [*Pouring wine*]
70 When did I see thee so put down?[12]
SIR ANDREW. Never in your life, I think, unless you see canary
    put me down. Methinks sometimes I have no more wit than a

---

1 To deal with. Maria deliberately takes him literally in her reply.
2 By (the Virgin) Mary (a mild oath).
3 I may think what I like (proverbial; here, an equivalent of the modern "you said
it, not me").
4 Maria has taken the hand he offered, and in many performances brings it to
her breasts, usually to Sir Andrew's consternation. The buttery bar is the jutting
ledge of the buttery half-door serving-hatch (French *bouteillerie*, bottle store-room).
5 Why? Sir Andrew has not understood the "metaphor."
6 (1) Thirsty, (2) sexually insufficient (a moist hand was a sign of amorousness
and fertility).
7 Generally taken to refer to the proverb "Fools have wit enough to come in out
of the rain"; but "hand" is specific, and Sir Andrew may simply be proud of not
splashing himself when he "make[s] water" (1.3.110, TLN 238).
8 (1) Insipid (cf. 1.5.34, TLN 333), (2) ironical, (3) Sir Andrew's dry hand (which
she still holds).
9 (1) Always ready, (2) in my hand (which she is about to "let go").
10 (1) Unproductive, (2) empty of jests (having let go of Sir Andrew's hand which
made her "full of them").
11 Probably "stand in need of," though in production Sir Toby often refills a glass
already in use. Canary is a sweet wine originally from the Canary Islands.
12 (1) Defeated in repartee, (2) rendered legless (from drink).

Christian[1] or an ordinary man[2] has. But I am a great eater of
beef,[3] and I believe that does harm to my wit.

SIR TOBY. No question.   75

SIR ANDREW. An I thought that, I'd forswear it. I'll ride home
tomorrow, Sir Toby.

SIR TOBY. *Pourquoi*,[4] my dear knight?

SIR ANDREW. What is *pourquoi*? "Do," or "not do"? I would I had
bestowed that time in the tongues[5] that I have in fencing, danc- 80
ing, and bear-baiting. O had I but followed the arts!

SIR TOBY. Then hadst thou had an excellent head of hair.

SIR ANDREW. Why, would that have mended my hair?

SIR TOBY. Past question, for thou see'st it will not curl by nature.[6]

SIR ANDREW. But it becomes me well enough, dost not?   85

SIR TOBY. Excellent! It hangs like flax on a distaff;[7] and I hope to
see a housewife take thee between her legs, and spin[8] it off.

SIR ANDREW. Faith, I'll home tomorrow, Sir Toby. Your niece will
not be seen, or if she be, it's four to one she'll none of me.[9] The
count[10] himself here hard by woos her.   90

SIR TOBY. She'll none o'th'count. She'll not match above her degree,
neither in estate, years,[11] nor wit; I have heard her swear't. Tut,
there's life in't, man.

---

1 I.e., "an ordinary man."
2 (1) Typical, (2) one who eats at an "ordinary" (a cheap fixed-price eating house).
Hence Sir Andrew's reference to "beef."
3 Believed to dull the brain, though possibly to instill valor.
4 Why (French). See 1.3.22, TLN 144.
5 (1) Foreign languages (Sir Andrew's meaning), (2) tongs for curling hair (Sir
Toby's meaning). Pronunciation was the same.
6 In comparison to "arts" (1.3.81, TLN 208).
7 Sir Andrew is compared to the thin staff held upright between the knees to
hold the straw-colored strands of flax ready for spinning.
8 A housewife would spin flax, but the pronunciation "hussif" also suggests
"hussy" or prostitute, who might take Sir Andrew between her legs and give him
venereal disease, leading to his hair falling out.
9 (She'll have) nothing to do with me.
10 Orsino, earlier described as a duke. In the next speech Sir Toby says Olivia (a
countess) will not marry "above her degree," so Shakespeare is still thinking of
Orsino as of higher rank than Olivia. See A Note on the Text, p. 65, for discussion
of the inconsistency of rank.
11 Implies that Orsino is older, but that Sir Andrew is much the same age as
Olivia.

SIR ANDREW. I'll stay a month longer. I am a fellow o'th'strangest
95 mind i'th'world. I delight in masques and revels[1] sometimes
altogether.

SIR TOBY. Art thou good at these kickshawses,[2] knight?

SIR ANDREW. As any man in Illyria, whatsoever he be, under the
degree of my betters;[3] and yet I will not compare with an old
100 man.[4]

SIR TOBY. What is thy excellence in a galliard, knight?

---

1 Courtly presentations in which some members of the audience joined in the
dancing.
2 Trifles, (little) somethings (French, *quelque choses*).
3 "betters" = of higher rank, but the entire phrase is a foolish backtracking from
meaning.
4 Perhaps "experienced," or a clumsy compliment to the older Sir Toby, or simply
a further exception from comparison.

1.3.101–18: GALLIARDS AND CUTTING
A CAPER (TLN 228–48)

Sir Toby's encouragement of Sir Andrew to dance draws on a vocabulary
familiar to Elizabethans, including reference to the coranto, jig, and
cinquepace. "What is thy excellence in a galliard," he asks, referring to a
lively dance of "four movements [steps], then a *saut majeur*...." (Thoinot
Arbeau, *Orchésographie* [Langres: 1589], trans. Cyril W. Beaumont
[London: C.W. Beaumont, 1925], p. 80). The *saut majeur* ("high leap")
is sometimes translated as "caper" (in the next line), and certainly the
general English sense of "caper" (French *capriole*) is "a frolicsome leap";
but Arbeau has a more technical definition: "there are many dancers so
agile that, in making the *saut majeur*, they move their legs in the air, and
this shaking is called *capriole*...." Possibly Sir Andrew demonstrates at
this point, leaping high and scissoring his long thin legs back and forth
several times before landing. But when he boasts about his "back-trick"
(1.3.104, TLN 231) we are less certain what he means. A 1606 play, *The
Return from Parnassus*, refers in 2.6 to a "back-caper" (see OED), and this
is what Cesare Negri's *Nuove Inventioni di Balli* describes as a *salto* (again,
a "leap") that finishes with the leg behind. It is no wonder Sir Toby ends
the scene exhorting Sir Andrew to "caper ... higher!"

SIR ANDREW. Faith, I can cut a caper. [*He dances.*]

SIR TOBY. And I can cut the mutton[1] to it.

SIR ANDREW. And I think I have the back-trick[2] simply as strong as
any man in Illyria. [*He demonstrates.*]   105

SIR TOBY. Wherefore are these things hid? Wherefore have these
gifts a curtain before 'em? Are they like to take dust, like Mistress
Moll's picture?[3] Why dost thou not go to church in a galliard, and
come home in a coranto?[4] My very walk should be a jig;[5] I would

---

1   Sir Toby quibbles on "cut," and on "caper" as a pickle to eat with "mutton"
(which may also suggest "prostitute").
2   Possibly with a sexual quibble, given "mutton," and the association of a strong
back with male sexual capacity.
3   Paintings were often protected by curtains.
4   A fast "running" (Italian) dance.
5   Another fast dance.

A dance back-step from Cesare Negri, *Nuove Inventioni di Balli* (Milan: 1604), fol F4b
(p. 68), in the collection of the Folger Shakespeare Library; photograph by David
Carnegie. Illustrations from Arbeau are available at TLN 229 on the ISE website
(<http://internetshakespeare.uvic.ca>).

110   not so much as make water but in a cinquepace![1] What dost thou
mean! Is it a world to hide virtues in? I did think by the excellent
constitution of thy leg, it was formed under the star of a galliard.[2]

SIR ANDREW. Ay, 'tis strong, and it does indifferent[3] well in a flame-
colored[4] stock. Shall we set about some revels?

115 SIR TOBY. What shall we do else? Were we not born under Taurus!

SIR ANDREW. Taurus? That's sides and heart.

SIR TOBY. No, sir, it is legs and thighs. Let me see thee caper.

[Sir Andrew dances.]

Ha, higher! Ha, ha, excellent!

Exeunt.

[1.4]

Enter Valentine, and Viola in man's attire [as Cesario].

VALENTINE. If the Duke continue these favors towards you, Cesario,
you are like to be much advanced. He hath known you but three
days,[5] and already you are no stranger.

VIOLA. You either fear his humor,[6] or my negligence, that you call
5   in question the continuance of his love. Is he inconstant, sir, in
his favors?

VALENTINE. No, believe me.

Enter Orsino, Curio, and Attendants.

VIOLA. I thank you. Here comes the count.[7]

ORSINO. Who saw Cesario, ho?

10 VIOLA. On your attendance, my lord, here.

ORSINO. *[To the Courtiers]* Stand you awhile aloof. *[All but Viola
stand apart.]* Cesario,
Thou know'st no less but all; I have unclasped

---

1   A dance of "five steps" (French).

2   Astrology favorable to dancing.

3   Moderately.

4   In Folio Sir Andrew's stocking ("stock") is "dam'd colored," but the profane
intensifier seems unlikely.

5   For the double time scheme, see 5.1.86–92, TLN 2246–54.

6   Capriciousness.

7   In the first line of this scene "Duke"; see p. 75, note 1 and A Note on the Text,
p. 65.

TAURUS! ... IT IS LEGS
                   AND THIGHS (TLN 246–47)

The twelve signs of the zodiac were thought to govern individual health
and personality according to both the current date and when someone
was born. Various signs were believed to be especially associated with
particular parts of the body, as contemporary almanac woodcuts illustrate. Phillip Stubbes's *Anatomy of Abuses* (1583) provides a critical contemporary view:

> So far infatuate are these busy-headed astronomers, and curious
> searching astrologers, that they attribute every part of man's
> body to one particular sign or planet. And therefore to Aries
> they have assigned the government of the head and face. To
> Taurus the neck and throat. To Gemini the shoulders, the arms,
> and the hands. To Leo the heart and back. To Cancer the breast,
> stomach, and lungs. To Libra the reins [kidneys] and loins. To
> Virgo the guts and belly. To Scorpio the privy parts and bladder.
> To Sagittarius the thighs. To Capricorn the knees. To Aquarius
> the legs. To Pisces the feet. And thus they do bear the world in
> hand that the whole body of man, both intern and extern, within
> and without, is ruled and governed by their signs, by stars and
> planets, not by God only.

Because the astrological information was constant, the same woodcut
would appear year after year in annual almanacs that listed holy days in
the church calendar, dates for planting crops or seeking medical attention,
astrological calculations, weather forecasts, and other useful information, so the image and its associated signs of the zodiac were known to
everyone.

Sir Toby justifies setting about revels by saying he and Sir Andrew
were "born under Taurus." Taurus (the Bull), as woodcuts show, governs
the neck, so perhaps Sir Toby is thinking about drinking; in John Lyly's
Galathea, an astronomer advises, "Then the Bull for the throat" (cited in
Arden 2). Sir Andrew, however, mistakenly identifies Taurus with "sides
and heart," so Sir Toby (mis-) corrects him to "legs and thighs," but there
is no way of knowing whether Sir Toby's mistake is deliberate (which

(continued)

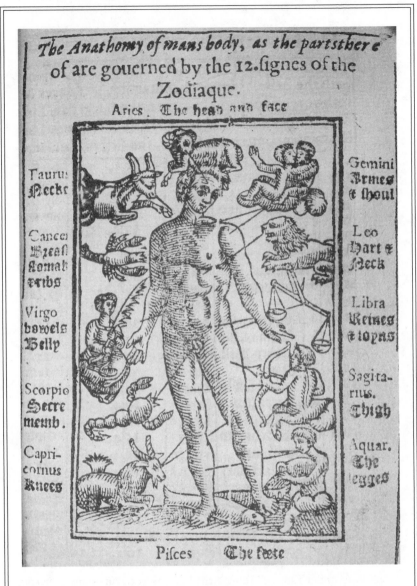

The Anathomy of mans body, as the partsthere of are gouerned by the 12.fignes of the Zodiaque.

Aries. The head and face

Taurus Necke

Cancer Breast stomak ribs

Virgo bowels Belly

Scorpio Secre memb.

Capricornus Knees

Gemini Armes & shoul

Leo Hart & Neck

Libra Reines & Lopns

Sagitarius. Thigh

Aquar. The legges

Pisces The feete

seems likely, since his first use of Taurus was entirely appropriate) or a further error. Either way, the choice of "legs and thighs" encourages Sir Andrew to "caper ... higher" as they leave.

ABOVE: Zodiacal man, from E. Pond, *A New Almanac for the Year of our Lord ... 1609*, in the collection of the Folger Shakespeare Library; photograph by David Carnegie.

To thee the book even of my secret soul.
Therefore, good youth, address thy gait° unto her,   *direct your steps*
Be not denied access,[1] stand at her doors,   15
And tell them, there thy fixèd foot shall grow°   *be planted*
Till thou have audience.
VIOLA.   Sure, my noble lord,
If she be so abandoned to her sorrow
As it is spoke, she never will admit me.
ORSINO. Be clamorous, and leap all civil bounds,°   *usual polite limits* 20
Rather than make unprofited return.
VIOLA. Say I do speak with her, my lord, what then?
ORSINO. O then unfold the passion of my love,
Surprise[2] her with discourse of my dear° faith;   *loving*
It shall become thee well to act my woes,   25
She will attend° it better in thy youth,   *attend to*
Than in a nuncio's[3] [*indicating Valentine*] of more grave aspect.[4]
VIOLA. I think not so, my lord.
ORSINO.   Dear lad, believe it;
For they shall yet belie thy happy years[5]
That say thou art a man. Diana's lip   30
Is not more smooth, and rubious;[6] thy small pipe°   *high voice*
Is as the maiden's organ, shrill, and sound;[7]
And all is semblative[8] a woman's part.°   *resembles*
I know thy constellation[9] is right apt
For this affair. [*To the Courtiers*] Some four or five attend him—   35
All, if you will, for I myself am best
When least in company. Prosper well in this,
And thou shalt live as freely as thy lord

---

1 Stressed on the second syllable.
2 Capture by surprise attack.
3 Messenger's.
4 Serious expression, with implication of age. Accent is on the second syllable of
"aspect."
5 "Misrepresent your fortunate youthfulness" (Arden 2).
6 Ruby-colored (a Shakespearean coinage).
7 High-pitched and unbroken.
8 Resembles.
9 Character, as determined by the configuration of the "stars" (i.e., planets) at
one's birth; see extended note on pp. 93–94.

To call his fortunes thine.[1]

VIOLA.   I'll do my best
To woo your lady.

[Exit Orsino.]

40   *[To the audience]* Yet a barful strife;[2]
Whoe'er I woo, myself would be his wife.

Exeunt [Viola, Courtiers, and Attendants].

[1.5]

Enter Maria, and Clown.

MARIA. Nay, either tell me where thou hast been, or I will not open
my lips so wide as a bristle may enter, in way of thy excuse. My
lady will hang thee[3] for thy absence.

CLOWN. Let her hang me; he that is well hanged in this world needs
5   to fear no colors.[4]

MARIA. Make that good.°   *explain the logic of that*

CLOWN. He shall see none to fear!

MARIA. A good lenten[5] answer. I can tell thee where that saying was
born, of "I fear no colors."

10 CLOWN. Where, good Mistress Mary?

MARIA. In the wars; and that may you be bold to say in your foolery.

CLOWN. Well, god give them wisdom that have it;[6] and those that
are fools, let them use their talents.[7]

MARIA. Yet you will be hanged for being so long absent; or to be
15   turned away[8]—is not that as good as a hanging to you?

---

1   Either (1) be as free as your lord is to control his fortune, or (2) live in the same
freedom as your lord, and share his fortune.

2   (Internal) conflict full of obstacles.

3   An exaggeration: whipping was the standard punishment for fools.

4   Need not fear the battle flags (of any enemy). The Clown puns on "collar" =
noose for hanging.

5   Dull, thin (like food during Lent, a period of fasting).

6   Apparently nonsensical (since those who have wisdom are not in need of it).

7   (1) Professional skills, (2) unit of weight of gold or silver; hence, money. See
Matthew 25:14–29.

8   Dismissed (with a pun on "turned off" = hanged).

ENTER CLOWN (TLN 296)

The Clown was almost certainly played by Robert Armin. Armin joined the Lord Chamberlain's men as their clown in 1599, replacing Will Kemp, who was best known for extemporaneous jests and for dancing and jigs; he even danced from London to Norwich for a dare (seen in the well-known title-page woodcut to his *Kemp's Nine Days' Wonder* [1600]). Armin was better known for his singing, which may explain the number of songs in *Twelfth Night*, and perhaps why Viola's intention to offer her services as a singer in Orsino's court never materializes. He also specialized in ventriloquistic double acts such as his portrayal of both himself and "Sir Topaz" in 4.2. A similar scene for himself is written into one of his own plays, *The Two Maids of More-clacke* (1609). The title-page woodcut shows Armin himself in role, but wearing the long coat of an idiot, whereas he probably played Feste (also a "natural" fool) in the traditional jester's motley and cockscomb (see p. 99, note 9). For more on Robert Armin, see Gurr 1992, pp. 84–90; C.S. Felver, *Robert Armin, Shakespeare's Fool* (Kent, OH: Kent State UP, 1961); and Wiles.

The woodcut of Kemp's jig to Norwich (including a servant playing on pipe and tabor as at the start of 3.1) is available at TLN 1213 on the ISE website (<http://internet-shakespeare.uvic.ca>).

RIGHT: Robert Armin in his play *The Two Maids of More-clacke* (1609), in the collection of the Folger Shakespeare Library; photograph by David Carnegie.

CLOWN. Many a good hanging prevents a bad marriage; and for turning away, let summer bear it out.[1]

MARIA. You are resolute, then?

CLOWN. Not so neither, but I am resolved on two points—[2]

20 MARIA. That if one break, the other will hold; or if both break, your gaskins[3] fall!

CLOWN. Apt in good faith, very apt. Well, go thy way;[4] if Sir Toby would leave drinking, thou wert as witty a piece of Eve's flesh[5] as any in Illyria.

25 MARIA. Peace, you rogue,[6] no more o'that!

Enter Lady Olivia, with Malvolio [and Gentlemen and Ladies].[7]

Here comes my lady. Make your excuse wisely, you were best.

CLOWN. [*To the audience*] Wit,[8] an't be thy will, put me into good fooling! Those wits that think they have thee, do very oft prove fools; and I, that am sure I lack thee, may pass for a wise man.

30 For what says Quinapalus?[9] "Better a witty fool, than a foolish wit." [*To Olivia*] God bless thee, lady!

OLIVIA. [*To the Gentlemen*] Take the fool away.

CLOWN. Do you not hear, fellows? Take away the lady.

OLIVIA. Go to,[10] y'are a dry[11] fool; I'll no more of you. Besides, you

35 grow dishonest.[12]

---

1 Make it (i.e., dismissal) endurable (because summer will make food easy to find and shelter unnecessary).

2 (1) Matters, (2) laces with metal "points" to tie breeches ("gaskins") up to the doublet.

3 Wide knee-length slops (breeches).

4 Do things in your own manner, go about your business.

5 "Eve's flesh" = woman.

6 Maria stops the Clown either to prevent further comment on Sir Toby, or because she sees Olivia entering.

7 Like Orsino, Olivia is well attended. She is likely to be in mourning black.

8 Intelligence, wisdom (in contrast to "will" = desire).

9 A philosopher probably invented on the spot; cf. "Pigrogromitus" (2.3.20, TLN 723).

10 An expression of impatience, like "Come, come."

11 Insipid. The Clown, like Maria earlier (1.3.62, TLN 187), plays on both meanings.

12 Dishonorable (because absent).

CLOWN. Two faults, madonna,[1] that drink and good counsel will amend: for give the dry fool drink, then is the fool not dry. Bid the dishonest man mend himself:[2] if he mend, he is no longer dishonest; if he cannot, let the botcher[3] mend him. Anything that's mended is but patched;[4] virtue that transgresses is but patched 40
with sin, and sin that amends is but patched with virtue. If that this simple syllogism[5] will serve, so; if it will not, what remedy? As there is no true cuckold but calamity, so beauty's a flower. The lady bade take away the fool,[6] therefore I say again, take her away.

OLIVIA. Sir, I bade them take away you. 45

CLOWN. Misprision[7] in the highest degree! Lady, *cucullus non facit monachum*[8]—that's as much to say, as "I wear not motley[9] in my brain." Good madonna, give me leave to prove you a fool.

OLIVIA. Can you do it?

CLOWN. Dexteriously,[10] good madonna. 50

OLIVIA. Make your proof.

CLOWN. I must catechize[11] you for it, madonna. Good my mouse of virtue,[12] answer me.

OLIVIA. Well sir, for want of other idleness,[13] I'll bide[14] your proof.

CLOWN. Good madonna, why mourn'st thou? 55

OLIVIA. Good fool, for my brother's death.

---

1   My lady (Italian), used often by the Clown as an endearment.
2   (1) Amend, reform, (2) repair.
3   Patcher, mender of clothes or shoes.
4   (1) Repaired, (2) ? clothed in the motley of a jester.
5   A proposition in logic; in this case the conclusion (that sin and virtue are much the same) is nonsense, but the implication that all life is a mixture of the two is important.
6   Olivia, currently "wedded to calamity" (*Romeo and Juliet* 3.3.3, TLN 1801), will eventually be unfaithful to calamity (i.e., will cheer up); but her beauty, like a flower, will fade (cf. 2.3.43–48, TLN 747–52; and 2.4.38–41, TLN 926–29; she would do better to love and marry now). Therefore to insist on seven years' mourning is folly.
7   (1) Misunderstanding, (2) action wrong in law (intensified by "in the highest degree").
8   (Wearing) a cowl does not make (a man) a monk (Latin proverb).
9   The parti-colored garment and cap worn by professional jesters, and emblematically signaling folly. See extended note, p. 114.
10 Dextrously (an Elizabethan form).
11 Question (as a priest teaches religious belief by question and answer).
12 My good virtuous mouse.
13 Pastime (not pejorative).
14 (1) Abide, await, (2) endure.

CLOWN. I think his soul is in hell, madonna.

OLIVIA. I know his soul is in heaven, fool.

CLOWN. The more fool, madonna, to mourn for your brother's soul,
60   being in heaven. [*To the Gentlemen*] Take away the fool, gentlemen.

OLIVIA. What think you of this fool, Malvolio? Doth he not mend?[1]

MALVOLIO. Yes,[2] and shall do, till the pangs of death shake him:
    infirmity, that decays the wise, doth ever make the better fool.

CLOWN. God send you, sir, a speedy infirmity, for the better increas-
65   ing your folly: Sir Toby will be sworn that I am no fox,[3] but he will
    not pass[4] his word for twopence[5] that you are no fool.

OLIVIA. How say you to that, Malvolio?

MALVOLIO. I marvel your ladyship takes delight in such a barren[6]
    rascal. I saw him put down[7] the other day with an ordinary[8] fool,
70   that has no more brain than a stone.[9] Look you now, he's out of
    his guard[10] already. Unless you laugh and minister occasion[11] to
    him, he is gagged. I protest I take these wise men,[12] that crow[13] so
    at these set[14] kind of fools, no better than the fools' zanies.[15]

OLIVIA. Oh, you are sick of self-love, Malvolio, and taste with a
75   distempered[16] appetite. To be generous, guiltless, and of free[17]
    disposition, is to take those things for bird-bolts[18] that you deem

---

1 Improve.

2 In performance, this single reluctant first word can reveal so much of
Malvolio's antipathy to the Clown as to raise a laugh.

3 I.e., not crafty (in antithesis to "fool").

4 Pledge.

5 Pronounced "tuppence."

6 Empty (of jests; cf. 1.3.68, TLN 193).

7 Defeated in repartee (cf. 1.3.70, TLN 195).

8 (1) Undistinguished, (2) who performs at an eating house ("ordinary"; cf. p. 89,
note 2).

9 Probably alluding to Stone, a popular "tavern fool" (cf. "ordinary fool").

10 OED defines as "off guard," but Malvolio seems to be observing ("Look you
now") the Clown abandoning the contest.

11 Supply opportunities (as a comedy straight man).

12 Persons of good judgment.

13 Laugh loudly (as perhaps Olivia has done).

14 Not spontaneous (possibly implying "memorized," or simply "formulaic").

15 Subordinate comic performers who assist the act (from the Italian *zanni*, comic
servants in the commedia dell'arte).

16 Diseased.

17 Magnanimous, noble.

18 Blunt arrows or quarrels for shooting birds.

cannon bullets. There is no slander in an allowed[1] fool, though
he do nothing but rail; nor no railing in a known discreet man,[2]
though he do nothing but reprove.

CLOWN. Now Mercury endue thee with leasing,[3] for thou speak'st   80
well of fools.

Enter Maria.

MARIA. Madam, there is at the gate a young gentleman much
desires to speak with you.

OLIVIA. From the Count Orsino, is it?

MARIA. I know not, madam. 'Tis a fair young man, and well   85
attended.[4]

OLIVIA. Who of my people hold him in delay?

MARIA. Sir Toby, madam, your kinsman.

OLIVIA. Fetch him off, I pray you, he speaks nothing but madman.[5]
Fie on him!   90

          [Exit Maria.]

Go you, Malvolio; if it be a suit from the count, I am sick, or not
at home. What you will, to dismiss it.

          Exit Malvolio.

Now you see, sir, how your fooling grows old,[6] and people dislike it.

CLOWN. Thou hast spoke for us, madonna, as if thy eldest son should   95
be a fool; whose skull Jove cram with brains, for—

Enter Sir Toby [drunk].

here he comes—[7] one of thy kin has a most weak pia mater.[8]

OLIVIA. By mine honor, half drunk. What is he at the gate, cousin?

---

1 Licensed, allowed to jest.
2 Presumably with reference to Malvolio.
3 The god of cheating give you the gift of lying ("leasing") (which you will need if
you praise fools).
4 See 1.4.35–36, TLN 287–88.
5 I.e., madman's talk.
6 Stale.
7 The punctuation adopted here emphasizes the difference between Olivia's
potential "eldest son," and another of her "kin" whom the Clown sees
approaching.
8 Brain (physiologically, an enclosing membrane).

SIR TOBY. A gentleman.

100 OLIVIA. A gentleman? What gentleman?

SIR TOBY. 'Tis a gentleman here—[*belching*] a plague o'these pickle herring! [*To Clown*] How now, sot!¹

CLOWN. Good Sir Toby!

OLIVIA. Cousin, cousin, how have you come so early by this lethargy?²

105 SIR TOBY. Lechery? I defy lechery! There's one at the gate.

OLIVIA. Ay, marry, what is he?

SIR TOBY. Let him be the devil an he will, I care not; give me faith, say I. Well, it's all one.³

Exit.

OLIVIA. What's a drunken man like, fool?

110 CLOWN. Like a drowned man, a fool, and a madman: one draught⁴ above heat⁵ makes him a fool, the second mads him, and a third drowns him.

OLIVIA. Go thou and seek the coroner, and let him sit⁶ o'my coz, for he's in the third degree of drink: he's drowned. Go look after him.

115 CLOWN. He is but mad yet, madonna, and the fool shall look to the madman.

[*Exit.*]

Enter Malvolio.

MALVOLIO. Madam, yond young fellow swears he will speak with you. I told him you were sick; he takes on him to understand so much, and therefore comes to speak with you. I told him you

120 were asleep; he seems to have a foreknowledge of that too, and therefore comes to speak with you. What is to be said to him, lady? He's fortified against any denial.

OLIVIA. Tell him he shall not⁷ speak with me.

---

1 (1) Fool, (2) drunkard.

2 Torpor. This indicates the symptoms of Sir Toby's drunkenness, and perhaps why he mishears the word.

3 It doesn't matter (a phrase repeated elsewhere in the play).

4 Drink.

5 I.e., above normal body temperature (wine was thought to heat the blood).

6 Convene his court (to pass judgment).

7 Olivia uses the emphatic form (rather than the simple "will not").

MALVOLIO. He has been told so; and he says he'll stand at your door
  like a sheriff's post,[1] and be the supporter[2] to a bench, but he'll   125
  speak with you.
OLIVIA. What kind o'man is he?
MALVOLIO. Why, of mankind.[3]
OLIVIA. What manner of man?
MALVOLIO. Of very ill manner: he'll speak with you, will you or no.   130
OLIVIA. Of what personage and years is he?
MALVOLIO. Not yet old enough for a man, nor young enough for a
  boy: as a squash[4] is before 'tis a peascod, or a codling[5] when 'tis
  almost an apple. 'Tis with him in standing water[6] between boy
  and man. He is very well-favored,[7] and he speaks very shrewishly;[8]   135
  one would think his mother's milk were scarce out of him.
OLIVIA. Let him approach. Call in my gentlewoman.
MALVOLIO. [Calling offstage] Gentlewoman, my lady calls.

                                                        Exit.

Enter Maria.
OLIVIA. Give me my veil.[9] Come, throw it o'er my face.

                                              [She is veiled.]

We'll once more hear Orsino's embassy.   140

Enter Viola [as Cesario].
VIOLA. The honorable lady of the house, which is she?
OLIVIA. Speak to me, I shall answer for her.[10] Your will?
VIOLA. Most radiant, exquisite, and unmatchable beauty—[To Maria
  or a Gentleman] I pray you tell me if this be the lady of the house,
  for I never saw her. I would be loath to cast away my speech; for   145

---

1 One of the pair of large painted posts set up by the door of a sheriff, probably
for displaying public notices.
2 Support, prop.
3 I.e., ordinary.
4 Immature pea-pod ("peascod").
5 Immature apple.
6 At the turn of the tide, between ebb and flow.
7 Good-looking.
8 Sharply (but also perhaps "shrill," as at 1.4.32, TLN 284).
9 Probably a short light veil, already attached to her headdress.
10 Deliberate equivocation: (1) act as her deputy, or (2) reply for myself.

besides that it is excellently well penned,[1] I have taken great pains to con[2] it. [*Olivia and others laugh.*] Good beauties,[3] let me sustain[4] no scorn; I am very comptible, even to the least sinister usage.[5]

OLIVIA. Whence came you, sir?

150 VIOLA. I can say little more than I have studied, and that question's out of my part.[6] Good gentle one, give me modest[7] assurance if you be the lady of the house, that I may proceed in my speech.

OLIVIA. Are you a comedian?[8]

VIOLA. No, my profound heart;[9] and yet—by the very fangs of mal-
155 ice I swear—I am not that[10] I play. Are you the lady of the house?

OLIVIA. If I do not usurp myself, I am.

VIOLA. Most certain, if you are she, you do usurp yourself,[11] for what is yours to bestow is not yours to reserve.[12] But this is from my commission.[13] I will on with my speech in your praise, and then
160 show you the heart of my message.

OLIVIA. Come to what is important in't, I forgive you[14] the praise.

VIOLA. Alas, I took great pains to study it, and 'tis poetical.

OLIVIA. It is the more like to be feigned,[15] I pray you keep it in. I heard you were saucy at my gates, and allowed your approach
165 rather to wonder at you, than to hear you. If you be not mad, be

---

1 Written, composed.

2 Memorize (see "studied" in Viola's next speech).

3 Most likely Olivia and all her gentlewomen; but smaller productions have only Olivia and Maria.

4 Suffer.

5 Context suggests "sensitive even to the smallest discourtesy."

6 Not in my script.

7 Moderate, appropriate.

8 Actor (not necessarily comic).

9 A mild oath, like "by my faith" (not a jocular form of address to Olivia).

10 I.e., that which.

11 Viola responds to Olivia's joke about supplanting herself ("usurp") with a more serious sense of the word—to appropriate a power wrongfully. See next note.

12 That which is your right to give where you choose (i.e., yourself in marriage) is not yours to withhold altogether. See Introduction, p. 15.

13 Outside, beyond, my instructions.

14 Excuse you (from delivering)

15 (1) Invented, "poetical" (line 162, TLN 489), (2) deceitful.

gone. If you have reason, be brief. 'Tis not that time of moon[1]
with me to make one in so skipping[2] a dialogue.

MARIA. Will you hoist sail, sir? Here lies your way.

VIOLA. [*To Maria*] No, good swabber,[3] I am to hull[4] here a little longer. [*To Olivia*] Some mollification for your giant,[5] sweet lady! Tell   170
me your mind, I am a messenger.[6]

OLIVIA. Sure you have some hideous matter to deliver, when the
courtesy of it is so fearful.[7] Speak your office.

VIOLA. It alone concerns your ear. I bring no overture[8] of war, no
taxation of homage.[9] I hold the olive[10] in my hand. My words are   175
as full of peace as matter.[11]

OLIVIA. Yet you began rudely. What are you? What would you?

VIOLA. The rudeness that hath appeared in me, have I learned from
my entertainment.[12] What I am, and what I would, are as secret as
maidenhead:[13] to your ears, divinity;[14] to any others', profanation.   180

OLIVIA. Give us the place alone; we will hear this divinity.

> [*Exeunt Maria, Gentlemen, and Ladies.*]

Now sir, what is your text?[15]

VIOLA. Most sweet lady—

OLIVIA. A comfortable[16] doctrine, and much may be said of it. Where
lies your text?   185

VIOLA. In Orsino's bosom.

OLIVIA. In his bosom! In what chapter[17] of his bosom?

---

1 Period of lunacy.
2 Erratic, going from one thing to another.
3 A low-ranked sailor who washes ("swabs") the decks.
4 Lie with sails furled.
5 Please pacify your huge protector.
6 Tell me your views, and I shall report them back.
7 Terrible, inspiring fear.
8 Preliminary declaration.
9 Demand for payment due to a feudal superior.
10 I.e., olive branch (symbol of peace).
11 Substance.
12 Viola refers to her reception by Sir Toby and Malvolio (and possibly Maria).
13 Virginity.
14 Religious discourse.
15 Chosen passage (from the bible, as theme for a sermon).
16 Strengthening.
17 As of the bible.

VIOLA. To answer by the method,[1] in the first[2] of his heart.

OLIVIA. O, I have read it. It is heresy. Have you no more to say?

190 VIOLA. Good madam, let me see your face.

OLIVIA. Have you any commission from your lord to negotiate with my face? You are now out of your text.[3] But we will draw the curtain,[4] and show you the picture.

[*She unveils.*]

Look you, sir, such a one I was this present.[5] Is't not well done?

195 VIOLA. Excellently done, if god did all.[6]

OLIVIA. 'Tis in grain,[7] sir, 'twill endure wind and weather.

VIOLA. 'Tis beauty truly blent,° whose red and white   blended
Nature's own sweet and cunning hand laid on.
Lady, you are the cruel'st she alive

200 If you will lead these graces to the grave,
And leave the world no copy.[8]

OLIVIA. O sir, I will not be so hard-hearted. I will give out divers schedules[9] of my beauty. It shall be inventoried, and every particle and utensil labeled to my will:[10] as, item,[11] [*indicating*] two lips,

205 indifferent[12] red; item, two grey eyes, with lids to them; item, one neck; one chin; and so forth. Were you sent hither to praise[13] me?

VIOLA. I see you what you are, you are too proud;
But if you were the devil,[14] you are fair.
My lord and master loves you. O, such love

---

1 I.e., catechetical style (being adopted by Olivia, as earlier by the Clown; see p. 99, note 11).

2 I.e., first chapter.

3 Straying from your script.

4 Unveil.

5 Just now, today.

6 I.e., if nature has not been assisted by cosmetics.

7 Fast dyed, indelible.

8 I.e., a child (though in her reply, Olivia twists the meaning to "list, inventory").

9 Various lists.

10 Every small portion and part of my body will be listed and attached as a codicil to my will (quibbling on Viola's "leave" as "bequeath").

11 Also (a Latin term, used to introduce each new entry in a formal list or inventory).

12 Moderately.

13 Appraise (for an inventory).

14 Lucifer was beautiful, but fell from heaven through being "proud."

Could be but recompensed,[1] though you were crowned   210
   The nonpareil° of beauty.   *unmatchable person*
OLIVIA.   How does he love me?[2]
VIOLA. With adorations, fertile° tears,[3]   *abundant*
   With groans that thunder love, with sighs of fire.
OLIVIA. Your lord does know my mind, I cannot love him.
   Yet I suppose him virtuous, know him noble,   215
   Of great estate, of fresh and stainless youth;
   In voices well divulged,[4] free,[5] learn'd, and valiant,
   And in dimension, and the shape of nature,°   *physically*
   A gracious° person. But yet I cannot love him.   *graceful*
   He might have took his answer long ago.   220
VIOLA. If I did love you in my master's flame,[6]
   With such a suff'ring, such a deadly° life,   *deathly*
   In your denial I would find no sense;
   I would not understand it.
OLIVIA.   Why, what would you?
VIOLA. Make me a willow[7] cabin at your gate,   225
   And call upon my soul° within the house;   *i.e., Olivia*
   Write loyal cantos° of contemnèd love,   *songs*
   And sing them loud even in the dead of night;
   Hallow[8] your name to the reverberate° hills,   *reverberating*
   And make the babbling gossip° of the air   *the nymph Echo*   230
   Cry out "Olivia!" O you should not rest
   Between the elements of air and earth,
   But you should pity me.
OLIVIA.   You might do much!
   What is your parentage?
VIOLA. Above my fortunes, yet my state° is well: *status, rank*   235
   I am a gentleman.

---

1   Could be no more than requited (even if ...).
2   Olivia's more serious interest in what Viola says is signaled here by her completing the blank verse line, and then continuing in verse.
3   The short (four beat) line may suggest a pause in the middle or at the end.
4   Well spoken of (or possibly "well spoken of as: ...").
5   Generous, magnanimous.
6   With Orsino's burning passion.
7   Associated with rejected love.
8   Halloo, shout.

OLIVIA.   Get you to your lord.
I cannot love him. Let him send no more,
Unless, perchance, you come to me again,
To tell me how he takes it. Fare you well.
240   [*Offering a purse*] I thank you for your pains. Spend this for me.
VIOLA. I am no fee'd post,[1] lady; keep your purse.
My master, not myself, lacks recompense.
Love[2] make his heart of flint, that you shall love,
And let your fervor, like my master's, be
245   Placed in contempt. Farewell, fair cruelty.
                                                        Exit.

OLIVIA. "What is your parentage?"
"Above my fortunes, yet my state is well:
I am a gentleman." I'll be sworn thou[3] art!
Thy tongue, thy face, thy limbs, actions, and spirit,
250   Do give thee five-fold blazon.[4] Not too fast! Soft, soft![5]
Unless the master were the man.[6] How now!
Even so quickly may one catch the plague?
Methinks I feel this youth's perfections
With an invisible and subtle stealth
255   To creep in at mine eyes. Well, let it be.
[*Calling*] What ho, Malvolio!

Enter Malvolio.
MALVOLIO.   Here, madam, at your service.
OLIVIA. Run after that same peevish° messenger,   *perverse, obstinate*
The county's[7] man. He left this ring[8] behind him,
    [*Having secretly taken a ring from her finger, she gives it to Malvolio.*]
Would I° or not. Tell him I'll none of it.   *whether I wanted it*
260   Desire him not to flatter with° his lord,   *encourage*
Nor hold him up with hopes; I am not for him.

---

1   Messenger requiring a tip.
2   May the god of love (Cupid) ...
3   Olivia shifts to the more intimate singular form of address.
4   Coat of arms (indicating a gentleman).
5   Take it slowly!
6   Unless Orsino were (like) his servant Cesario.
7   Count's (Orsino's).
8   Since Viola left no ring, Olivia must quickly provide one.

If that the youth will come this way tomorrow,
I'll give him reasons for't. Hie thee,° Malvolio.   *hasten*
MALVOLIO. Madam, I will.

                                            Exit.

OLIVIA. [*To the audience*] I do I know not what, and fear to find   265
Mine eye too great a flatterer for my mind.¹
Fate, show thy force, ourselves we do not owe;°   *own*
What is decreed must be; and be this so.²

                                            [*Exit.*]

[2.1]

*Enter Antonio³ and Sebastian.*⁴

ANTONIO. Will you stay⁵ no longer? Nor will you not⁶ that I go with
you?
SEBASTIAN. By your patience,⁷ no. My stars shine darkly⁸ over me.
The malignancy⁹ of my fate might perhaps distemper¹⁰ yours;
therefore I shall crave of you your leave that I may bear my evils¹¹   5
alone. It were a bad recompense for your love to lay any of them
on you.
ANTONIO. Let me yet know of you whither you are bound.

---

1 That my eye will over-praise (Cesario) and my reason be persuaded too easily
(of his worth).
2 Like Viola at 1.2.61 (TLN 112), Olivia expresses an openness to events. The
rhyming couplets, as at the end of many scenes, emphasize the completion of a
movement of the play.
3 Antonio's profession, as with the Captain who rescued Viola, will be evident
from his costume, probably including the "sea-cap" he later discards (3.4.295,
TLN 1847, and extended note).
4 Sebastian will be instantly identifiable because his clothes (and in some
productions, physical appearance and hair) are identical to Viola's (see 3.4.348–53,
TLN 1900–05, and note).
5 As we learn later (5.1.69–89, TLN 2228–49), Antonio has rescued Sebastian and
looked after him.
6 Do you not wish.
7 If you will be so indulgent.
8 Ominously.
9 Evil influence.
10 Infect.
11 Misfortunes.

SEBASTIAN. No, sooth,[1] sir. My determinate voyage is mere extrava-
10 gancy.[2] But I perceive in you so excellent a touch of modesty that
you will not extort from me what I am willing to keep in; therefore it charges me in manners the rather to express myself.[3] You
must know of me then, Antonio, my name is Sebastian (which
I called Roderigo). My father was that Sebastian of Messaline[4]
15 whom I know you have heard of. He left behind him myself and
a sister, both born in an hour.[5] If the heavens had been pleased,
would we had so ended! But you, sir, altered that, for some hour
before you took me from the breach[6] of the sea was my sister
drowned.
20 ANTONIO. Alas the day!
SEBASTIAN. A lady, sir, though it was said she much resembled me,
was yet of many accounted beautiful. But though I could not with
such estimable wonder[7] overfar believe that, yet thus far I will
boldly publish[8] her: she bore a mind that envy could not but call
25 fair. [*Weeping*] She is drowned already, sir, with salt water, though
I seem to drown her remembrance again with more.
ANTONIO. Pardon me, sir, your bad entertainment.[9]
SEBASTIAN. O good Antonio, forgive me your trouble.[10]
ANTONIO. If you will not murder me for my love, let me be your
30 servant.[11]
SEBASTIAN. If you will not undo what you have done—that is, kill[12]
him whom you have recovered[13]—desire it not. Fare ye well at

---

1   (in) truth, really.
2   My travel plan is just to wander.
3   I observe in you so much politeness that you will not try to force from me what
I wish to keep hidden; therefore good manners require me the more to reveal who
I am.
4   Evidently a personage of high standing, whose children can eventually marry a
duke and a countess (see 5.1.254, TLN 2430, "right noble is his blood"). Messaline
is geographically unknown; possibly Marseilles, Messina, or Mytilene.
5   I.e., they are twins.
6   Breaking waves, surf.
7   Admiring judgment.
8   Proclaim.
9   Poor hospitality.
10 The inconvenience I have put you to.
11 The social gulf between them is fully established; see p. 109, note 3.
12 Intensity of feeling becomes elaborate courtesy as each claims he will die unless
he can be of service to the other.
13 Rescued, restored to life.

once; my bosom is full of kindness, and I am yet so near the manners of my mother[1] that upon the least occasion more mine eyes will tell tales[2] of me. I am bound to the Count Orsino's court; 35 farewell.

Exit.

ANTONIO. The gentleness of all the gods go with thee!
I have many enemies in Orsino's court,
Else would I very shortly see thee there.
But come what may, I do adore thee so   40
That danger shall seem sport, and I will go.

Exit [following Sebastian].

[2.2]

Enter Viola [as Cesario] and Malvolio [with the ring], at several[3] doors.
MALVOLIO. Were not you even now with the Countess Olivia?
VIOLA. Even now, sir; on a moderate pace, I have since arrived but hither.
MALVOLIO. She returns this ring to you, sir. You might have saved me my pains to have taken it away yourself. She adds, moreover, 5 that you should put your lord into a desperate assurance[4] she will none of[5] him. And one thing more: that you be never so hardy[6] to come again in his affairs, unless it be to report your lord's taking of this. [*Offering the ring*] Receive it so.
VIOLA. She took the ring[7] of me; I'll none of it.   10
MALVOLIO. Come, sir, you peevishly threw it[8] to her; and her will is, it should be so returned. [*Throwing the ring down*] If it be worth stooping for, there it lies, in your eye;[9] if not, be it his that finds it.

Exit.

---

1   Womanly readiness to cry.
2   Betray (by crying, again).
3   Separate (two different stage doors).
4   Certainty beyond hope.
5   Have nothing to do with.
6   Bold.
7   Viola quick-wittedly covers for Olivia.
8   This is embroidery; Malvolio's capacity for fancy will be his undoing.
9   View, sight.

VIOLA. [*To the audience, picking up the ring*] I left no ring with her.
    What means this lady?
15   Fortune forbid my outside° have not charmed[1] her!   *appearance*
    She made good view of me; indeed so much
    That methought her eyes had lost her tongue,
    For she did speak in starts distractedly.[2]
    She loves me, sure; the cunning° of her passion   *craftiness*
20   Invites me in° this churlish messenger.   *solicits me by means of*
    None of my lord's ring? Why, he sent her none;
    I am the man!° If it be so, as 'tis,   *i.e., whom she loves*
    Poor lady, she were better love a dream.
    Disguise, I see thou art a wickedness,
25   Wherein the pregnant enemy° does much.   *inventive Satan*
    How easy is it for the proper false[3]
    In women's waxen hearts to set their forms.[4]
    Alas, our frailty is the cause, not we,
    For such as we are made of, such we be.[5]
30   How will this fadge?° My master loves her dearly,   *turn out*
    And I, poor monster,[6] fond° as much on him,   *dote*
    And she, mistaken, seems to dote on me.
    What will become of this? As I am man,
    My state is desperate for my master's love;
35   As I am woman—now alas the day—
    What thriftless° sighs shall poor Olivia breathe?   *unprofitable*
    O time, thou must untangle this, not I,
    It is too hard a knot for me t'untie.

                                                        [*Exit.*]

---

1   Enchanted (see 3.1.102, TLN 1325).
2   I.e., looking at Viola distracted her from coherent speech.
3   Handsome deceivers (men, or in this case, Viola).
4   To impress their (handsome) images into women's receptive affections (as a seal imprints soft wax).
5   Since women are made of weak material, it is not our fault we are weak.
6   Because both a man and a woman, as she then explains.

[2.3]

Enter Sir Toby and Sir Andrew.

SIR TOBY. Approach, Sir Andrew. Not to be abed after midnight, is to be up betimes; and *diluculo surgere*,[1] thou know'st.

SIR ANDREW. Nay, by my troth, I know not; but I know to be up late is to be up late.

SIR TOBY. A false conclusion.[2] I hate it as an unfilled can.[3] To be up   5 after midnight, and to go to bed then, is early; so that to go to bed after midnight, is to go to bed betimes. Does not our lives consist of the four elements?[4]

SIR ANDREW. Faith, so they say, but I think it rather consists of eating and drinking.   10

SIR TOBY. Th'art a scholar; let us therefore eat and drink. [*Calling*] Marian,[5] I say, a stoup[6] of wine!

Enter Clown.

SIR ANDREW. Here comes the fool, i'faith.

CLOWN. How now, my hearts! Did you never see the picture of "We Three"?   15

SIR TOBY. Welcome, ass. Now let's have a catch.[7]

SIR ANDREW. By my troth, the fool has an excellent breast.[8] I had rather than forty shillings[9] I had such a leg,[10] and so sweet a breath to sing, as the fool has. In sooth, thou wast in very gracious fooling last night, when thou spok'st of Pigrogromitus, of the Vapians   20

---

1   "T'arise betimes in the morning" (is the most wholesome thing in the world). So says William Lily's Latin grammar, known to every Elizabethan schoolboy (except Sir Andrew, as his reply indicates). Sir Toby probably carries a candle.
2   Faulty logic.
3   Empty drinking vessel.
4   I.e., fire, air, water, earth, thought to be the basic components of all matter, including the human body ("our lives").
5   A diminutive form of Mary or Maria.
6   A large tankard, usually about a quart (approximately one liter).
7   Round—a popular song with successive overlapping of parts.
8   Singing voice.
9   Two pounds sterling.
10   Although this could simply refer to the Clown's well-turned leg, more likely it indicates that he dances (with "leg" a metonym for dancing) as well as sings, or possibly that he bows ("makes a leg") before or after his songs.

"We three" is a picture or an inn sign showing two fools or asses. The riddling caption can only be solved by the observer admitting to being the third. The Clown thus identifies the knights as fools like him, and Sir Toby responds in kind with "Welcome, ass." Robert Armin, the Clown in Shakespeare's company, played Feste, a "fool natural" (i.e., someone mentally subnormal from birth; see extended note, p. 97) who is a jester or "allowed fool." The traditional fool's costume is motley: parti-colored garments in contrasting colors, probably gaskins (breeches; see p. 98, note 3) and doublet or short coat. The coat was often of extravagant cut (sometimes with four sleeves), usually with bells at the elbows. The most instantly recognizable feature was the fool's cap. This originated in the medieval cowl or hood (see 1.5.46–47, TLN 347–48: "*cucullus non facit monachum*"), to which were added ass's ears (often with bells at the end) or a representation of a cock's head. Sometimes both features were found together, and sometimes the cock's head was reduced to just the comb (hence "coxcomb" for a fool), or simply to a conical hat with a bell on the end. Armin may have carried a bauble, which might be a bladder on a stick (a comic club, like a child's balloon now), or a truncheon, slap-stick, wooden dagger or the like, or a "*marotte*." The marotte was a short stick with a carved image of the fool's head, complete with fool's cap, on it, allowing a fool to carry on a mock dialogue with himself as represented by the marotte. His arrival will almost certainly be accompanied by the jin-gling of bells on his costume and hat. Many of these features, including a marotte, can be seen in the painting "We Three" below.

"We Three Loggerheads," showing two court jesters (probably Tom Derry and either Archie Armstrong or Muckle John) from an early seventeenth-century oil on board painting, by permission of the Shakespeare Birthplace Trust. A color reproduction may be seen on the ISE website (<http://internetshakespeare. uvic.ca>).

passing the equinoctial of Queubus.[1] 'Twas very good, i'faith. I
sent thee sixpence[2] for thy leman[3]—hadst it?

CLOWN. I did impeticos[4] thy gratillity:[5] for Malvolio's nose is no
whipstock,[6] my lady[7] has a white hand, and the Myrmidons[8] are
no bottle-ale houses.[9]   25

SIR ANDREW. Excellent! Why, this is the best fooling, when all is
done. Now a song!

SIR TOBY. [To Clown, giving money] Come on, there is sixpence for
you. Let's have a song.

SIR ANDREW. [Giving sixpence] There's a testril[10] of me too. If one   30
knight give a—

CLOWN. Would you have a love song, or a song of good life?[11]

SIR TOBY. A love song, a love song.

SIR ANDREW. Ay, ay. I care not for good life.

                                                    Clown sings.

CLOWN.

O mistress mine, where are you roaming?   35
O stay and hear, your true love's coming,
    That can sing both high and low.
Trip° no further, pretty sweeting,   *tread nimbly*
Journeys end in lovers meeting,
    Every wise man's son[12] doth know.   40

SIR ANDREW. Excellent good, i'faith.

SIR TOBY. Good, good.

---

1 Probably invented mock-astronomy; cf. 1.5.30, TLN 329. ("Queubus" is pronounced "cue-bus.")
2 A small silver coin worth half a shilling, commonly used as a tip.
3 Sweetheart, lover.
4 A burlesque word, like much of the nonsense that follows. It suggests
pocketing the money in a petticoat, a joke perhaps on the Clown's wide gaskins
(see 1.5.21, TLN 319).
5 Another burlesque word, suggesting "little gratuity."
6 Handle of a whip.
7 Olivia (not his "leman").
8 The personal troops of the Homeric warrior Achilles.
9 Perhaps (1) low taverns selling mere bottled ale, or (2) establishments selling
bottled ale for consumption at the theater or elsewhere.
10 Sixpence.
11 Probably "a drinking song," but Sir Andrew misunderstands as a moral song or
hymn.
12 I.e., fool ("a wise man commonly has foolish children"; proverbial).

CLOWN.

What is love? 'Tis not hereafter,
Present[1] mirth hath present laughter;
45   What's to come is still° unsure.   *always*
In delay there lies no plenty,
Then come kiss me, sweet and twenty;[2]
Youth's a stuff will not endure.

SIR ANDREW. A mellifluous voice, as I am true knight.

50 SIR TOBY. A contagious° breath.   *infectious, noxious*

SIR ANDREW. Very sweet and contagious, i'faith.

SIR TOBY. To hear by the nose, it is dulcet in contagion. But shall
we make the welkin[3] dance indeed? Shall we rouse the night-owl
in a catch that will draw three souls out of one weaver?[4] Shall we
55   do that?

SIR ANDREW. An you love me, let's do't! I am dog at[5] a catch.

CLOWN. By'r lady, sir, and some dogs will catch well.

SIR ANDREW. Most certain. Let our catch be "Thou Knave."[6]

CLOWN. "Hold thy peace, thou knave," knight? I shall be constrained[7]
60   in't to call thee knave, knight.

SIR ANDREW. 'Tis not the first time I have constrained one to call
me knave. Begin, fool. It begins, [*Singing*] "Hold thy peace."

CLOWN. I shall never begin if I hold my peace.[8]

SIR ANDREW. Good, i'faith! Come, begin.

                                                    Catch sung.[9]

---

1   Immediate (in occurrence and effect).

2   Dear one, twenty times dear (or possibly "you darling twenty-year-old"; cf.
modern "sweet sixteen").

3   Sky, heavens (cf. 3.1.51, TLN 1269).

4   Music was said to "hale souls out of men's bodies" (*Much Ado About Nothing*
2.3.58–59, TLN 894–96) with ecstasy, but to draw three souls from one man would
be a triumph. Weavers were known for singing as they worked, but Calvinist
psalms rather than catches (rounds in which each successive singer has to take up
or "catch" his part in time).

5   Good at (proverbial).

6   Each of the three singers in turn tells another to be silent ("hold thy peace"),
and calls him a knave.

7   Forced.

8   In a recent New Zealand production, the Clown remained silent until Sir
Andrew finally got the joke.

9   In performance, the singing is likely to be rowdy ("caterwauling," line 65, TLN
771), and may include much stage business. Some effort may be required from
Maria to make herself noticed or heard when she enters.

Enter Maria[1] [interrupting the song].

MARIA. What a caterwauling do you keep here! If my lady have   65
not called up her steward Malvolio, and bid him turn you out of
doors, never trust me.

SIR TOBY. My lady's a Cathayan,[2] we are politicians,[3] Malvolio's
a Peg-a-Ramsay,[4] and [*Singing*] "Three merry men[5] be we"! Am
not I consanguineous?[6] Am I not of her blood? Tilly-vally,[7] lady!   70
[*Singing*] "There dwelt a man in Babylon, lady, lady"![8]

CLOWN. Beshrew me,[9] the knight's in admirable fooling.

SIR ANDREW. Ay, he does well enough if he be disposed, and so do
I too.[10] He does it with a better grace, but I do it more natural.[11]

SIR TOBY. [*Singing*] "O'the twelfth day of December—"[12]   75

MARIA. For the love o'god, peace!

Enter Malvolio.[13]

MALVOLIO. My masters, are you mad! Or what are you? Have you
no wit, manners, nor honesty,[14] but to gabble like tinkers[15] at this
time of night? Do ye make an alehouse of my lady's house, that
ye squeak out your coziers' catches[16] without any mitigation or   80

---

1   She probably carries a candle, and may well appear "as from bed," i.e., in her
shift.
2   A person from China (Cathay).
3   Amoral intriguers.
4   A popular tune, and probably a ribald reference to the Peggy of the title. The
meanings of the terms in this speech are much debated. All three are generally
pejorative at this time, so the intention may be to reject Maria's criticism by
inflating it to a ludicrous degree ("Olivia is a foreign barbarian, we are dangerous
intriguers, and Malvolio is the naughty woman of a popular song").
5   The final phrase of what was evidently a very popular song.
6   Of her blood; kin.
7   Expression of contempt; "fiddle-faddle."
8   The opening line and refrain of a popular song, here chosen by Sir Toby for the
reiteration of "Lady." See A Note on Music and Songs, pp. 70–71.
9   Curse me (a mild oath).
10   The first of many comic/pathetic "me too"-isms.
11   (1) Naturally, (2, unintended by Sir Andrew) like a "natural" or idiot (cf. 1.3.24,
TLN 145).
12   No music has been certainly identified for this.
13   He probably carries a candle (see p. 113, note 1; and note 1 above).
14   Common sense, good manners, nor decency.
15   Often vagrants, with a reputation for drunken singing.
16   Cobblers' rounds. Cf. "tinkers" (2.3.78, TLN 787) and "weaver" (2.3.54,
TLN 759).

remorse[1] of voice? Is there no respect of place, persons, nor time in you?

SIR TOBY. We did keep time, sir, in our catches. Sneck up![2]

MALVOLIO. Sir Toby, I must be round[3] with you. My lady bade
85   me tell you that, though she harbors[4] you as her kinsman, she's nothing allied[5] to your disorders. If you can separate yourself and your misdemeanors, you are welcome to the house. If not, an it would please you to take leave of her, she is very willing to bid you farewell.

90 SIR TOBY. [Singing, to Maria] "Farewell, dear heart, since I must needs be gone."[6]

MARIA. Nay, good Sir Toby.

CLOWN. [Singing] "His eyes do show his days are almost done."

MALVOLIO. Is't even so?

95 SIR TOBY. [Singing] "But I will never die."

CLOWN. [Singing] "Sir Toby, there you lie."[7]

MALVOLIO. This is much credit to you.

SIR TOBY. [Singing, indicating Malvolio] "Shall I bid him go?"

CLOWN. [Singing] "What an[8] if you do?"

100 SIR TOBY. [Singing] "Shall I bid him go, and spare not?"

CLOWN. [Singing] "O no, no, no, no, you dare not!"

SIR TOBY. [To Malvolio] Out o'tune,[9] sir? Ye lie! Art any more than a steward? Dost thou think because thou art virtuous there shall be no more cakes and ale?[10]

---

1   Considerate lowering (of volume).
2   Go hang (yourself).
3   Plain-spoken, blunt.
4   Provides lodging for.
5   In no way related, not kin.
6   Sir Toby and the Clown improvise on a popular song to make its words apply to the situation with Malvolio. See A Note on Music and Songs, pp. 70–71.
7   In some productions Sir Toby lies on the stage in mock death, in addition to telling an untruth about being immortal, but there is a danger of breaking the musical rhythm of the exchange.
8   A metrical filler, anticipating and emphasizing "if."
9   (1) Musically off pitch, (2) out of order or harmony.
10 Traditional at church festivals, disapproved of by Puritans.

CLOWN. Yes, by Saint Anne,[1] and ginger[2] shall be hot i'th'mouth too. 105
SIR TOBY. Th'art i'th'right. [To Malvolio] Go, sir, rub your chain with
    crumbs.[3] A stoup of wine,[4] Maria!
MALVOLIO. Mistress Mary, if you prized my lady's favor at anything
    more than contempt, you would not give means[5] for this uncivil
    rule.[6] She shall know of it, by this hand. 110

    Exit.

MARIA. Go shake your ears![7]
SIR ANDREW. 'Twere as good a deed as to drink when a man's
    a-hungry,[8] to challenge him the field, and then to break promise
    with him, and make a fool[9] of him.
SIR TOBY. Do't, knight. I'll write thee a challenge; or I'll deliver thy 115
    indignation to him by word of mouth.
MARIA. Sweet Sir Toby, be patient for tonight. Since the youth of
    the count's was today with my lady, she is much out of quiet. For
    Monsieur[10] Malvolio, let me alone with him. If I do not gull[11] him
    into a nayword,[12] and make him a common recreation,[13] do not 120
    think I have wit enough to lie straight in my bed. I know I can
    do it.
SIR TOBY. Possess us,[14] possess us, tell us something of him.
MARIA. Marry, sir, sometimes he is a kind of Puritan.[15]

---

1 Mother of the Virgin Mary; because she is not a biblical figure, this oath was
particularly repugnant to puritans.
2 Used to spice ale, but also regarded as an aphrodisiac.
3 I.e., polish your steward's insignia (which Malvolio may be wearing). He is
being reminded of his subordinate position.
4 Sir Toby not only defies Malvolio, but puts Maria on the spot; stage business
sometimes makes clear her choice.
5 I.e., wine.
6 Disorderly conduct.
7 A contemptuous dismissal, proverbially implying someone is an ass. The line is
usually directed at Malvolio's just-departed back, since Maria (in her next speech)
wishes the others to be "patient for tonight."
8 This addition makes nonsense of the proverbial "as good a deed as to drink."
9 By challenging Malvolio to a duel, then dishonorably failing to show up, Sir
Andrew would in fact be the "fool."
10 A mocking use of the French form of address, here equivalent to "his high and
mightiness."
11 Trick.
12 Byword (for foolishness).
13 Source of general amusement.
14 Put us in possession (of your scheme).
15 An extreme Protestant, morally strict; see Appendix G, p. 279.

125 SIR ANDREW. Oh, if I thought that, I'd beat him like a dog!
SIR TOBY. What, for being a Puritan? Thy exquisite[1] reason, dear
knight?
SIR ANDREW. I have no exquisite reason for't, but I have reason
good enough.
130 MARIA. The devil a Puritan that he is, or anything constantly[2] but a
time-pleaser,[3] an affectioned[4] ass, that cons[5] state[6] without book,
and utters it by great swaths.[7] The best persuaded[8] of himself, so
crammed, as he thinks, with excellencies, that it is his grounds[9]
of faith that all that look on him love him; and on that vice in him
135 will my revenge find notable cause to work.
SIR TOBY. What wilt thou do?
MARIA. I will drop in his way some obscure epistles of love, wherein
by the color of his beard, the shape of his leg, the manner of his
gait, the expressure[10] of his eye, forehead, and complexion, he
140 shall find himself most feelingly personated.[11] I can write very like
my lady your niece; on a forgotten matter we can hardly make
distinction of our hands.[12]
SIR TOBY. Excellent, I smell a device.[13]
SIR ANDREW. I have't in my nose too.
145 SIR TOBY. He shall think by the letters that thou wilt drop that they
come from my niece, and that she's in love with him.
MARIA. My purpose is indeed a horse of that color.
SIR ANDREW. And your horse now would make him an ass.
MARIA. Ass,[14] I doubt not.

---

1 Ingeniously devised.
2 Consistently.
3 Time-server.
4 Affected.
5 Learns by heart ("without book").
6 Matter appropriate to high rank.
7 The wide sweeps covered by the swing of the scythe.
8 Having the highest opinion.
9 Foundation (of all that he believes in).
10 Expression.
11 Justly or vividly described.
12 When we no longer remember which of us wrote something, it is almost impossible to tell by the handwriting.
13 Sense a stratagem.
14 Maria repeats the punch line of this rare example of Sir Andrew's wit so that she can address him as "Ass," or for a pun on "As."

SIR ANDREW. Oh, 'twill be admirable! 150

MARIA. Sport royal, I warrant you. I know my physic[1] will work with him. I will plant you two, and let the fool make a third,[2] where he shall find the letter. Observe his construction[3] of it. For this night, to bed,[4] and dream on the event.[5] Farewell.

Exit.

SIR TOBY. Good night, Penthesilea![6] 155

SIR ANDREW. Before me,[7] she's a good wench.

SIR TOBY. She's a beagle[8] true bred, and one that adores me. What o'that?

SIR ANDREW. I was adored once,[9] too.

SIR TOBY. Let's to bed, knight. Thou hadst need send for more 160 money.

SIR ANDREW. If I cannot recover[10] your niece, I am a foul way out.[11]

SIR TOBY. Send for money, knight. If thou hast her not i'th'end, call me cut.[12]

SIR ANDREW. If I do not, never trust me, take it how you will.[13] 165

SIR TOBY. Come, come, I'll go burn some sack;[14] 'tis too late to go to bed now. Come, knight, come, knight.

Exeunt.

---

1 Medicine (to purge Malvolio of conceit).

2 It is not clear whether the Clown is still present (he might have exited earlier in the scene), nor why he is, in 2.5, replaced by Fabian.

3 Construing, interpretation.

4 Maria's prime purpose is to stop them partying (in the Armfield film she takes their gin bottle away).

5 Outcome.

6 Queen of the warrior Amazon women (joking again about Maria's small stature).

7 A mild oath that substitutes "me" for "god."

8 A small breed of hound (perhaps loyal, perhaps "on the scent" of Malvolio).

9 This unexpected glimpse of Sir Andrew's unlikely past is usually both comic and, after a pause, poignant. Alternatively, it may be another "me-too"-ism, even resentful.

10 Obtain (and thereby retrieve expenses).

11 Either (1) grievously out of pocket, or (2) lost in my purpose.

12 Proverbial abuse: a "cut" is a curtal, a horse with its tail docked (cut short). Possibly also a cut (gelded) horse.

13 A typically confused complication by Sir Andrew; this defiance makes no sense when Sir Toby has already given permission.

14 Mull some wine.

[2.4]

Enter Orsino, Viola [as Cesario], Curio, and others.

ORSINO. [*To the Musicians*] Give me some music. [*To the Courtiers*]
   Now good morrow, friends;
   Now, good Cesario—but that piece of song,[1]
   That old and antique[2] song we heard last night;
5   Methought it did relieve my passion much,
   More than light airs and recollected terms[3]
   Of these most brisk and giddy-pacèd times.
   Come, but one verse.
CURIO. He is not here, so please your lordship, that
10   should sing it.
ORSINO. Who was it?
CURIO. Feste[4] the jester, my lord, a fool that the Lady Olivia's father
   took much delight in. He is about the house.
ORSINO. Seek him out, and [*To the Musicians*] play the tune the
   while.

   [*Exit Curio.*]
   Music plays.[5]

15   Come hither,[6] boy. If ever thou shalt love,
   In the sweet pangs of it, remember me.
   For such as I am, all true lovers are:
   Unstaid and skittish in all motions° else,   impulses, emotions
   Save in the constant image of the creature
20   That is beloved. How dost thou like this tune?
VIOLA. It gives a very echo to the seat

---

1   Orsino apparently commands music, greets his attendant lords, Cesario particularly, then returns his attention to the musicians. He is not asking Cesario to
sing.
2   Old, quaint (at the time pronounced and often spelled "antic").
3   Frivolous tunes and artificial phrases. Instead Orsino wants an "antique" folk
song, "old and plain" as he says at line 43 (TLN 932).
4   The only mention of the Clown's name.
5   There is no SD for the music to stop, although there is a renewed direction for
the musicians to play at line 50 (TLN 939) Clearly a production decision is needed.
6   As at 1.3.11 (TLN 261), Viola's special attraction for Orsino is emphasized by
their spatial separation from the other courtiers.

Where love is throned.[1]

ORSINO.   Thou dost speak masterly;
My life upon't, young though thou art, thine eye
Hath stayed upon some favor° that it loves.   *face*
Hath it not, boy?

VIOLA.   A little, by your favor.[2]   25

ORSINO. What kind of woman is't?

VIOLA.   Of your complexion.[3]

ORSINO. She is not worth thee then. What years, i'faith?

VIOLA. About your years, my lord.

ORSINO. Too old, by heaven! Let still the woman take
An elder than her self; so wears she[4] to him,   30
So sways she level° in her husband's heart.   *she adjusts to (him)*
For, boy, however we do praise ourselves,
Our fancies[5] are more giddy and unfirm,
More longing, wavering, sooner lost and worn,°   *worn out*
Than women's are.

VIOLA.   I think it well,[6] my lord.   35

ORSINO. Then let thy love be younger than thyself,
Or thy affection cannot hold the bent;[7]
For women are as roses, whose fair flower[8]
Being[9] once displayed,[10] doth fall that very hour.

VIOLA. And so they are. Alas, that they are so: 40
To die, even[11] when they to perfection grow.

Enter Curio and Clown.

---

1 Returns an exact reflection (to the heart, "the seat / Where love is throned");
cf. 1.1.36–37 (TLN 43–44).
2 If you please (with the hidden sense of "like your face").
3 (1) Coloring, (2) temperament.
4 She adapts (like clothes to the wearer).
5 Affections (cf. 1.1.14–15, TLN 18–19).
6 The irony of her agreement will be understood by both Viola and the audience.
7 Maintain its intensity (a metaphor from archery of a bow retaining its
springiness).
8 Elided to one syllable for the meter, and to rhyme with "hour."
9 Elided to one syllable for the meter.
10 (1) Unfolded, (2) open to view.
11 Just. Again the audience knows, with Viola, that her response to Orsino is rich
in irony.

ORSINO. Oh, fellow, come, the song we had last night.
    Mark it, Cesario, it is old and plain;
    The spinsters[1] and the knitters in the sun,
45   And the free[2] maids that weave their thread with bones,[3]
    Do use[4] to chant it. It is silly sooth,°   *simple truth*
    And dallies[5] with the innocence of love,
    Like the old age.[6]
CLOWN. Are you ready, sir?[7]
50 ORSINO. Ay,[8] prithee sing.   *Music.*[9]

The Song.[10]
CLOWN. [*Singing*]
    Come away, come away, death,
    And in sad cypress[11] let me be laid.
    Fie away,[12] fie away, breath,
    I am slain by a fair cruel maid.
55   My shroud of white, stuck all with yew,
      O prepare it.
      My part of death no one so true
      Did share it.[13]

    Not a flower,[14] not a flower sweet,

---

1 Spinners (nearly always female, whence the modern usage).

2 Innocent, unconstrained.

3 Make lace with bone bobbins.

4 Have the custom.

5 Speaks, plays (amorously).

6 I.e., golden age, olden times of ideal pastoral innocence and virtue.

7 In performance, the Clown sometimes asks this with heavy irony, thus lightly drawing attention to Orsino's intense involvement with Viola.

8 Since this is spelled "I" in Folio, it is possible that Orsino does not reply to the Clown, but simply says "I pray you to sing."

9 The stage direction implies the play's musicians, although in modern productions the Clown often accompanies himself.

10 Probably an old song, but no music survives; see A Note on Music and Songs, pp. 69–70.

11 I.e., coffin of cypress wood (associated, like "yew" three lines later, with mourning).

12 I.e., begone. Earlier editors often emended unnecessarily to "fly away."

13 No one as faithful (as I) has ever shared my allotted portion, death.

14 The meter requires elision to "flow'r" both times, as at 2.4.38, TLN 926.

On my black coffin let there be strewn.   60
Not a friend, not a friend greet
My poor corpse, where my bones shall be thrown.
   A thousand, thousand sighs to save,
   Lay me O where
   Sad true lover never find[1] my grave,   65
   To weep there.

ORSINO. [*Giving money*] There's for thy pains.
CLOWN. No pains, sir; I take pleasure in singing, sir.
ORSINO. I'll pay thy pleasure then.
CLOWN. Truly, sir, and pleasure will be paid,[2] one time or another.   70
ORSINO. Give me now leave to leave[3] thee.
CLOWN. Now the melancholy god[4] protect thee, and the tailor make
   thy doublet of changeable taffeta,[5] for thy mind is a very opal.[6] I
   would have men of such constancy put to sea, that their business
   might be everything, and their intent everywhere; for that's it that   75
   always makes a good voyage of nothing.[7] Farewell.

                                                                    Exit.

ORSINO. Let all the rest give place.
               [*All the Courtiers except Viola stand apart.*]
                                Once more, Cesario,
Get thee to yond same sovereign cruelty.
Tell her my love, more noble than the world,[8]
Prizes not quantity of dirty lands;   80
The parts° that Fortune hath bestowed upon her,   *possessions*
Tell her I hold as giddily[9] as Fortune;

---

1 I.e., will never find.
2 I.e., paid for with pain (proverbial).
3 A courteous and witty dismissal.
4 Saturn (the planet ruling those of a melancholy disposition).
5 Shot silk ("changeable")—like a lover—when viewed from different angles,
because the warp and woof are of different colors).
6 A semi-precious stone whose color changes with differences in light and angle
of view.
7 I.e., men of no fixed purpose should be seafaring merchants, so that either (1)
they will get some pleasure from wasting their time (cf. the proverb, "He that is
everywhere is nowhere"), or (2) by being all over the place, they can be opportunis-
tic and make a profit where none was expected.
8 Society (with worldly values).
9 Lightly (as the fickle goddess Fortune).

But 'tis that miracle and queen of gems[1]
That Nature pranks° her in, attracts my soul.   *adorns*

85 VIOLA. But if she cannot love you, sir?

ORSINO. I cannot[2] be so answered.

VIOLA.   Sooth, but you must.
Say that some lady, as perhaps there is,
Hath for your love as great a pang of heart
As you have for Olivia. You cannot love her.

90 You tell her so. Must she not then be answered?

ORSINO. There is no woman's sides
Can bide° the beating of so strong a passion   *endure, bear*
As love doth give my heart; no woman's heart
So big, to hold so much. They lack retention.[3]

95 Alas, their love may be called appetite,
No motion of the liver, but the palate,
That suffers surfeit, cloyment, and revolt;[4]
But mine is all as hungry as the sea,
And can digest as much. Make no compare

100 Between that love a woman can bear me,
And that I owe° Olivia.   *have for*

VIOLA.   Ay, but I know—[5]

ORSINO. What dost thou know?

VIOLA. Too well what love women to men may owe.
In faith, they are as true of heart as we.

105 My father had a daughter loved a man
As it might be perhaps, were I a woman,
I should your lordship.

ORSINO.   And what's her history?

VIOLA. A blank,[6] my lord. She never told° her love,   *i.e., told of*

---

1   Her beauty (or more generally, her being, which is an enduring gift of Nature rather than a temporary whim of Fortune).

2   Folio's "It cannot" (= your suit cannot) makes sense in Orsino's half-line, but matches neither "you must," nor "Must she not" in Viola's reply.

3   Power to retain (a physiological metaphor, as becomes clearer in the lines following).

4   Mere appetite, not a true emotion of the liver (one of the seats of love; see p. 79, note 2), just a greedy taste which is sated and sickened by excess.

5   It is a production decision whether Viola stops herself just in time, or is cut off by Orsino.

6   (1) A void, (2) a vacant space yet to be filled in (i.e., a "history" not yet complete).

But let concealment like a worm i'th'bud[1]
Feed on her damask cheek.[2] She pined in thought,   110
And with a green and yellow melancholy[3]
She sat like Patience on a monument,
Smiling at grief. Was not this love indeed?
We men may say more, swear more, but indeed
Our shows are more than will:[4] for still° we prove   *always*   115

---

1   The contraction preserves the meter.
2   She permitted secrecy, like an insect larva (cankerworm) in a rosebud, to eat
away at her healthy pink cheek. A "damask" is a pink and white rose.
3   Love sickness (specifically chlorosis, a form of anemia in teenage girls which
gives a greenish tinge to the skin, and was thought to result from love melancholy;
and pale or jaundiced skin).
4   Our displays are greater than our passions.

2.4.112:   PATIENCE ON
            A MONUMENT (TLN 1003)

Patience (*Patientia*) is one of the seven heavenly virtues in Christian
thinking, closely associated (and sometimes conflated or confused)
with Fortitude. Viola here personifies her, just as she appears in art and
emblem books; an elaborate iconography usually signals her emblematic role as suffering with great endurance ("smiling at grief"). The
"monument" is sometimes a squared plinth, sometimes simply a rock,
on which she sits or leans, and to which she is often chained. Sometimes
she bears a symbolic yoke of oppression on her shoulders, or thorns
under her bare feet. The difficulties facing her may be less specific, such
as the grotesquely deformed and frightening world surrounding her in
"Patience," created by the artist Pieter Breugel the Elder as part of his
sixteenth-century depiction of "The Seven Virtues." A more brutally
political and military set of horrors to be endured is depicted here
in Hans Collaert's engraving "The Spanish Fury," in which Catholic
Spanish troops in the Netherlands are sacking Antwerp. Patience sits
with great forbearance as slaughter and flames engulf her. She is, as
often in the iconography, holding a cross. In *Pericles*, the king says of
his long-lost daughter, "thou dost look / Like Patience smiling on kings'
graves, and smiling / Extremity out of act" (5.1.140–42).   *(continued)*

Much in our vows, but little in our love.

ORSINO. But died thy sister of her love, my boy?

VIOLA. I am all the daughters of my father's house,
And all the brothers too; and yet I know not—
Sir, shall I to this lady?

120 ORSINO.   Ay, that's the theme.
To her in haste; [*Giving a jewel*] give her this jewel;[1] say
My love can give no place,[2] bide no denay.[3]

                             Exeunt[, Viola a different way].

---

1   Probably a ring or pendant.

2   Cede no priority (to anyone or anything else).

3   Denial, refusal. The older spelling retains the rhyme for the final couplet of the scene.

Patience in Hans Collaert's engraving, "The Spanish Fury" (1577). From the Wikimedia Commons, <http://commons.wikimedia.org>. Images of Patience by Breughel and by Cesare Ripa may be seen at TLN 1003 on the ISE website (<http://internetshakespeare. uvic.ca>).

[2.5]

Enter Sir Toby, Sir Andrew, and Fabian.[1]

SIR TOBY. Come thy ways,[2] Signor Fabian.

FABIAN. Nay,[3] I'll come! If I lose a scruple[4] of this sport, let me be boiled to death with melancholy.[5]

SIR TOBY. Wouldst thou not be glad to have the niggardly[6] rascally sheep-biter[7] come by some notable shame? 5

FABIAN. I would exult, man! You know he brought me out o'favor with my lady, about a bear-baiting[8] here.

SIR TOBY. To anger him we'll have the bear again, and we will fool him black and blue[9]—shall we not, Sir Andrew?

SIR ANDREW. An we do not, it is pity of our lives.[10] 10

Enter Maria [with a letter].

SIR TOBY. Here comes the little villain![11] How now, my metal of India?[12]

MARIA. Get ye all three into the box-tree.[13] Malvolio's coming down this walk; he has been yonder i'the sun practicing behavior to his own shadow this half hour. Observe him, for the love of mock- 15
ery, for I know this letter will make a contemplative idiot of him.

---

1 Fabian replacing the Clown (cf. 2.3.152, TLN 864–865) is never explained.
2 Come along. Evidently Sir Toby enters before this new character.
3 An intensifier, like modern "don't worry."
4 Tiniest portion (literally, a very small unit of weight—20 grains—or of time).
5 A double joke, since (1) melancholy was a cold humor, and (2) "boil" was pronounced "bile," and black bile was thought to be the source of melancholy.
6 Mean, stingy.
7 Literally, a dog that savages sheep, but generally used of a malicious or sneaking fellow.
8 A sport particularly condemned by Puritans (cf. 2.3.124, TLN 833).
9 I.e., he will be bruised by their planned foolery.
10 We do not deserve to live.
11 Playful abuse, and another reference to Maria's small size.
12 (1) Gold, (2) mettle, spirit.
13 A small evergreen tree or shrub much used for ornamental garden hedges, and, in its dwarf variety, for borders. Although Elizabethan theater companies did have property trees for a few plays, and stage posts, this hedge may be imaginary in performance. See Introduction, pp. 28–29.

Close,[1] in the name of jesting! [*The men hide.*] Lie thou there; [*Placing the letter on the stage*] for here comes the trout that must be caught with tickling.[2]

Exit.

Enter Malvolio.

20 MALVOLIO. [*To the audience*] 'Tis but fortune,[3] all is fortune. Maria once told me she[4] did affect[5] me, and I have heard herself[6] come thus near, that should she fancy,[7] it should be one of my complexion.[8] Besides, she uses me with a more exalted respect than anyone else that follows her.[9] What should I think on't? [*He struts about the stage.*]

25 SIR TOBY. [*Aside to Sir Andrew and Fabian, and to the audience.*] Here's an overweening rogue![10]

FABIAN. [*Aside*] Oh, peace! Contemplation makes a rare turkey-cock[11] of him; how he jets[12] under his advanced[13] plumes!

SIR ANDREW. [*Aside*] 'Slight,[14] I could so beat the rogue!

30 SIR TOBY. [*Aside*] Peace, I say!

MALVOLIO. To be Count Malvolio!

SIR TOBY. [*Aside*] Ah, rogue!

SIR ANDREW. [*Aside*] Pistol[15] him, pistol him!

SIR TOBY. [*Aside*] Peace, peace!

---

1   An urgent command to keep close, hide. The hiding may be real, or stage convention; see p. 129, note 13.

2   Trout in shallow water can be caught by "tickling," i.e., gently stroking the belly until the fish can be hooked out by the gills with thumb and fingers. Hence a proverbial image of flattery and gulling.

3   Malvolio is indulging a fantasy of a higher life if Fortune were less fickle.

4   I.e., Olivia.

5   Feel fond of.

6   Olivia.

7   Fall in love (but see p. 77, note 1).

8   Coloring (as at 2.3.139 and 2.4.26, TLN 850 and 913).

9   Is in her service.

10 Neither this nor the subsequent interjections are heard by Malvolio, but this need not mean they are quiet; see Introduction, p. 18.

11 Proverbially vain.

12 Struts.

13 Raised, displayed.

14 By god's light (an oath).

15 Shoot (with a pistol).

MALVOLIO. There is example for't: the Lady of the Strachy married   35
the yeoman of the wardrobe.[1]

SIR ANDREW. [*Aside*] Fie on him, Jezebel![2]

FABIAN. [*Aside*] Oh, peace, now he's deeply in.[3] Look how imagination blows[4] him.

MALVOLIO. Having been three months married to her, sitting in my   40
state—[5]

SIR TOBY. [*Aside*] Oh, for a stone-bow[6] to hit him in the eye!

MALVOLIO. —calling my officers about me, in my branched[7] velvet
gown,[8] having come from a day-bed,[9] where I have left Olivia
sleeping—   45

SIR TOBY. [*Aside*] Fire and brimstone!

FABIAN. [*Aside*] Oh, peace, peace!

MALVOLIO. —and then to have the humor of state,[10] and after a
demure travel of regard[11]—telling them I know my place, as I
would they should do theirs—to ask for my kinsman Toby.[12]   50

SIR TOBY. [*Aside*] Bolts[13] and shackles!

FABIAN. [*Aside*] Oh, peace, peace, peace! [*Malvolio walks near the letter.*] Now, now![14]

---

1 A woman of birth married a social inferior (who looked after the clothes in a great household). Attempts to identify an historical lady called, or from, Strachy, and a specific yeoman, have not been persuasive.

2 A biblical example of shamelessness. Only Sir Andrew might fail to realize he is speaking of a woman, the wicked wife of King Ahab (2 Kings 9:30–37).

3 Absorbed.

4 Inflates, puffs up.

5 Throne (canopied with the cloth of state).

6 A crossbow modified to shoot small stones (rather than arrows).

7 Embroidered with foliage or flowers.

8 A dignified full length garment worn by a man of high social standing.

9 A bed for use during the day (in his fantasy, with Olivia).

10 Temperament of high rank.

11 Grave looking about (at all present).

12 Malvolio, imagining himself of higher rank, familiarly drops the "Sir" here and at line 57, TLN 1076.

13 Fetters (equivalent to "shackles").

14 Fabian presumably draws their attention to Malvolio approaching the letter; if so, his failure to see it will heighten their frustration.

MALVOLIO. Seven of my people, with an obedient start,[1] make out[2]
55   for him. I frown the while, and perchance wind up my watch,[3] or
play with my— [*Realizing he is playing with his steward's chain*] some
rich jewel. Toby approaches; curtsies[4] there to me—
SIR TOBY. [*Aside*] Shall this fellow live!
FABIAN. [*Aside*] Though our silence be drawn from us with cars,[5] yet
60   peace!
MALVOLIO. —I extend my hand to him, thus;[6] quenching my familiar[7] smile with an austere regard of control—[8]
SIR TOBY. [*Aside*] And does not Toby[9] take[10] you a blow o'the lips
then?
65 MALVOLIO. —saying, "Cousin Toby, my fortunes having cast me on
your niece give me this prerogative of speech—"
SIR TOBY. [*Aside*] What, what!
MALVOLIO. "—you must amend your drunkenness."
SIR TOBY. [*Aside*] Out, scab![11]
70 FABIAN. [*Aside*] Nay, patience, or we break the sinews of our plot!
MALVOLIO. "Besides, you waste the treasure of your time with a
foolish knight—"
SIR ANDREW. [*Aside*] That's me, I warrant you.
MALVOLIO. "—one Sir Andrew."
75 SIR ANDREW. [*Aside*] I knew 'twas I, for many do call me fool.
MALVOLIO. [*Seeing and then taking up the letter*] What employment[12]
have we here?

---

1 (1) Sudden display of energy, (2) rush.
2 Go forth.
3 Watches were large and usually richly ornamented, so Malvolio is no doubt
imagining an ostentatious display of winding it.
4 Bows low, makes a "courtesy."
5 Chariots (or carts) and horses. Cf. *The Two Gentlemen of Verona* 3.1.265–66, TLN
1333–34, "a team of horse shall not pluck that from me."
6 Probably lowering his hand to indicate that Sir Toby would have to kneel to
kiss it.
7 Friendly.
8 Commanding gaze.
9 Sir Toby mimics Malvolio's earlier familiarity (see above, p. 131, note 12).
10 Strike.
11 A common term of abuse.
12 Business.

FABIAN. [*Aside*] Now is the woodcock near the gin.[1]

SIR TOBY. [*Aside*] Oh, peace, and the spirit of humors intimate read-
ing aloud[2] to him.   80

MALVOLIO. [*To the audience, as he examines the outside of the letter*] By
my life, this is my lady's hand: these be her very C's, her U's, and
her T's,[3] and thus makes she her great P's.[4] It is, in contempt of
question,[5] her hand.

SIR ANDREW. [*Aside*] Her C's, her U's, and her T's—why that?[6]   85

MALVOLIO. [*Reading*] "To the unknown beloved, this, and my good
wishes." Her very phrases! [*Starting to break the seal*] By your leave,
wax.[7] [*Pausing*] Soft![8] And the impressure her Lucrece,[9] with
which she uses to seal.[10] 'Tis my lady! To whom should this be?
                    [*He breaks the seal and opens the letter.*]

FABIAN. [*Aside*] This wins him, liver and all.[11]   90

MALVOLIO. "Jove knows I love,

But who?

Lips, do not move,

No man must know."

"No man must know." What follows? The numbers[12] altered. "No   95
man must know." If this should be thee, Malvolio!

SIR TOBY. [*Aside*] Marry, hang thee, brock![13]

MALVOLIO. [*Reading*] "I may command, where I adore,

---

1   Snare, trap. Woodcocks were proverbially stupid birds, and therefore easy to
trap.

2   May the god of eccentricity suggest to him that he read aloud.

3   A bawdy pun on "cut" as vulva. Malvolio is likely to be mystified by the audience laughter.

4   (1) Capital P's, (2) copious urinations (pees from the "cut.")

5   Beyond doubt.

6   Sir Andrew's naivety extends the joke; in performance, one of the others sometimes whispers in his ear, and he looks shocked or intrigued.

7   I.e., sealing wax to hold the letter closed.

8   Not too fast (be cautious). Cf. 1.5.250, TLN 588.

9   I.e., the imprint (in the wax) is of her seal, an image of the Roman Lucretia (a
model of chastity who killed herself because she had been raped; see Shakespeare's
poem *The Rape of Lucrece*).

10 Habitually seals.

11 Totally. The liver is the seat of the passions; see p. 79, note 2.

12 Meter.

13 Badger (often "stinking brock").

But silence, like a Lucrece knife,[1]
100 With bloodless stroke my heart doth gore;
M.O.A.I.[2] doth sway my life."
FABIAN. [*Aside*] A fustian[3] riddle.
SIR TOBY. [*Aside*] Excellent wench, say I.
MALVOLIO. "M.O.A.I. doth sway my life." Nay, but first let me see,
105 let me see, let me see.
FABIAN. [*Aside*] What dish o'poison has she dressed[4] him!
SIR TOBY. [*Aside*] And with what wing the staniel checks at it![5]
MALVOLIO. "I may command, where I adore." Why, she may command me: I serve her, she is my lady. Why, this is evident to any
110 formal capacity.[6] There is no obstruction[7] in this. And the end—
what should that alphabetical position[8] portend? If I could make
that resemble something in me! Softly. "M.O.A.I."
SIR TOBY. [*Aside*] Oh, ay,[9] make up[10] that! He is now at a cold scent.[11]
FABIAN. [*Aside*] Sowter will cry upon't for all this, though it be as
115 rank as a fox.[12]
MALVOLIO. "M." Malvolio! "M," why that begins my name!
FABIAN. [*Aside*] Did not I say he would work it out? The cur is excellent at faults.[13]

---

1 I.e., the knife with which she committed suicide.
2 As the comments in the next two lines make clear, these letters have no obvious meaning (though some ingenious suggestions have been made), but are designed to persuade Malvolio they have.
3 High-sounding gibberish (literally, a coarse substitute cloth).
4 Prepared (for).
5 How quickly the kestrel (a small hawk, lightly regarded in falconry) adjusts his flight to follow this distraction.
6 Fully formed (i.e., normal) intelligence.
7 Obstacle, difficulty.
8 Arrangement.
9 Echoing "O.I."
10 Complete, make sense of.
11 I.e., no longer able to be followed by the hounds. The terminology here switches from falconry to hunting.
12 I.e., the hound Sowter will (pick up the scent again and) give tongue, even though our bait stinks (of deception) as much as a fox.
13 The dog is good at (finding the right trail again where there are) breaks in the scent (because he is too poor a hunter to change direction at the fault).

STAND-UP COMEDY
(TLN 1129–45)

Comic actors in Shakespeare's time, in an open-air theater, tightly surrounded by the audience on three or even four sides, could acknowledge the audience and play directly to them. This style of playing fell out of favor during the nineteenth and twentieth centuries, as realism became the acting norm, with actors expected to behave as if the characters they were playing were real people within a real environment. And it is rare in film, which still tends to realism in acting and design. But the conventions of stand-up comedy have never entirely disappeared, and the growing popularity of open stages and even reconstructed Elizabethan theaters during the twentieth century has led to a resurgence of playing comic scenes to the audience.

When Malvolio's letter scene in 2.5 is played in this way, as it often has been in the last two decades, the dynamic with the audience can be joyfully intense, and the actor may deliberately slow the pace of the scene in order to build suspense. Here is a short section, with stage directions added to suggest how this manner of playing works.

MALVOLIO [*perhaps assuring the audience that he will work it out*] Softly! [*pronouncing individually each of the letters*] "M. O. A. I." [*perhaps spelling it out again silently as Sir Toby and Fabian comment; then realizing it might mean him*] "M" [*sharing his realization with the audience*]—Malvolio! [*making sure the audience understands the implication*] "M"! Why, that begins my name! [*He checks that the audience has understood, returns to the letter as* FABIAN *comments, then complains to the audience.*] "M"—But then there is no consonancy in the sequel; that suffers under probation: [*perhaps showing the letter to the audience*] "A" should follow, but "O" does. [*Getting little comfort from the audience, he checks the letter again.* FABIAN *and* SIR TOBY *both comment.* MALVOLIO *demonstrates to the audience, perhaps again showing the place in the letter, further proof of what he has been saying, possibly in confusion or with a sense of grievance.*] And then "I" comes behind. [*He returns to the letter to try again, as Fabian comments. He may then spell the letters out again, and/or try to pronounce* "moai" *as if it were a word, possibly in several different ways*] "M. O. A. I." [*He may peer at the audience to see if any of them think he is on the right track. And so on.*]

MALVOLIO. "M." But then there is no consonancy in the sequel. That
120   suffers under probation:[1] "A" should follow, but "O" does.
FABIAN. [*Aside*] And "O" shall end,[2] I hope.
SIR TOBY. [*Aside*] Ay, or I'll cudgel him, and make him cry "O"!
MALVOLIO. And then "I" comes behind.
FABIAN. [*Aside*] Ay, an you had any eye[3] behind you, you might see
125   more detraction[4] at your heels than fortunes before you.
MALVOLIO. "M.O.A.I." This simulation[5] is not as the former; and yet
    to crush this a little, it would bow to me, for every one of these
    letters are in my name. Soft, here follows prose.

                                           [*Reading*]

"If this fall into thy hand, revolve.[6] In my stars[7] I am above thee,
130   but be not afraid of greatness. Some are born great, some achieve
    greatness, and some have greatness thrust upon 'em. Thy fates
    open their hands,[8] let thy blood and spirit embrace them; and to
    inure[9] thyself to what thou art like to be, cast thy humble slough,[10]
    and appear fresh. Be opposite[11] with a kinsman, surly with ser-
135   vants; let thy tongue tang arguments of state;[12] put thyself into
    the trick of singularity.[13] She thus advises thee, that sighs for thee.
    Remember who commended thy yellow stockings, and wished to
    see thee ever cross-gartered.[14] I say remember. Go to,[15] thou art
    made if thou desir'st to be so. If not, let me see thee a steward

---

1   No consistency in what follows; that breaks down under testing.
2   It will conclude with a groan (punning on the letter "O," which possibly also
suggests a hangman's noose).
3   Echoing "Ay," and "I" in the riddle; a repeat of the play on "O."
4   Disparagement (possibly with additional reference to stage business of the
eavesdroppers behind Malvolio).
5   Counterfeit (or a code to be broken).
6   Turn (it) over in your mind. If the actor seeks an easy laugh by physically turning around, he risks losing the primary sense.
7   Astrological determinants at birth (hence rank and fortune).
8   Are being generous.
9   Accustom.
10 Throw off your lowly behavior (as a snake its old skin; pronounced "sluff").
11 Antagonistic (to Sir Toby).
12 Ring out (like a bell) with high political matter. Cf. 2.3.131–32, TLN 841.
13 Affectation of idiosyncrasy.
14 See extended note, pp. 155–56.
15 Well then.

still, the fellow of servants, and not worthy to touch Fortune's   140
fingers. Farewell.
    She that would alter services[1] with thee,
    The Fortunate-Unhappy."
Daylight and champaign[2] discovers[3] not more! This is open.[4] I
will[5] be proud, I will read politic authors,[6] I will baffle[7] Sir Toby,   145
I will wash off gross acquaintance, I will be point-device[8] the very
man. I do not now fool myself, to let imagination jade[9] me; for
every reason excites to[10] this, that my lady loves me. She did com-
mend my yellow stockings of late, she did praise my leg being
cross-gartered, and in this she manifests herself to my love, and   150
with a kind of injunction drives me to these habits[11] of her liking.
I thank my stars, I am happy.[12] I will be strange, stout,[13] in yellow
stockings, and cross-gartered, even with the swiftness of putting
on. Jove[14] and my stars be praised! Here is yet a postscript.
                                      [Reading]

"Thou canst not choose but know who I am. If thou entertain'st[15]   155
my love, let it appear in thy smiling; thy smiles become thee well.
Therefore in my presence still[16] smile, dear my sweet, I prithee."

Jove, I thank thee. I will smile, I will do everything that thou wilt
have me.
                                               Exit.

---

1   Exchange duties (by raising him from servant to husband and master).
2   Open country. The first syllable is stressed and pronounced as in "champion."
3   Reveals.
4   Clear, evident.
5   Malvolio uses the emphatic "will," not the standard "shall," here and in the
following lines.
6   I.e., from whom he can learn "arguments of state."
7   (1) Confound, (2) display to the world as disgraced.
8   Precisely (i.e., in every detail).
9   Trick (as a deceitful horse—a jade—would).
10 Induces (belief in).
11 (1) Clothes, (2) behavior.
12 Fortunate.
13 Aloof, proud, as instructed in the letter (line 134–35, TLN 1154–55).
14 Malvolio is perhaps echoing Olivia's apparent choice of pagan god in the letter
(line 91, TLN 1109) here and in 3.4.
15 Receive, accept. He now uses the intimate singular pronoun as lovers do.
16 Always.

160 FABIAN. I will not give my part of this sport for a pension of thou-
        sands to be paid from the Sophy.°   *the Shah of Persia (modern Iran)*
    SIR TOBY. I could marry this wench for this device—
    SIR ANDREW. So could I too.
    SIR TOBY. —and ask no other dowry with her, but such another jest.
165 SIR ANDREW. Nor I neither.

    Enter Maria.
    FABIAN. Here comes my noble gull-catcher.°   *trapper of fools*
    SIR TOBY. [*Abasing himself on the stage*] Wilt thou set thy foot o'my
        neck?°   *a traditional symbol of supremacy*
    SIR ANDREW. Or o'mine either?
170 SIR TOBY. Shall I play[1] my freedom at tray-trip,[2] and become thy
        bondslave?
    SIR ANDREW. I'faith, or I either?
    SIR TOBY. Why, thou hast put him in such a dream that when the
        image of it leaves him he must run mad.
175 MARIA. Nay, but say true, does it work upon him?
    SIR TOBY. Like aqua-vitae[3] with a midwife.
    MARIA. If you will then see the fruits of the sport, mark his first
        approach before my lady. He will come to her in yellow stock-
        ings, and 'tis a color she abhors, and cross-gartered, a fashion
180   she detests; and he will smile upon her, which will now be so
        unsuitable to her disposition, being addicted to a melancholy as
        she is, that it cannot but turn him into a notable contempt.[4] If
        you will see it, follow me.   [*Exit.*]
    SIR TOBY. To the gates of Tartarus,[5] thou most excellent devil of wit!
                                                [*Exit following Maria.*]
185 SIR ANDREW. I'll make one too.[6]
                                                [*Exit following them both.*]

---

1 Wager, play for.
2 A dice game needing a three ("tray") thrown to win.
3 Brandy (or other spirits).
4 Public subject of scorn.
5 The classical hell.
6 Sir Andrew's fifth "me too"-ism since line 163 (TLN 1185) is reinforced by a fear
of being left behind as they exit following Maria.

[3.1]

Enter [from different ways] Viola [as Cesario] and Clown [playing on tabor].

VIOLA. Save thee,[1] friend, and thy music. Dost thou live by[2] thy
tabor?

CLOWN. No, sir, I live by° the church.   *live beside*

VIOLA. Art thou a churchman?[3]

CLOWN. No such matter, sir. I do live by the church, for I do live at   5
my house, and my house doth stand by the church.

VIOLA. So thou mayst say the king lies by[4] a beggar, if a beggar dwell
near him; or the church stands by[5] thy tabor, if thy tabor stand
by the church.

CLOWN. You have said,[6] sir. [*To the audience as well as Viola*] To see   10
this age! A sentence[7] is but a cheverel[8] glove to a good wit: how
quickly the wrong side may be turned outward!

VIOLA. Nay, that's certain: they that dally nicely[9] with words may
quickly make them wanton.°   *(1) capricious, equivocal, (2) lascivious*

CLOWN. I would therefore my sister had had no name, sir.   15

VIOLA. Why, man?

CLOWN. Why, sir, her name's a word, and to dally with that word
might make my sister wanton. But indeed, words are very rascals
since bonds[10] disgraced them.

VIOLA. Thy reason, man?   20

---

1 God preserve you. Viola as a matter of course uses the singular pronoun to
a social inferior; cf. the more formal greetings later in the scene (lines 62–64,
TLN 1282–84).

2 Make a living by.

3 Since the Clown is in motley, Viola is ironic or continuing the joke.

4 (1) Dwells by, (2) sleeps with.

5 (1) Is near, (2) is maintained by.

6 The Clown appears to accept Viola's skill with words, as he did Maria's at 1.5.22
(TLN 320), but goes on to make that the subject for further jesting.

7 A pithy form of words, an aphorism (Latin *sententia*, whence modern
"sententious").

8 Kid leather (noted for pliancy and capability of being stretched; pronounced
"shevril").

9 Play or flirt subtly.

10 Either (1) words are regarded as rogues, now that legal contracts ("bonds")
have made a person's word distrusted; or (2) words are dishonored since so many
promises have been broken.

Viola's reference to the Clown's "tabor" (a small drum used chiefly to accompany a pipe or trumpet), and mention of "thy music," indicates that Robert Armin was certainly playing a drum, and probably a pipe as well, one with each hand. An earlier Elizabethan clown, Richard Tarlton, is pictured in a manuscript drawing doing just that, and a woodcut of *Kemp's Nine Days' Wonder* (1600) shows Thomas Sly, Kemp's taborer, playing both instruments as he accompanies Kemp's famous jig from London to Norwich. See also extended note on p. 97, and R.A. Foakes, *Illustrations of the English Stage 1580–1642* (London: Scolar P, 1985), 44–45 and 150. The woodcut of Sly playing on pipe and tabor is available at TLN 1213 on the ISE website (<http://internetshakespeare. uvic.ca>).

Drawing of Richard Tarlton by John Scottowe, British Library Harleian MS 3885, f. 19, reproduced here from *Shakespeare's England* (Oxford: Clarendon, 1916), Vol. II, facing p. 258; photograph by David Carnegie.

CLOWN. Troth, sir, I can yield you none without words, and words
are grown so false I am loath to prove reason with them.

VIOLA. I warrant thou art a merry fellow and car'st for nothing.

CLOWN. Not so, sir, I do care for something; but in my conscience,
sir, I do not care for you: if that be to care for nothing, sir, I would   25
it would make you invisible.

VIOLA. Art not thou the Lady Olivia's fool?

CLOWN. No indeed, sir! The Lady Olivia has no folly. She will keep
no fool, sir, till she be married; and fools are as like husbands as
pilchards[1] are to herrings: the husband's the bigger. I am indeed   30
not her fool, but her corrupter of words.

VIOLA. I saw thee late[2] at the Count Orsino's.

CLOWN. Foolery, sir, does walk about the orb[3] like the sun, it
shines everywhere. I would be sorry, sir, but the fool should be
as oft with your master as with my mistress:[4] I think I saw your   35
wisdom° there.   *a mocking title, = "fool."*

VIOLA. Nay, an thou pass upon me,[5] I'll no more with thee. Hold,
[*Giving him a coin*] there's expenses for thee.

CLOWN. Now Jove, in his next commodity[6] of hair, send thee a beard.

VIOLA. By my troth, I'll tell thee, I am almost sick for one, [*To the*   40
audience] though I would not have it grow on my chin.[7] [*To the
Clown.*] Is thy lady within?

CLOWN. [*Indicating the coin*] Would not a pair of these have bred,[8] sir?

VIOLA. Yes, being kept together, and put to use.[9]

CLOWN. I would play Lord Pandarus of Phrygia, sir, to bring a   45
Cressida to [*Displaying the coin*] this Troilus.[10]

VIOLA. I understand you, sir, 'tis well begged. [*Gives another coin.*]

---

1 Small fish very similar to herrings.

2 Lately.

3 Around the earth. In the Ptolemaic system, the sun was thought to circle the
earth, the center of the universe.

4 I.e., it would be a pity if (1) I, (2) you, (3) folly, were not to spend as much time
with Orsino as with Olivia.

5 Jest at (from fencing, "thrust") me.

6 Consignment.

7 A riddling answer: she is lovesick for Orsino.

8 (1) Produced offspring, (2) earned interest.

9 (1) Copulation, (2) usury, earning interest. Viola, as usual, extends the Clown's
jest.

10 Pandarus of Troy acted as "pander" to his niece Cressida and Troilus.

CLOWN. The matter, I hope, is not great, sir, begging but a beggar:[1]
Cressida was a beggar. My lady is within, sir. I will conster[2] to
50 them whence you come; who you are, and what you would, are
out of my welkin—I might say element, but the word is overworn.
Exit.

VIOLA. [*To the audience*] This fellow is wise enough to play the fool,
And to do that well craves a kind of wit.
He must observe their mood on whom he jests,
55 The quality[3] of persons, and the time;
And like the haggard, check at every feather[4]
That comes before his eye. This is a practice°   *profession, skill*
As full of labor as a wise man's art:
For folly that he wisely shows, is fit;°   *appropriate*
60 But wise men, folly-fall'n,[5] quite taint their wit.[6]

Enter Sir Toby and Sir Andrew.

SIR TOBY. Save you, gentleman.
VIOLA. And you, sir.
SIR ANDREW. *Dieu vous garde, monsieur.*°   *"God save you, sir" (French)*
VIOLA. *Et vous aussi; votre serviteur.*[7]
65 SIR ANDREW. I hope, sir, you are, and I am yours.[8]
SIR TOBY. Will you encounter[9] the house? My niece is desirous you
should enter, if your trade[10] be to her.
VIOLA. I am bound[11] to your niece, sir; I mean, she is the list[12] of my
voyage.

---

1   I.e., the coin he has begged is a beggar because Cressida was traditionally
portrayed as developing leprosy and therefore reduced to begging.
2   Construe, explain (to those within).
3   (1) Nature, (2) rank.
4   Like an untamed adult hawk, fly at every lure (that the trainer swings) in its
view.
5   Who have fallen into folly.
6   Infect their (reputation for) intelligence.
7   "And you also; [I am] your servant" (French).
8   Since Sir Andrew's phrase is memorized ("without book," 1.3.22, TLN 144), he
is comically at a loss when Viola replies in French.
9   Either (1) confront as an adversary, or (2) go to meet.
10 Business. Perhaps contemptuous.
11 (1) Bound for (nautical, following "trade"), (2) obliged to (for the invitation), (3)
tied to.
12 Boundary (hence, "destination").

SIR TOBY. Taste[1] your legs, sir, put them to motion.   70

VIOLA. My legs do better understand[2] me, sir, than I understand
  what you mean by bidding me taste my legs.

SIR TOBY. I mean to go, sir, to enter.

VIOLA. I will answer you with gait and entrance—

Enter Olivia and [Maria].

  But we are prevented.[3] *[To Olivia]* Most excellent accomplished   75
  lady, the heavens[4] rain odors on you.[5]

SIR ANDREW. *[To the audience]* That youth's a rare courtier: "rain
  odors"—well.[6]

VIOLA. My matter hath no voice, lady, but to your own most pregnant[7] and vouchsafed[8] ear.   80

SIR ANDREW. *[Writing]* "Odors," "pregnant," and "vouchsafed": I'll
  get 'em all three all ready.[9]

OLIVIA. Let the garden door[10] be shut, and leave me to my hearing.
            *[Exeunt Maria and Sir Toby, followed by Sir Andrew
                        looking back to observe Olivia.]*
  Give me your hand, sir.

VIOLA. My duty, madam, and most humble service.[11]   85

OLIVIA. What is your name?

VIOLA. Cesario is your servant's name, fair princess.

OLIVIA. My servant,[12] sir? 'Twas never merry world[13]
  Since lowly feigning° was called compliment.   *pretended humility*
  Y'are servant to the Count Orsino, youth.   90

---

1 Try. Cf. 3.4.218, TLN 1762.

2 (1) Stand under, (2) comprehend.

3 Anticipated, forestalled.

4 May the heavens.

5 In production, Viola may present Orsino's jewel (2.4.121, TLN 1013) at this
point. Shakespeare makes no mention of it here.

6 Probably meaning "that's good" (rather than "good heavens!").

7 Receptive.

8 Bestowed (i.e., attentive); probably pronounced vouchsafèd.

9 Perhaps memorizing, but more likely by writing them in his table-book, which
he may now be doing.

10 I.e., the door into the private walled garden where they are now imagined to be.

11 Although Olivia offers her hand, as to an equal, Viola emphasizes her page's
role, probably kneeling and kissing the hand.

12 (1) Attendant, (2) suitor, lover.

13 I.e., things have never been good since.

VIOLA. And he is yours, and his[1] must needs be yours:
　　Your servant's servant is your servant, madam.
OLIVIA. For him, I think not on him; for his thoughts,
　　Would they were blanks,° rather than filled with me.　　*blank pages*
95　VIOLA. Madam, I come to whet your gentle thoughts
　　On his behalf.
OLIVIA.　　　Oh, by your leave, I pray you![2]
　　I bade you never speak again of him;
　　But would you undertake another suit,
　　I had rather hear you to solicit that
100　Than music from the spheres.[3]
VIOLA. Dear lady—
OLIVIA.　　　　Give me leave, beseech you. I did send,[4]
　　After the last enchantment you did here,
　　A ring in chase of you. So did I abuse°　　　　　*wrong*
　　Myself, my servant, and I fear me, you.
105　Under your hard construction° must I sit,　　*harsh interpretation*
　　To force that on you in a shameful cunning
　　Which you knew none of yours. What might you think?
　　Have you not set mine honor at the stake,
　　And baited it with all th'unmuzzled thoughts
110　That tyrannous heart can think?[5] To one of your receiving[6]
　　Enough is shown; a cypress, not a bosom,
　　Hides my heart.[7] So, let me hear you speak.
VIOLA. I pity you.
OLIVIA.　　　　That's a degree° to love.　　　　　*step*

1　I.e., his servants.
2　Olivia's completion of the blank verse line started by Viola suggests urgency and interruption.
3　I.e., the celestial music, inaudible to mortals, created by the rotation of the crystalline spheres supporting the planets and fixed stars.
4　Whether Viola's beginning and Olivia's interruption constitute two short lines or a shared hexameter, the metrical disruption clearly signals Olivia's urgency and breach of decorum.
5　The image is from bear-baiting, with Olivia's honor chained to a stake like the bear, and baited (bitten, hence wounded) by Cesario's contemptuous thoughts (like unmuzzled dogs).
6　Perception.
7　I.e., transparent gauze, not flesh, covers my heart (therefore you can see my feelings).

VIOLA. No, not a grece:[1] for 'tis a vulgar[2] proof
  That very oft we pity enemies.[3]   115
OLIVIA. Why then, methinks 'tis time to smile again.
  O world, how apt the poor are to be proud![4]
  If one should be a prey, how much the better
  To fall before the lion than the wolf![5]

                                            Clock strikes.[6]

  The clock upbraids me with the waste of time.   120
  Be not afraid, good youth, I will not have you;
  And yet when wit and youth is come to harvest,[7]
  Your wife is like to reap a proper[8] man.
  There lies your way, due west.[9]
VIOLA.   Then westward ho![10]
  Grace and good disposition[11] attend your ladyship.   125
  You'll nothing, madam, to my lord by me?
OLIVIA. Stay!
  I prithee tell me what thou[12] think'st of me?
VIOLA. That you do think you are not what you are.
OLIVIA. If I think so, I think the same of you.[13]   130

---

1 This obsolete word tends to be used for shallow ceremonial steps raising a throne, altar, etc., and does not have the more general meanings of "degree." Pronounced "greece."
2 Common, generally accepted.
3 Viola gently returns Olivia's ring at this point in the Nunn film.
4 Either (1) isn't it typical that, though rejected, I am still proud, or (2) look at him, poor but too proud to accept me.
5 Either (1) Cesario rather than anyone base, or (2) Orsino, a king among men, rather than the cruel Cesario. The first is more likely, because Olivia is a victim ("prey") to Cesario, but never offers herself to Orsino.
6 Since this unusual stage direction serves no plot function, the thematic importance to Shakespeare of time passing deserves notice.
7 I.e., when you reach maturity.
8 (1) Worthy, excellent, (2) handsome.
9 Perhaps non-specific, perhaps metaphorically "into the sunset, out of my life"; or Shakespeare may simply be setting up Viola's next line.
10 The familiar Thames watermen's cry seeking passengers going upriver to the court at Westminster (perhaps suggesting Orsino's court) from the City (or the theaters).
11 God's grace, and peace of mind.
12 Here and in her ensuing speeches Olivia switches from "you" to "thou" as she declares her love; see also p. 137, note 15.
13 I.e., that you are more than you appear (perhaps noble in disguise; cf. 1.5.247–50, TLN 585–88).

VIOLA. Then think you right: [*Including the audience*] I am not what
    I am.[1]

OLIVIA. I would you were as I would have you be.

VIOLA. Would it be better, madam, than I am?
    I wish it might,° for now I am your fool![2]   *(be better)*

135 OLIVIA. [*To the audience*] Oh, what a deal of scorn looks beautiful
    In the contempt and anger of his lip!
    A murd'rous guilt shows not itself more soon,
    Than love that would seem hid. Love's night is noon.[3]
    [*To Viola*] Cesario, by the roses of the spring,[4]

140   By maidhood, honor, truth, and everything,
    I love thee so, that maugre[5] all thy pride,
    Nor wit nor reason can my passion hide.
    Do not extort thy reasons from this clause,
    For that I woo, thou therefore hast no cause;

145   But rather reason thus with reason fetter:[6]
    Love sought is good, but giv'n unsought is better.

VIOLA. By innocence I swear, and by my youth,
    I have one heart, one bosom,[7] and one truth,
    And that no woman has; nor never none

150   Shall mistress be of it, save I alone.
    And so adieu, good madam; never more
    Will I my master's tears to you deplore.[8]

OLIVIA. Yet come again—for thou perhaps mayst move
    That heart, which now abhors, to like his love.

                        Exeunt [*different ways*].

---

1   Viola's rueful self-awareness about her situation again means more to the audience than to the person addressed.

2   I.e., being made a fool of by you.

3   A proverb meaning "love cannot be hid." Olivia's passion is about to declare
itself in full light.

4   The 14-line rhyming-couplet sonnet which starts here heightens the intensity
of this passionate declaration and reply. Cf. *Romeo and Juliet* 1.5.94–107, TLN
670–85.

5   Despite (pronounced "mauger": "au" as in "taught").

6   I.e., do not squeeze out arguments from this proposition, that because I love
you therefore you should not love me; instead, restrain that reasoning with this, as
follows.

7   (1) Seat of affection (i.e., the heart), (2) repository of secrets.

8   I.e., tell you sadly about Orsino's love-grief.

[3.2]

Enter Sir Andrew, [followed by] Sir Toby and Fabian.

SIR ANDREW. No, faith, I'll not stay a jot longer!

SIR TOBY. Thy reason, dear venom, give thy reason.

FABIAN. You[1] must needs yield your reason, Sir Andrew!

SIR ANDREW. Marry, I saw your niece do more favors to the count's serving-man than ever she bestowed upon me. I saw't 5 i'th'orchard.[2]

SIR TOBY. Did she see thee the while,[3] old boy, tell me that?

SIR ANDREW. As plain as I see you now.

FABIAN. This was a great argument[4] of love in her toward you.

SIR ANDREW. 'Slight,[5] will you make an ass o'me? 10

FABIAN. I will prove it legitimate, sir, upon the oaths of judgment and reason.

SIR TOBY. And they have been grand-jurymen[6] since before Noah was a sailor.

FABIAN. She did show favor to the youth in your sight only to 15 exasperate you, to awake your dormouse[7] valor, to put fire in your heart, and brimstone[8] in your liver. You should then have accosted[9] her, and with some excellent jests, fire-new from the mint,[10] you should have banged the youth into dumbness. This was looked for at your hand, and this was balked.[11] The double 20 gilt[12] of this opportunity you let time wash off, and you are now sailed into the north[13] of my lady's opinion, where you will hang

---

1 Sir Toby uses, as always, the familiar second person singular, Fabian the respectful plural.
2 Garden (not necessarily for fruit trees).
3 During that time.
4 Proof.
5 By god's light (as at 2.5.29, TLN 1048).
6 Judgment and Reason are personified as members of a grand jury, who decide whether evidence is sufficient to send a case to trial.
7 (1) Hibernating, (2) timid.
8 Sulphur.
9 The audience, and even Sir Andrew, may recall Sir Toby's definition at 1.3.47–48, TLN 171–72.
10 I.e., like a coin freshly minted from molten metal.
11 Let slip.
12 I.e., "golden opportunity," since gilded twice over.
13 Cold and distant region.

like an icicle on a Dutchman's beard,[1] unless you do redeem it by
some laudable attempt, either of valor or policy.[2]

25 SIR ANDREW. An't be any way, it must be with valor, for policy I
hate. [*To the audience*] I had as lief[3] be a Brownist,[4] as a politician.[5]

SIR TOBY. Why then, build me[6] thy fortunes upon the basis of valor.
Challenge me the count's youth to fight with him, hurt him in
eleven places. My niece shall take note of it; and assure thyself,
30 there is no love-broker[7] in the world can more prevail in man's
commendation with woman than report of valor.

FABIAN. There is no way but this, Sir Andrew.

SIR ANDREW. Will either of you bear me a challenge to him?

SIR TOBY. Go, write it in a martial hand.[8] Be cursed[9] and brief. It
35 is no matter how witty, so it be eloquent, and full of invention.[10]
Taunt him with the license of ink.[11] If thou "thou'st"[12] him some
thrice, it shall not be amiss; and as many lies[13] as will lie in thy
sheet of paper, although the sheet were big enough for the bed
of Ware[14] in England, set 'em down. Go, about it! Let there be
40 gall[15] enough in thy ink; though thou write with a goose-pen,[16] no
matter. About it!

SIR ANDREW. Where shall I find you?

---

1 The Arctic expedition of Willem Barents in 1596–97 would have lent topicality
to this use of "north": see extended note, p. 150.

2 (1) Strategy, (2) scheming (derogatory; see "politician" in next speech and
2.3.68, TLN 774).

3 Rather.

4 Protestant sect named for Robert Browne (1550–1633), a founder of the
Congregationalist movement; in Sir Andrew's mind, likely a kind of Puritan.

5 Amoral intriguer.

6 The ethical dative, meaning "for me," but principally acting as an intensifier for
Sir Toby's close involvement, as also in the next sentence.

7 Go-between.

8 No such style of handwriting is known; Sir Toby has probably made it up
(although editors have suggested a careless scrawl, or aggressive flourishes).

9 Malignant, disagreeable (usually spelt at the time, as in Folio, "curst").

10 The major divisions of rhetoric, equivalent to style and content.

11 Freedom conferred by writing (not face to face).

12 I.e., rudely use "thou" rather than "you."

13 I.e., iterations of "thou liest," an accusation that would provoke a duel.

14 This bed, an Elizabethan tourist attraction at an inn in Ware, measures over 3
meters square, and is preserved in the Victoria and Albert Museum, London.

15 (1) Oak-gall (used in making ink), (2) bitterness.

16 (1) Goose quill, (2) pen used by a goose (fool).

SIR TOBY. We'll call thee at thy *cubiculo*.[1] Go!

Exit Sir Andrew.

FABIAN. This is a dear manikin[2] to you, Sir Toby.

SIR TOBY. I have been dear[3] to him, lad, some two thousand[4] strong, 45
or so.

FABIAN. We shall have a rare letter from him—but you'll not
deliver't?

SIR TOBY. Never trust me[5] then; and by all means[6] stir on the youth
to an answer. I think oxen and wainropes[7] cannot hale them 50
together. For Andrew, if he were opened[8] and you find so much
blood in his liver[9] as will clog[10] the foot of a flea, I'll eat the rest
of th'anatomy.

FABIAN. And his opposite, the youth, bears in his visage no great
presage[11] of cruelty. 55

Enter Maria.

SIR TOBY. Look where the youngest wren of nine[12] comes.

MARIA. If you desire the spleen,[13] and will laugh yourselves into
stitches, follow me. Yond gull Malvolio is turned heathen, a very
renegado;[14] for there is no Christian that means to be saved by
believing rightly can ever believe such impossible passages of 60
grossness.[15] He's in yellow stockings!

SIR TOBY. And cross-gartered?

---

1 Bedchamber (a humorous or affected use of Latin or Italian).
2 Little man (i.e., "you are fond of this plaything").
3 Expensive (punning on previous line).
4 Either ducats (see p. 85, note 2) or pounds.
5 (... if I do not). But Sir Toby changes his mind after reading the challenge: see
3.4.164–68, TLN 1701–06.
6 Probably (1) in every possible way, but possibly (2) certainly (i.e., used
permissively).
7 Oxen and their wagon ("wain") harness.
8 Dissected.
9 A "liver white and pale"—i.e., lacking in blood (courage)—is "the badge of ...
cowardice" (*Henry IV, Part Two* 4.3.103–04, TLN 2341–42).
10 (1) Encumber, clag (in something sticky), (2) provide with clogs (wooden shoes).
11 Sign, portent.
12 I.e., the last hatched, and therefore tiniest, of a brood of nine of the smallest
bird (another reference to Maria's size).
13 Amusement (laughter was thought to be controlled by the spleen).
14 Spanish form of "renegade"; traitor to Christianity.
15 Either (1) acts of absurdity, or (2) grossly unbelievable statements (i.e., "passages" of Maria's letter).

MARIA. Most villainously,[1] like a pedant that keeps a school
i'th'church.[2] I have dogged him like his murderer. He does obey
65   every point of the letter that I dropped to betray him. He does
smile his face into more lines than is in the new map with the
augmentation of the Indies; you have not seen such a thing as
'tis. I can hardly forbear hurling things at him; I know my lady
will strike him. If she do, he'll smile, and take't for a great favor.
70   SIR TOBY. Come, bring us, bring us where he is!

Exeunt.

---

1   Abominably.
2   Like a schoolmaster who has to use the church for lack of his own schoolroom.

3.2.66:   THE NEW MAP (TLN 1458)

Maria's description of Malvolio's smile creating "more lines than is in
the new map with the augmentation of the Indies" seems to refer to
the diagonal "rhumb lines" printed on maps and charts as navigation
courses. They can be seen in the particular map Maria is probably referring to, Hakluyt's map of the world published in 1599 or 1600. The criss-
crossing diagonal lines create a vivid image of a smiling face crinkling
into laugh lines. The map's "augmentation of the Indies" evidently refers
to a very much more detailed depiction of the East Indies than in earlier
maps (just above one of the first extensive outlines of northern Australia).
The other new feature on this map is the detail around the western and
northern coasts of the island of Novaya Zemlya north of Russia. That
the Dutch Arctic expedition under William Barents (hence Barents Sea)
was still in the popular imagination is evident in Fabian's warning to Sir
Andrew that "you are now sailed into the north of my lady's opinion,
where you will hang like an icicle on a Dutchman's beard ..." (3.2.21–23,
TLN 1404–07, and n.). Detail from this map is available at TLN 1458 on
the ISE website (<http://internetshakespeare.uvic.ca>). See also Arthur
M. Hind, *Engraving in England in the Sixteenth and Seventeenth Centuries*,
Part I (Cambridge: Cambridge UP, 1952), Plates 100, 101.

[3.3]

Enter Sebastian and Antonio.

SEBASTIAN. I would not by my will have troubled you,
   But since you make your pleasure of your pains,
   I will no further chide you.
ANTONIO. I could not stay behind you. My desire,
   More sharp than filèd steel, did spur me forth;   5
   And not all° love to see you—though so much   *only*
   As might have drawn one to a longer voyage—
   But jealousy° what might befall your travel,   *anxiety*
   Being skilless in° these parts, which to a stranger,   *ignorant of*
   Unguided and unfriended, often prove   10

"Hakluyt's Map of the World in Projection" (also known as "A Chart of the World on Mercator's Projection" and as the "Wright-Molyneux Map"), c. 1599–1600. Facsimile courtesy of the Alexander Turnbull Library, Wellington, New Zealand, callmark qREng HAK Prin 1598 vol. 1.

Rough and unhospitable.[1] My willing love,
The rather[2] by these arguments of fear,
Set forth in your pursuit.

SEBASTIAN.　　　　　My kind Antonio,
I can no other answer make but thanks,

15　And thanks, and ever thanks; and oft[3] good turns
Are shuffled off° with such uncurrent[4] pay.　　　　　*evaded*
But were my worth, as is my conscience,[5] firm,
You should find better dealing. What's to do?
Shall we go see the relics[6] of this town?

20　ANTONIO. Tomorrow, sir; best first go see your lodging.
SEBASTIAN. I am not weary, and 'tis long to night.
I pray you, let us satisfy our eyes
With the memorials and the things of fame
That do renown this city.

ANTONIO.　　　　　Would you'd pardon me.[7]

25　I do not without danger walk these streets.
Once in a sea-fight 'gainst the count his° galleys　　　　　*Count's*
I did some service, of such note indeed
That were I ta'en here it would scarce be answered.[8]
SEBASTIAN. Belike° you slew great number of his people.　　　　　*I suppose*

30　ANTONIO. Th'offence is not of such a bloody nature,
Albeit the quality° of the time and quarrel　　　　　*nature*
Might well have given us bloody argument.[9]
It might have since been answered in repaying
What we took from them, which for traffic's sake[10]

35　Most of our city did. Only myself stood out,

1　Shakespeare may be thinking of local pirates (cf. *Henry VI, Part Two* 4.1.108,
TLN 2276: "Bargulus the strong Illyrian pirate").
2　More speedily (the original meaning).
3　Folio ("thanks: and ever oft") is defective in meter and sense.
4　Worthless (because not legal money, not "currency").
5　Awareness of being indebted.
6　Antiquities (as in his next speech).
7　Possibly completing an irregular verse line.
8　I.e., if I were captured, it would be virtually impossible for me to defend
myself (under their law). Since reparation would not now be accepted (as Antonio
explains in his next speech), his life would be in danger.
9　Reason justifying bloodshed.
10　For the sake of trade.

For which, if I be lapsèd° in this place,   *apprehended (an unusual usage)*
I shall pay dear.
SEBASTIAN.   Do not then walk too open.°   *openly, publicly*
ANTONIO. It doth not fit[1] me. Hold, sir, here's my purse.
In the south suburbs at the Elephant[2]
Is best to lodge; I will bespeak our diet,[3]   40
Whiles you beguile the time, and feed your knowledge
With viewing of the town. There shall you have me.°   *find me*
SEBASTIAN. Why I your purse?
ANTONIO. Haply° your eye shall light upon some toy[4]   *perhaps*
You have desire to purchase; and your store,   45
I think, is not for idle markets,[5] sir.
SEBASTIAN. I'll be your purse-bearer,[6] and leave you for
An hour.
ANTONIO. To th'Elephant.
SEBASTIAN.   I do remember.

                    Exeunt [different ways].

[3.4]

Enter Olivia and Maria.
OLIVIA. [*To the audience*] I have sent after him; he says[7] he'll come.
How shall I feast him? What bestow of° him?   *on*
For youth is bought more oft than begged or borrowed.[8]
I speak too loud—
[*To Maria*] Where's Malvolio? He is sad and civil,[9]   5

---

1 Is not appropriate for.
2 There was an inn with this common name very close to the Globe in the "south suburbs" of London.
3 Order our meals (note "feed" in the next line).
4 Trifle.
5 Your supply of money is not enough for unnecessary expenditure.
6 Sebastian is joking about a formal appointment as official in charge of payments.
7 I.e., suppose he says. The servant sent after Cesario does not return until line 50.1, TLN 1578.
8 Olivia turns the proverb "better to buy than to beg or borrow" to a wryly cynical meaning.
9 Grave and circumspect.

And suits well for a servant with my fortunes.[1]
Where is Malvolio?

MARIA. He's coming, madam, but in very strange manner. He is
sure possessed,° madam.   *i.e., by the devil; mad*

10 OLIVIA. Why, what's the matter? Does he rave?

MARIA. No, madam, he does nothing but smile. Your ladyship were
best to have some guard about you if he come, for sure the man
is tainted in's wits.

OLIVIA. Go call him hither. [*To the audience*] I am as mad as he,

15 If sad and merry madness equal be.

*Enter Malvolio [smiling, in cross-gartered yellow stockings, and kissing
his hand repeatedly to Olivia].[2]*

How now, Malvolio!

MALVOLIO. Sweet lady, ho, ho!

OLIVIA. Smil'st thou? I sent for thee upon a sad[3] occasion.

MALVOLIO. Sad, lady? I could be sad. This does make some obstruc-

20 tion in the blood,[4] this cross-gartering; but what of that? If it
please the eye of one,[5] it is with me as the very true sonnet[6] is,
[*Singing*] "Please one, and please all."

OLIVIA. Why, how dost thou, man? What is the matter with thee?

MALVOLIO. Not black in my mind,[7] though yellow[8] in my legs.

25 [*Holding up letter*] It did come to his hands, and commands shall
be executed. I think we do know the sweet roman hand.[9]

OLIVIA. Wilt thou go to bed,[10] Malvolio?

---

1 (1) Her bereavement, (2) her love melancholy.

2 Since Malvolio's extraordinary appearance usually provokes loud laughter
(often Olivia's prompt to turn and see him), theaters seldom retain the Folio entry
direction prior to her aside, as Malvolio would upstage her.

3 (1) Serious (Olivia's sense), (2) melancholy (Malvolio's sense in the next line).

4 Which would cause melancholy.

5 I.e., of Olivia.

6 Song (not exclusively a 14-line poem).

7 Melancholy (thought to be caused by black bile; see also note 4).

8 Although yellow might be the color for a lover (see extended note, p. 155),
"Black and Yellow" was also a popular sad song.

9 I.e., Olivia's fashionable italic (Italian) handwriting (not the old-fashioned
English Secretary hand).

10 (1) To rest and recover (Olivia's sense), (2) for sex (Malvolio's sense in the next
line).

3.4.15.1:   IN YELLOW STOCKINGS,
            AND CROSS-GARTERED (TLN 1535)

Maria has already forewarned us of Malvolio's appearance (2.5.78–80, TLN 1201–03). Some critics have suggested that the point about his stockings being yellow is that the color had become unfashionable, but costume histories do not support this view: yellow remained a popular color, both in general use and at court, into the seventeenth century. It was often associated with love and marriage (and marital jealousy), and such a light color was evidently fashionable for young (and therefore marriageable) men, or for those seeking to relive their youth, rather than for older men. What is fashionable for a young man may appear surprising or even shocking on an older man, or on a character such as Malvolio whose usual dress is probably dark and sober in style and color, in keeping with the hint of Puritanism (2.3.130–35, TLN 833–40). And of course for Olivia, "'tis a color she abhors" (2.5.179, TLN 1202).

The purpose of garters was to support a man's stockings. Cross-gartering involved placing a ribbon below the front of the knee, passing the ends behind the knee, giving them a cross twist, then bringing them forward above the knee and tying them in a bow at the side or in front. This flamboyant style was still in fashion at the time of *Twelfth Night* (though some critics dispute this), but, like yellow stockings, it seems to have been a fashion more appropriate for the young and stylish than for an older and graver man. "As rare an old youth as ever walked cross-gartered" (John Ford, *The Lover's Melancholy* [1629], 3.1.2) describes a man seeking to dress younger than his age. The combination of yellow stockings and cross-gartering displays the usually soberly dressed Malvolio as a lover to Olivia.

See M. Channing Linthicum, "Malvolio's Cross-Gartered Yellow Stockings," *Modern Philology* 25 (1927–28): 87–93, *Costume in the Drama of Shakespeare and His Contemporaries* (Oxford: Clarendon, 1936); and C. Willett and Phillis Cunnington, *Handbook of English Costume in the Sixteenth Century* (London: Faber and Faber, 1954) and *Handbook of English Costume in the Seventeenth Century* (London: Faber and Faber, 1955).

Further views of cross-gartering are available at TLN 1535 on the ISE website (<http://internetshakespeare.uvic.ca>).

(continued)

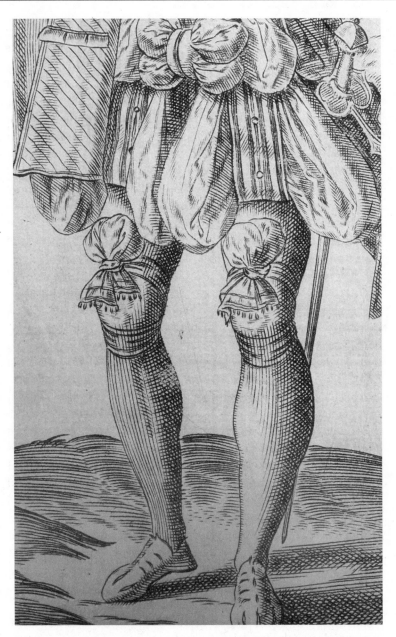

A German cavalier cross-gartered, from *Omnium Pene Europae ... Gentium Habitus* (Antwerp, 1581), in the collection of the Folger Shakespeare Library; photograph by David Carnegie.

MALVOLIO. To bed! [*Singing*] "Ay, sweetheart, and I'll come to thee."
OLIVIA. God comfort thee! Why dost thou smile so, and kiss thy
    hand¹ so oft?   30
MARIA. How do you, Malvolio?
MALVOLIO. At your request? Yes, nightingales answer daws!²
MARIA. Why appear you with this ridiculous boldness before my
    lady?
MALVOLIO. [*To Olivia*] "Be not afraid of greatness": 'twas well writ. 35
OLIVIA. What mean'st thou by that, Malvolio?
MALVOLIO. "Some are born great—"
OLIVIA. Ha?
MALVOLIO. "—some achieve greatness—"
OLIVIA. What say'st thou?   40
MALVOLIO. "—and some have greatness thrust upon them."
OLIVIA. Heaven restore thee!
MALVOLIO. "Remember who commended thy yellow stockings—"
OLIVIA. Thy yellow stockings?
MALVOLIO. "—and wished to see thee cross-gartered."   45
OLIVIA. Cross-gartered?
MALVOLIO. "Go to, thou art made, if thou desir'st to be so—"
OLIVIA. Am I made?³
MALVOLIO. "—if not, let me see thee a servant still."
OLIVIA. [*To the audience*] Why, this is very midsummer madness.⁴   50

Enter Servant.
SERVANT. Madam, the young gentleman of the Count Orsino's is
    returned; I could hardly⁵ entreat him back. He attends your lady-
    ship's pleasure.
OLIVIA. I'll come to him. [*Exit Servant.*] Good Maria, let this fellow
    be looked to. Where's my cousin Toby? Let some of my people   55

---

1 A gentlemanly courtesy to a lady.
2 Apparently sarcastic: he (the prized singing nightingale) refuses to answer
Maria (a stupid noisy jackdaw).
3 Olivia is astonished at Malvolio's rude ("thou") offer of a position she already
holds ("made" = assured of success in life).
4 Proverbial. Cf., in a different context, *Romeo and Juliet* 3.1.4, TLN 1434–35,
"now, these hot days, is the mad blood stirring."
5 Only with difficulty.

have a special care of him; I would not have him miscarry[1] for the half of my dowry.

Exit [following Servant, Maria a different way].

MALVOLIO. Oh ho, do you come near[2] me now? [*To the audience*] No worse man than Sir Toby to look to me! This concurs directly with
60   the letter. She sends him on purpose, that I may appear stubborn to him; for she incites me to that in the letter. "Cast thy humble slough," says she, "be opposite with a kinsman, surly with servants, let thy tongue tang with arguments of state, put thyself into the trick of singularity"; and consequently[3] sets down the
65   manner how: as, a sad face, a reverend carriage, a slow tongue, in the habit[4] of some sir of note,[5] and so forth. I have limed[6] her, but it is Jove's[7] doing, and Jove make me thankful. And when she went away now, "Let this fellow[8] be looked to." "Fellow!" Not Malvolio, nor after my degree,[9] but "fellow." Why, every-
70   thing adheres together, that no dram of a scruple, no scruple of a scruple,[10] no obstacle, no incredulous or unsafe[11] circumstance— what can be said? Nothing that can be can come between me and the full prospect of my hopes. Well Jove, not I, is the doer of this, and he is to be thanked.

Enter Sir Toby, Fabian, and Maria.

75   SIR TOBY. [*Pretending not to see Malvolio*] Which way is he, in the name of sanctity? If all the devils of hell be drawn[12] in little,[13] and Legion[14] himself possessed him, yet I'll speak to him.

---

1 Come to harm.
2 Begin to understand.
3 Subsequently.
4 (1) Clothing, (2) manner.
5 Distinguished gentleman.
6 Caught (as birds ensnared with sticky birdlime).
7 See p. 137, note 14.
8 (1) Equal (cf. "fellow of servants," 2.5.140, TLN 1161), (2) inferior person (cf. 5.1.91, TLN 2253). Malvolio understands (1), whereas Olivia clearly means (2).
9 Rank (as steward).
10 Not a tiny measure ("dram") of doubt ("scruple"), not even a third of a dram ("scruple") of doubt ("scruple").
11 Incredible or unreliable.
12 (1) Assembled (as an army), (2) painted.
13 In miniature.
14 In Mark 5:1–20, the "unclean spirits" possessing a man replied to Jesus, "My name is Legion: for we are many" (a Roman legion was about 6000 men).

FABIAN. Here he is, here he is. [*To Malvolio*] How is't with you, sir?
How is't with you, man?

MALVOLIO. Go off, I discard you. Let me enjoy my private.[1] Go off!   80

MARIA. [*To Sir Toby and Fabian, aloud, to be overheard*] Lo, how hollow
the fiend speaks within[2] him! Did not I tell you? Sir Toby, my lady
prays you to have a care of him.

MALVOLIO. [*Aside*] Ah ha! Does she so?

SIR TOBY. [*To them, aloud*] Go to, go to. Peace, peace, we must deal   85
gently with him. Let me alone.[3] [*Approaching Malvolio*] How do
you, Malvolio? How is't with you? What, man, defy the devil; consider, he's an enemy to mankind.

MALVOLIO. Do you know what you say?

MARIA. [*To them, aloud*] La you,[4] an you speak ill of the devil, how   90
he takes it at heart! Pray god he be not bewitched!

FABIAN. [*To them, aloud*] Carry his water[5] to th'wise woman.[6]

MARIA. [*To them, aloud*] Marry, and it shall be done tomorrow morning[7] if I live. My lady would not lose him for more than I'll say.

MALVOLIO. How now, mistress?   95

MARIA. [*To them, aloud*] Oh, lord!

SIR TOBY. [*To them, aloud*] Prithee hold thy peace, this is not the way.
Do you not see you move him?[8] Let me alone with him.

FABIAN. [*To them, aloud*] No way but gentleness; gently, gently. The
fiend is rough, and will not be roughly used.   100

SIR TOBY. [*Approaching Malvolio*] Why, how now, my bawcock?[9] How
dost thou, chuck?

MALVOLIO. Sir!

---

1   Privacy.
2   This sequence depends on everything Malvolio says being taken as the voice of
the devil possessing him (see 3.4.76–77, TLN 1608, and notes).
3   Leave it to him.
4   Look you. Malvolio has evidently reacted strongly to Sir Toby's implication
that he is in league with the devil.
5   Urine (for diagnosis by a physician or a "wise woman").
6   A woman skilled in cures (and perhaps in undoing witchcraft).
7   The prospect of Maria's interest in his full chamber-pot will further outrage
Malvolio.
8   Raise his emotions.
9   Fine bird (in this context a comic term of endearment, like "chuck" and "biddy"
that follow). Possibly Sir Toby is clucking to call Malvolio.

SIR TOBY. Ay, biddy, come with me. What, man, 'tis not for gravity[1]
105   to play at cherry-pit[2] with Satan. Hang him, foul collier![3]

MARIA. [*To them, aloud*] Get him to say his prayers, good Sir Toby,
   get him to pray.

MALVOLIO. My prayers, minx![4]

MARIA. [*To them, aloud*] No, I warrant you, he will not hear of
110   godliness.

MALVOLIO. Go hang yourselves all! You are idle,[5] shallow things; I
   am not of your element.[6] You shall know more hereafter.

                                             Exit.

SIR TOBY. Is't possible?

FABIAN. [*Including the audience*] If this were played upon a stage now,
115   I could condemn it as an improbable fiction!

SIR TOBY. His very genius[7] hath taken the infection of the device,
   man.

MARIA. Nay, pursue him now, lest the device take air, and taint.[8]

FABIAN. Why, we shall make him mad indeed.

120 MARIA. The house will be the quieter.

SIR TOBY. Come, we'll have him in a dark room and bound.[9] My niece
   is already in the belief that he's mad. We may carry it thus[10] for our
   pleasure, and his penance, till our very pastime, tired out of breath,
   prompt us to have mercy on him; at which time we will bring the
125   device to the bar[11] and crown thee for a finder of madmen.[12]

Enter Sir Andrew [with a challenge].

   But see, but see!

FABIAN. More matter for a May morning![13]

---

1 (1) Dignified, (2) appropriate to Gravity, a personification of a dignified person.
2 A children's game throwing cherry stones into a hole.
3 Dirty coalman (referring to the devil's blackness).
4 Hussy, impertinent girl.
5 Foolish.
6 I.e., in your sphere (of existence). Cf. p. 77, note 5.
7 Spirit, soul.
8 Be exposed, and spoil (like food).
9 Standard treatment for madness.
10 Maintain this pretence.
11 I.e., court; hence, the verdict of public opinion.
12 (1) Discoverer of lunatics, (2) member of a jury which finds (declares) a person insane.
13 Sport fit for (1) May Day foolery, (2) a spring morning in the northern hemisphere (see Introduction, p. 12 and Appendix F9).

SIR ANDREW. Here's the challenge, read it. I warrant there's vinegar
and pepper in't.

FABIAN. Is't so saucy?°   *(1) spicy (with "vinegar and pepper"), (2) insolent*   130

SIR ANDREW. Ay, is't, I warrant him!¹ Do but read.

SIR TOBY. Give me. [*Taking the challenge and reading*] "Youth, whatsoever thou art, thou art but a scurvy fellow."²

FABIAN. [*To Sir Andrew*] Good, and valiant.

SIR TOBY. [*Reading*] "Wonder not, nor admire³ not in thy mind, why   135
I do call thee so, for I will show thee no reason for't."

FABIAN. [*To Sir Andrew*] A good note:⁴ that keeps you from the blow
of the law.°   *punishment (for a breach of the peace)*

SIR TOBY. [*Reading*] "Thou com'st to the Lady Olivia, and in my sight
she uses thee kindly. But thou liest in thy throat;⁵ that is not the   140
matter I challenge thee for."

FABIAN. Very brief, and to exceeding good sense—[*Aside*] less.⁶

SIR TOBY. [*Reading*] "I will waylay thee going home, where if it be
thy chance to kill me—"

FABIAN. Good.⁷   145

SIR TOBY. [*Reading*] "—thou kill'st me like a rogue and a villain."

FABIAN. [*To Sir Andrew*] Still you keep o'th'windy⁸ side of the law.
Good.

SIR TOBY. [*Reading*] "Fare thee well, and god have mercy upon one
of our souls. He may have mercy upon mine, but my hope is bet-   150
ter, and so look to thyself. Thy friend, as thou usest him,⁹ and
thy sworn enemy,
        Andrew Aguecheek."

SIR TOBY. If this letter move him not, his legs cannot. I'll giv't him.

---

1 Give him (Cesario) my word.

2 Sir Andrew has followed Sir Toby's instruction to be insulting (see 3.2.36–37,
TLN 1423–24).

3 Marvel, "wonder."

4 I.e., well said.

5 To "give the lie" in this emphatic form could only be answered by a duel, but Sir
Andrew withdraws the insult in the next phrase.

6 Because (1) Olivia using Cesario "kindly" is not a lie, and (2) Sir Andrew, having used it as provocation anyway, then says it is "not the matter."

7 Fabian's anticipation here may be comic if Sir Andrew realizes the implication.

8 I.e., windward (the safe side when sailing, or, for an animal, if being hunted).
Fabian is pointing out Sir Andrew's absurd avoidance of giving legal offense in his
challenge.

9 In so far as you treat me like (a friend).

155 MARIA. You may have very fit occasion for't; he is now in some commerce[1] with my lady, and will by and by depart.

SIR TOBY. Go, Sir Andrew; scout me[2] for him at the corner of the orchard like a bum-baily.[3] So soon as ever thou see'st him, draw. And as thou draw'st, swear horrible; for it comes to pass oft that a

160 terrible oath with a swaggering accent, sharply twanged off, gives manhood more approbation[4] than ever proof[5] itself would have earned him. Away!

SIR ANDREW. Nay, let me alone for swearing.

Exit.

SIR TOBY. Now will not I deliver his letter; for the behavior of the

165 young gentleman gives him out to be of good capacity[6] and breeding. His employment between his lord and my niece confirms no less. Therefore this letter, being so excellently ignorant, will breed no terror in the youth; he will find[7] it comes from a clodpoll.[8] But, sir, I will deliver his challenge by word of mouth, set upon

170 Aguecheek a notable report of valor, and drive the gentleman (as I know his youth will aptly receive it) into a most hideous opinion of his rage, skill, fury, and impetuosity. This will so fright them both that they will kill one another by the look, like cockatrices.[9]

Enter Olivia and Viola [as Cesario].

FABIAN. Here he comes with your niece; give them way[10] till he take

175 leave, and presently[11] after him.

SIR TOBY. I will meditate the while upon some horrid[12] message for a challenge.

[Exeunt Sir Toby, Fabian, and Maria.]

---

1 Dealing, communication.
2 Keep a look out. For "me" as an intensifier, see p. 148, note 6.
3 A contemptuous term for a sneaking bailiff who caught debtors "in the rear" (*OED*, bumbailiff).
4 Credit.
5 Testing, trial.
6 Intelligence.
7 Realize.
8 Blockhead.
9 I.e., basilisks, mythical monsters that could kill with a look.
10 Stay out of their way. It appears they do, since Olivia and Viola give no indication of seeing them.
11 Immediately.
12 Horrible, terrifying.

OLIVIA. I have said too much unto a heart of stone,
  And laid mine honor too unchary[1] on't;[2]
  There's something in me that reproves my fault,   180
  But such a headstrong potent fault it is,
  That it but mocks reproof.
VIOLA. With the same havior that your passion bears[3]
  Goes on my master's griefs.
OLIVIA. Here, wear this jewel for me, 'tis my picture[4]—   185
  Refuse it not, [*Giving the jewel*] it hath no tongue to vex you—
  And I beseech you come again tomorrow.
  What shall you ask of me that I'll deny,
  That, honor saved,[5] may upon asking give?
VIOLA. Nothing but this: your true love for my master.   190
OLIVIA. How with mine honor may I give him that
  Which I have giv'n to you?
VIOLA.   I will acquit[6] you.
OLIVIA. Well, come again tomorrow. Fare thee well,
  A fiend like thee might bear my soul to hell.

                                          [*Exit Olivia.*]

Enter Sir Toby and Fabian.
SIR TOBY. Gentleman, god save thee.   195
VIOLA. And you, sir.
SIR TOBY. That defense[7] thou hast, betake thee to't. Of what nature
  the wrongs are thou hast done him, I know not; but thy inter-
  ceptor, full of despite,[8] bloody as the hunter, attends thee at the

---

1 Unwarily, carelessly.
2 Either (1) on the "heart of stone" (imagined as an altar, or as a known stone in
a church where debts were paid), or (2) on what "I have said" (the idea is of wager-
ing honor).
3 Behavior that characterizes your emotional state.
4 A miniature portrait in a richly jeweled setting, probably a pendant on a gold
chain.
5 My virtue (i.e., chastity) excepted. Olivia's general sense is clear, that she (or
honor) will grant anything consistent with virtue.
6 Release, discharge (from a debt).
7 I.e., her sword.
8 Contempt and outrage.

200   orchard-end. Dismount thy tuck,[1] be yare[2] in thy preparation, for thy assailant is quick, skillful, and deadly.

VIOLA. You mistake, sir; I am sure no man hath any quarrel to me. My remembrance is very free and clear from any image of offense done to any man.

205 SIR TOBY. You'll find it otherwise, I assure you. Therefore, if you hold your life at any price, betake you to your guard; for your opposite hath in him what youth, strength, skill, and wrath can furnish man withal.°   *emphatic form of "with"*

VIOLA. I pray you, sir, what is he?

210 SIR TOBY. He is knight, dubbed with unhatched[3] rapier and on carpet consideration,[4] but he is a devil in private brawl. Souls and bodies hath he divorced three, and his incensement at this moment is so implacable that satisfaction can be none but by pangs of death and sepulcher. "Hob, nob"[5] is his word:[6] giv't or

215 take't.

VIOLA. I will return again into the house, and desire some conduct[7] of the lady. I am no fighter. I have heard of some kind of men that put quarrels purposely on others to taste[8] their valor; belike this is a man of that quirk.

[As Viola starts to exit, Sir Toby blocks her way.]

220 SIR TOBY. Sir, no. His indignation derives itself out of a very competent[9] injury; therefore get you on, and give him his desire. Back you shall not to the house, unless you undertake that with me which with as much safety you might answer him.[10] Therefore on, or strip your sword stark naked; for meddle[11] you must, that's

225 certain, or forswear to wear iron about you.[12]

---

1   Draw your rapier. "Dismount" is inflated language, since it properly applies to cannon.

2   Prompt.

3   Unhacked (i.e., the blade never nicked in battle).

4   I.e., dubbed at court, not kneeling on a battlefield: a carpet knight. "Consideration" may imply payment.

5   "Give't or take't" (i.e., death; literally, "have or have not").

6   Motto (written on a shield).

7   An escort.

8   Try, test.

9   Sufficient (in law to demand satisfaction).

10 I.e., a duel. Sir Toby's stance will no doubt indicate his readiness to draw his sword, and either he or Fabian will have blocked Viola's retreat.

11 Engage (in fighting).

12 I.e., admit your cowardice (cf. "never draw sword again," 1.3.54, TLN 177).

3.4.206:   BETAKE YOU TO YOUR GUARD
                    (TLN 1749)

Sir Toby employs specialized sword-fighting vocabulary as he prepares "Cesario" and Sir Andrew for their duel, in such terms as "pass," (l. 245, TLN 1793), "stuck," (l. 246, TLN 1794, and "duello" (l. 273, TLN 1823). Joseph Swetnam's manual *The School of the Noble and Worthy Science of Defence* (1617) is one among many books of instruction in the art of fighting, and a woodcut illustrates his description of the best *en garde* position for someone told to "betake you to your guard":

> Keep your rapier point something sloping towards your left shoulder, and your rapier hand so low as your girdlestead [waist], or lower, and bear out your rapier hand right at arm's end, so far as you can, and keep the point of your rapier something leaning outwards toward your enemy, keeping your rapier always on the outside of your enemy's rapier, but not joining with him, for you must observe a true distance at all weapons, that is to say, three feet betwixt the points of your weapons, and twelve foot distance with your fore-foot from your enemy's fore-foot. You must be careful that you frame your guard right, now you must not bear the rapier hand wide of the right side of your body, but right forward from your girdlestead, as before said. ("The true guard for the single Rapier," p. 117).

Joseph Swetnam, *The School of the Noble and Worthy Science of Defence* (1617), p. 118. From the Wikimedia Commons, <http://www.commons.wikimedia.org>.

VIOLA. [*To the audience*] This is as uncivil[1] as strange. [*To Sir Toby*] I beseech you, do me this courteous office, as to know of[2] the knight what my offense to him is. It is something of my negligence, nothing of my purpose.

230 SIR TOBY. I will do so.[3] [*To Fabian*] Signor Fabian, stay you by this gentleman till my return.

Exit [*Sir*] *Toby.*

VIOLA. Pray you, sir, do you know of this matter?

FABIAN. I know the knight is incensed against you, even to a mortal arbitrament,[4] but nothing of the circumstance more.

235 VIOLA. I beseech you, what manner of man is he?

FABIAN. Nothing of that wonderful promise, to read him by his form,[5] as you are like to find him in the proof of his valor. He is indeed, sir, the most skillful, bloody, and fatal opposite that you could possibly have found in any part of Illyria. Will you walk

240 towards him,[6] I will make your peace with him, if I can.

VIOLA. I shall be much bound to you for't. I am one that had rather go with sir priest[7] than sir knight; I care not who knows so much of my mettle.

Exeunt [*or withdraw*].[8]

Enter [*Sir*] *Toby and* [*Sir*] *Andrew.*

SIR TOBY. Why, man, he's a very devil, I have not seen such a virago.[9]

245 I had a pass[10] with him, rapier, scabbard,[11] and all, and he gives

---

1 Discourteous.

2 Enquire from.

3 Sir Toby can increase Viola's anxiety by an extended pause before he speaks.

4 Decision by (combat to the) death.

5 Outward appearance.

6 I.e., "If you will walk towards him," but in performance often a terrifying direct question.

7 Priests were normally called "sir," whether or not they had taken a university degree, which would also entitle them to this English translation of Latin *dominus*.

8 Probably to the back of the stage (at the Globe, near one of the doors), or to a front corner.

9 Female warrior. Possibly Sir Toby uses the term jokingly for the womanish-looking Cesario, unaware of its irony.

10 I.e., bout. Cf. "stuck in," and *Romeo and Juliet* 3.1.84, TLN 1516, "Come, sir, your *passado*."

11 Either a ludicrous embellishment, or for a practice bout, explaining Sir Toby's lack of injury.

me the stuck[1] in with such a mortal motion that it is inevitable;[2] and on the answer,[3] he pays[4] you as surely as your feet hits[5] the ground they step on. They say he has been fencer to the Sophy.[6]

SIR ANDREW. Pox on't, I'll not meddle with him! ·

SIR TOBY. Ay, but he will not now be pacified; [*Pointing towards Viola and Fabian*] Fabian can scarce hold him yonder.   250

SIR ANDREW. Plague on't, an I thought he had been valiant, and so cunning[7] in fence, I'd have seen him damned ere I'd have challenged him. Let him let the matter slip, and I'll give him my horse, gray Capilet.[8]   255

SIR TOBY. I'll make the motion.[9] Stand here, make a good show on't; this shall end without the perdition of souls.[10] [*Aside*] Marry, I'll ride your horse as well as I ride[11] you.

Enter Fabian and Viola [or they come forward].

[*To Fabian*] I have his horse to take up[12] the quarrel. I have persuaded him the youth's a devil.   260

FABIAN. [*Indicating Viola*] He is as horribly conceited[13] of him; and pants and looks pale, as if a bear were at his heels.

SIR TOBY. [*To Viola*] There's no remedy, sir; he will fight with you for's oath sake. Marry, he hath better bethought him of his quarrel, and he finds that now scarce to be worth talking of. Therefore   265 draw, for the supportance of his vow; he protests he will not hurt you.

---

1 Thrust (Italian *stoccata*). Cf. *Hamlet* 4.7.162, TLN 3152, "your venom'd stuck."
2 Not able to be parried.
3 Counter-thrust.
4 Kills. Cf. *Henry IV, Part One* 2.4.189, TLN 1151: "Two I am sure I have paid."
5 See 2.3.133 (TLN 843) for another example of a singular verb with a plural noun, not uncommon in Shakespeare.
6 Shah of Persia (see 2.5.162, TLN 1183).
7 Skillful.
8 Folio's spelling may represent the name Capulet, and it is possible that "Gray" should be part of the name.
9 Offer.
10 I.e., loss of life.
11 Make a fool of (punning on "ride your horse").
12 Settle.
13 Has as terrifying an idea.

VIOLA. [*To the audience*] Pray god defend me! A little thing would make me tell them how much I lack of a man.[1]

270 FABIAN. [*To Viola*] Give ground if you see him furious.

SIR TOBY. Come, Sir Andrew, there's no remedy, the gentleman will for his honor's sake have one bout with you. He cannot by the duello[2] avoid it. But he has promised me, as he is a gentleman and a soldier, he will not hurt you. [*To them both*] Come on, to't.

275 SIR ANDREW. Pray god he keep his oath!

Enter Antonio.

VIOLA. [*To Sir Andrew*] I do assure you, 'tis against my will.

ANTONIO. [*To Sir Andrew, drawing*] Put up your sword! If this
   young gentleman
Have done offense, I take the fault on me;
If you offend him, I for him defy you.[3]

280 SIR TOBY. You, sir? Why, what are you?

ANTONIO. One, sir, that for his love dares yet do more
Than you have heard him brag to you he will.

SIR TOBY. [*Drawing*] Nay, if you be an undertaker,[4] I am for you.[5]

Enter Officers.

FABIAN. O good Sir Toby, hold! Here come the officers.

285 SIR TOBY. [*To Antonio*] I'll be with you anon.[6]

[*They sheathe their swords.*]

VIOLA. [*To Sir Andrew*] Pray sir, put your sword up, if you please.

SIR ANDREW. Marry, will I, sir; [*Sheathing his sword*] and for that I promised you, I'll be as good as my word. He will bear you easily, and reins well.[7]

---

1 It would not take much to make me admit (1) how afraid I am, (2) that I am a woman (with a sexual quibble on the lack of "a little thing").

2 Code of dueling (available in published manuals).

3 Antonio probably interposes his body between Viola and Sir Andrew; the intrusion of the serious plot is also signaled by his speaking in verse.

4 (1) One who enters into combat with (see 1.3.50, TLN 173), (2) one who accepts responsibility (often, for another).

5 Ready for you.

6 Straight away. There is implicit agreement to conceal from the Officers any evidence of a duel.

7 Sir Andrew sheathes his sword in relief, and reaffirms his promise of his horse; Viola will be totally mystified.

FIRST OFFICER. [*To Second Officer*] This is the man; do thy office. 290

SECOND OFFICER. Antonio, I arrest thee at the suit
Of Count Orsino.

ANTONIO.   You do mistake me, sir.

FIRST OFFICER. No, sir, no jot. I know your favor[1] well, *face*
Though now you have no sea-cap on your head.
Take him away; he knows I know him well. 295

ANTONIO. I must obey.[2] [*To Viola*] This comes with seeking you;
But there's no remedy, I shall answer[3] it.
What will you do,[4] now my necessity
Makes me to ask you for my purse? It grieves me
Much more for what I cannot do for you 300
Than what befalls myself. You stand amazed,[5]
But be of comfort.

SECOND OFFICER. Come, sir, away.

ANTONIO. I must entreat of you some of that money.

VIOLA. What money, sir? 305
For the fair kindness you have showed me here,
And part° being prompted by your present trouble, *in part*
Out of my lean and low ability
I'll lend you something. My having is not much;
I'll make division of my present[6] with you. 310
Hold, [*Offering a few coins*] there's half my coffer.[7]

ANTONIO. [*Rejecting them*] Will you deny me now?[8]
Is't possible that my deserts° to you *deservings*
Can lack persuasion?[9] Do not tempt[10] my misery,
Lest that it make me so unsound[11] a man 315

---

1 Face.
2 At some point Antonio will surrender his sword, if it has not already been seized.
3 (1) Face the charge, (2) pay the penalty. See p. 152, note 8.
4 I.e., without enough money.
5 Bewildered. A much stronger word in Elizabethan English than now, as is evident from Antonio's concern.
6 I.e., such money as I have at present.
7 Strong-box (a rueful exaggeration of her nearly-empty purse).
8 Antonio's anger may lead him to strike the few coins from her hand.
9 Can lack power to move you (of all people).
10 Put to the test (by refusing me).
11 Morally weak (since kindness should be for its own sake, not for reward).

3.4.294:   SEA-CAP AND SAILORS (TLN 1847)

The exact nature of sailors' apparel in Shakespeare's time is not certain, but it seems to have been distinctive, as the Officer's identification of Antonio suggests. Possibly Antonio was wearing it when he first appeared in the play, prior to following Sebastian to Orsino's court. The "sea-cap" was probably a "Monmouth" thrummed "shaggy brimless hat or cap" with its very long pile designed to shed water, which went with "baggy breeches gathered in below the knee [and] a loose waist-length coat" (Phillis Cunnington and Catherine Lucas, *Occupational Costume in England* [London: Adam and Charles Black, 1967], p. 56). The breeches were likely made of canvas, possibly coated with tar (hence "tarpaulin"). Sailors often wore knives around their necks on a lanyard. Chaucer says of his Shipman, in the General Prologue, 392–93, that "A dagger on a lanyard falling free / Hung from his neck under his arm and down." In an illustration from Cesare Vecellio, *Habiti Antichi et Moderni di Tutto il Mondo* (Venice, 1598), a sailor in a thrummed sea-cap is carrying the additional identifier of a compass in its bowl, as does possibly the Captain who enters with his sailors at the start of the second scene of the play (TLN 50).

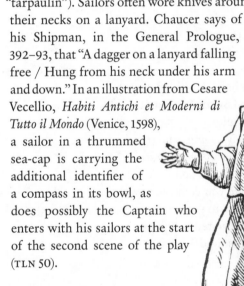

RIGHT: English sailor in thrummed sea-cap, from Cesare Vecellio, *Habiti Antichi et Moderni di Tutto il Mondo* (Venice, 1598), reproduced by permission from *Vecellio's Renaissance Costume Book* (New York: Dover, 1977); photograph by David Carnegie.

As to upbraid you with those kindnesses
That I have done for you.
VIOLA.   I know of none,
Nor know I you by voice or any feature.
I hate ingratitude more in a man
Than lying, vainness, babbling drunkenness,   320
Or any taint of vice whose strong corruption
Inhabits our frail blood.
ANTONIO.   O heavens themselves!
SECOND OFFICER. Come, sir, I pray you go.
ANTONIO. Let me speak a little. This youth that you see here
I snatched one half out of the jaws of death,   325
Relieved him with such sanctity of love,
And to his image,[1] which methought did promise
Most venerable° worth, did I devotion.[2]   *worthy of veneration*
FIRST OFFICER. What's that to us? The time goes by. Away!
ANTONIO. But O, how vile an idol proves this god!   330
[*To Viola*] Thou hast, Sebastian, done good feature shame.
In nature, there's no blemish but the mind;
None can be called deformed but the unkind.[3]
Virtue is beauty, but the beauteous evil[4]
Are empty trunks,[5] o'er-flourished[6] by the devil!   335
FIRST OFFICER. The man grows mad; away with him. [*To Antonio*]
Come, come, sir!
ANTONIO. Lead me on.
                                Exit [*Antonio guarded by Officers*].
VIOLA. [*To the audience*] Methinks his words do from such passion
fly
That he believes himself; so do not I.[7]   340
Prove true, imagination, O prove true,
That I, dear brother, be now ta'en for you!

---

1 (1) Appearance, (2) religious image (cf. "idol" in his next speech).
2 (1) Loyal service, (2) worship (cf. "god," 3.4.330, TLN 1885).
3 (1) Cruel, (2) unnatural.
4 See p. 82, note 2.
5 (1) Bodies, (2) household chests.
6 Painted with elaborate decoration.
7 I.e., I do not accept his belief (that I am Sebastian).

SIR TOBY. Come hither,[1] knight, come hither, Fabian. We'll whisper
o'er a couplet or two of most sage saws.[2]

[*They stand apart.*]

345 VIOLA. [*To the audience*] He named Sebastian! I my brother know
Yet living in my glass.[3] Even such and so
In favor was my brother, and he went
Still° in this fashion, color, ornament,   *always*
For him I imitate. O, if it prove,°   *prove true (that Sebastian is alive)*
350 Tempests are kind, and salt waves fresh[4] in love.

[*Exit.*]

SIR TOBY. A very dishonest[5] paltry boy, and more a coward than a
hare.[6] His dishonesty appears in leaving his friend here in necessity, and denying him; and for his cowardship, ask Fabian.

FABIAN. A coward, a most devout coward, religious in it.

355 SIR ANDREW. 'Slid,[7] I'll after him again, and beat him.

SIR TOBY. Do, cuff him soundly, but never draw thy sword.[8]

SIR ANDREW. An I do not—[9]

[*Exit following Viola.*]

FABIAN. Come, let's see the event.°   *outcome*

SIR TOBY. I dare lay any money 'twill be nothing yet.°   *after all*

Exit [*Sir Toby and Fabian, following Sir Andrew*].

[4.1]

Enter Sebastian and Clown [following].[10]

CLOWN. Will you make me believe that I am not sent for you?

SEBASTIAN. Go to, go to, thou art a foolish fellow,
Let me be clear of thee.

---

1   Shakespeare's purpose seems to be to give Viola most of the stage alone, to
emphasize her next speech.

2   Wise sayings.

3   In me as a mirror image (of him).

4   Sweet (drinkable), not salty.

5   Dishonorable.

6   Proverbial.

7   By god's eyelid (a mild oath).

8   Presumably Sir Toby realizes that Sir Andrew will lose his nerve if required to
draw sword again.

9   If I do not (cuff him soundly).

10 Sebastian, sightseeing as arranged at 3.3, enters trying to get clear of the Clown,
who has evidently been dogging him for some time.

CLOWN. Well held out[1] i'faith! No, I do not know you, nor I am
not sent to you by my lady, to bid you come speak with her; nor 5
your name is not Master Cesario; nor this is not my nose neither.
Nothing that is so, is so.

SEBASTIAN. I prithee vent thy folly somewhere else,
Thou know'st not me.

CLOWN. Vent my folly! [*To the audience*] He has heard that word of 10
some great man, and now applies it to a fool. Vent my folly! I
am afraid this great lubber the world will prove a cockney.[2] [*To
Sebastian*] I prithee now, ungird thy strangeness,[3] and tell me what
I shall vent to my lady. Shall I vent to her that thou art coming?

SEBASTIAN. I prithee, foolish Greek,[4] depart from me. [*Giving* 15
a coin]
There's money for thee; if you tarry longer,
[*Threatening a blow*] I shall give worse payment.°   *i.e., blows*

CLOWN. By my troth, thou hast an open hand.[5] [*To the audience*]
These wise men that give fools money get themselves a good
report—after fourteen years' purchase![6]   20

Enter Sir Andrew, Sir Toby, and Fabian.

SIR ANDREW. Now, sir, have I met you again? There's for you!
[*He strikes Sebastian.*]

SEBASTIAN. Why, there's for thee, and there, and there!
[*He beats Sir Andrew with the handle of his dagger.*][7]
[*To the audience*] Are all the people mad?

SIR TOBY. [*Seizing Sebastian*] Hold, sir, or I'll throw your dagger o'er
the house.   25

CLOWN. [*To the audience*] This will I tell my lady straight;[8] [*To them*]
I would not be in some of your coats for twopence.
[*Exit.*]

---

1 Kept up.
2 I.e., I fear the great clumsy world will turn out to be an affected townsman.
3 I.e., stop pretending you don't know me (literally, "unbelt your aloofness").
4 A "merry Greek" was a familiar term for a roisterer, a cheerful joker.
5 Generous (with money, and the threat of blows).
6 At the rate of calculation of the purchase price as fourteen years' rent, an
inflated price since twelve year's rent was the usual market value ("purchase").
A good reputation with fools is worthless anyway.
7 Cf. *Romeo and Juliet* 4.5.117–18, TLN 2695–96, "Then will I lay the serving-
creature's dagger on your pate."
8 Immediately.

SIR TOBY. Come on, sir, hold!

SIR ANDREW. Nay, let him alone. I'll go another way to work[1] with

30   him: I'll have an action of battery[2] against him, if there be any
law in Illyria. Though I struck him first, yet it's no matter for that.

SEBASTIAN. [*To Sir Toby*] Let go thy hand!

SIR TOBY. Come, sir, I will not let you go. Come, my young soldier,
put up your iron.[3] You are well fleshed.[4] Come on!

SEBASTIAN. I will be free from thee. [*He breaks free and draws his*

35   *sword.*]   What wouldst thou now?
If thou dar'st tempt° me further, draw thy sword.   *(1) test, (2) incite*

SIR TOBY. [*Drawing*] What, what! Nay then, I must have an ounce
or two of this malapert° blood from you.   *impudent*

Enter Olivia.

OLIVIA. Hold, Toby! On thy life I charge thee, hold!

40 SIR TOBY. Madam.

OLIVIA. Will it be ever thus? Ungracious wretch,
Fit for the mountains and the barbarous caves,
Where manners ne'er were preached! Out of my sight!
[*To Sebastian*] Be not offended, dear Cesario.
[*To Sir Toby*] Rudesby,[5] be gone!

                  [*Exeunt Sir Toby, Sir Andrew, and Fabian.*]

45   [*To Sebastian*] I prithee, gentle friend,
Let thy fair wisdom, not thy passion, sway°   *rule, bear sway*
In this uncivil and unjust extent[6]
Against thy peace. Go with me to my house,
And hear thou there how many fruitless pranks

50   This ruffian hath botched up,[7] that thou thereby
Mayst smile at this. Thou shalt not choose but go;
Do not deny. Beshrew his soul for me,°   *my curse upon him*

---

1   I'll use a different route for my purpose (proverbial).

2   Lawsuit for assault (which Sir Andrew goes on to admit has no basis in law).

3   Dagger. Cf. *Romeo and Juliet* 4.5.123–24, TLN 2702–03, "I will dry-beat you with
an iron wit, and put up my iron dagger."

4   Blooded, initiated into fighting.

5   Ruffian. Presumably they are amazed at Olivia's open display of affection for
"Cesario."

6   Assault (a legal term used here in a generalized sense).

7   Patched together (cf. 1.5.39, TLN 338–39).

He started one poor heart[1] of mine in thee.[2]

SEBASTIAN. [*To the audience*] What relish[3] is in this? How runs the
    stream?

    Or° I am mad, or else this is a dream.   *either*   55

    Let fancy still my sense in Lethe steep;[4]

    If it be thus to dream, still let me sleep!

OLIVIA. Nay, come, I prithee; would thou'dst be ruled by me![5]

SEBASTIAN. Madam, I will.

OLIVIA.   O say so, and so be.

                                    Exeunt.

[4.2]

Enter Maria [carrying a minister's gown and a false beard,] and Clown.

MARIA. Nay, I prithee put on this gown, and this beard;[6] make him
    believe thou art Sir Topaz the curate.[7] Do it quickly. I'll call Sir
    Toby the whilst.°   *in the meantime*

                                        [Exit.]

CLOWN. [*To the audience*] Well, I'll put it on, and I will dissemble
    myself[8] in't, and I would I were the first that ever dissembled in   5
    such a gown. I am not tall[9] enough to become the function well,
    nor lean enough to be thought a good student;[10] but to be said an

---

1   (1) Startled my heart, (2) roused from cover (a hunting term) a hart (deer;
cf. 1.1.20–22, TLN 26–28 and extended note).

2   She has given her heart to "Cesario," hence Sir Toby's attack was as if on her.

3   Taste (hence, "How do I identify what is going on?")

4   Let imagination continue to drown my rationality in the river of forgetfulness.

5   I.e., if only you would do as I wish.

6   False beards were standard in the theater; cf. *A Midsummer Night's Dream*
1.2.84–86 (TLN 354–56): "your straw-color beard, your orange-tawny beard, your
purple-in-grain beard, or your French-crown-color beard."

7   Although Chaucer and others had comic knights of this name, here he is a
priest (for the use of "sir," see p. 166, note 7). He is probably intended to be a
parish priest, or possibly an assistant curate (a minister appointed on a low salary
to act for a non-resident or incapacitated priest).

8   (1) Disguise, (2) act hypocritically.

9   Possibly "handsome," but more likely referring to a gown that is comically
large for him (see next note).

10 Divinity scholars (like other students) were regarded as prone to weight loss
and melancholy.

honest[1] man and a good housekeeper[2] goes as fairly as to say a careful[3] man and a great scholar.

Enter Sir Toby [and Maria].

10   The competitors° enter.   *confederates, partners*

SIR TOBY. Jove[4] bless thee, Master Parson.

CLOWN. *Bonos dies,*[5] Sir Toby: for as the old hermit of Prague,[6] that never saw pen and ink,[7] very wittily said to a niece of King Gorboduc,[8] "That that is, is";[9] so I, being Master Parson, am

15   Master Parson; for what is "that" but "that," and "is" but "is"?

SIR TOBY. To him, Sir Topaz!

CLOWN. *[In the voice of Sir Topaz]* What ho, I say. Peace in this prison.[10]

SIR TOBY. *[To the audience or Maria]* The knave counterfeits well: a good knave.

Malvolio within.

20   MALVOLIO. *[Within]* Who calls there?

CLOWN. Sir Topaz the curate, who comes to visit Malvolio the lunatic.

MALVOLIO. *[Within]* Sir Topaz, Sir Topaz, good Sir Topaz, go to my lady.

25   CLOWN. Out, hyperbolical fiend![11] How vexest thou this man! Talkest thou nothing but of ladies?

SIR TOBY. Well said, Master Parson!

---

1   Honorable.

2   Generous host.

3   Either (1) careworn (from study), or (2) conscientious.

4   Possibly Sir Toby substitutes a pagan "God" as a comment on the substitute parson.

5   Good day (bad Latin for *bonus dies*).

6   As at 1.5.30 (TLN 329), an invented mock-authority.

7   I.e., was illiterate.

8   A legendary British king, subject of the earliest English tragedy in blank verse (c. 1562). His unknown niece knitted bedsocks for the hermit of Prague.

9   Mock-learning from the mock-authority.

10 In the Elizabethan *Book of Common Prayer* (1559), "the Priest entering into the sick person's house, shall say 'Peace be in this house.'"

11 Fie, excessive devil (hyperbole, in rhetoric, is immoderate exaggeration of language).

The Folio stage direction reads "*Malvolio within*," and there is no direction for him to enter later in the scene, or ever be seen at all. On the Elizabethan stage he could have been behind a stage door or, more likely, behind an arras at the back of the stage. The visual focus would therefore have been on the disguised Clown's apparently improvised comic teasing of Malvolio. Maria's comment to the Clown that "Thou might'st have done this without thy beard and gown, he sees thee not" (4.2.61–62, TLN 2049–50) only makes sense if Malvolio is off-stage. Since the nineteenth century, however, it has been increasingly common to allow the audience to see Malvolio, or at least to see hands emerging from a trap door or through bars. The more of Malvolio they see, the more likely they are to feel sorry for him. Carried to an extreme, the character can be seen as tragic, as in Henry Irving's famous 1884 production (see Introduction, p. 40), and as in the 1709 illustration (not based on a specific production) from Rowe below. (See Carnegie, "*Maluolio within*.")

Malvolio within the "dark house." Detail from the frontispiece to *Twelfth Night* in Nicholas Rowe's edition of the *Works of Mr. William Shakespear* (1709), vol. 2. Courtesy of the Alexander Turnbull Library, Wellington, New Zealand, callmark REng SHAK Works 1709.

MALVOLIO. [*Within*] Sir Topaz, never was man thus wronged. Good
Sir Topaz, do not think I am mad: they have laid me here in hid-
30 eous darkness.

CLOWN. Fie, thou dishonest[1] Satan! I call thee by the most modest[2] terms— [*Including the audience*] for I am one of those gentle[3]
ones that will use the devil himself with courtesy—say'st thou
that house is dark?[4]

35 MALVOLIO. [*Within*] As hell, Sir Topaz.

CLOWN. Why, it hath bay windows transparent as barricadoes,[5] and
the clerestories[6] toward the south-north are as lustrous as ebony;
and yet complainest thou of obstruction?[7]

MALVOLIO. [*Within*] I am not mad, Sir Topaz; I say to you this house
40 is dark.

CLOWN. Madman, thou errest. I say there is no darkness but ignorance, in which thou art more puzzled[8] than the Egyptians in
their fog.[9]

MALVOLIO. [*Within*] I say this house is as dark as ignorance, though
45 ignorance were as dark as hell; and I say there was never man thus
abused. I am no more mad than you are. Make the trial of it in
any constant question.°   *consistent interrogation*

CLOWN. What is the opinion of Pythagoras[10] concerning wildfowl?[11]

MALVOLIO. [*Within*] That the soul of our grandam might haply[12]
50 inhabit a bird.

CLOWN. What think'st thou of his opinion?

---

1 Dishonorable.

2 Moderate.

3 Courteous, well-bred.

4 I.e., room is dark. Cf. *As You Like It* 3.2:390–92, TLN 1580–81: "Love … deserves
as well a dark house and a whip as madmen do."

5 Barricades (i.e., solid, like "ebony" in the next line).

6 Upper windows (especially in a church). Pronounced "clear-stories."

7 Blocking out (of light).

8 Confused.

9 One of the biblical plagues of Egypt was "thick" darkness "that may be felt"
(Exodus 10:21–23).

10 A classical philosopher whose belief in the kinship of all living beings led to
the frequently-mocked doctrine that the soul could migrate between humans and
animals.

11 Slang for whore.

12 Perhaps.

MALVOLIO. [*Within*] I think nobly of the soul, and no way approve his opinion.

CLOWN. Fare thee well. Remain thou still in darkness.¹ Thou shalt hold th'opinion of Pythagoras ere I will allow of thy wits,² and 55 fear to kill a woodcock³ lest thou dispossess the soul of thy grandam. [*Moving away*] Fare thee well.

MALVOLIO. [*Within*] Sir Topaz, Sir Topaz!

SIR TOBY. [*To Clown*] My most exquisite Sir Topaz!

CLOWN. Nay, I am for all waters.°   *versatile*   60

MARIA. Thou mightst have done this without thy beard and gown;⁴ he sees thee not.

SIR TOBY. [*To Clown*] To him in thine own voice, and bring me word how thou find'st him. I would we were well rid of this knavery. If he may be conveniently delivered,⁵ I would he were, for I am 65 now so far in offense with my niece that I cannot pursue with any safety this sport to the upshot.⁶ Come by and by to my chamber.

                           Exit [*Sir Toby and Maria*].

CLOWN. [*Singing*] Hey Robin,⁷ jolly Robin,
    Tell me how thy lady does.

MALVOLIO. [*Within*] Fool!   70

CLOWN. My lady is unkind, perdie.°   *by god (from French par Dieu)*

MALVOLIO. [*Within*] Fool!

CLOWN. Alas, why is she so?

MALVOLIO. [*Within*] Fool, I say!

CLOWN. She loves another—   75
    Who calls, ha?

MALVOLIO. [*Within*] Good fool, as ever thou wilt deserve well at my hand, help me to a candle, and pen, ink, and paper. As I am a gentleman, I will live to be thankful to thee for't.

---

1   (1) Without light, (2) theological ignorance.
2   Accept that you are sane.
3   Proverbial for stupidity; cf. 2.5.78, TLN 1097.
4   The Clown probably removes the disguise now, relying on changes of voice to bamboozle Malvolio for the rest of the scene.
5   Set free without trouble.
6   To its conclusion (archery term from the final shot in a match).
7   The Clown allows Malvolio to identify him by singing, in further mockery, a dialogue song about a lover who has lost to a rival (i.e., Malvolio to Cesario in the affections of Olivia).

80   CLOWN. Master Malvolio?

    MALVOLIO. [*Within*] Ay, good fool.

    CLOWN. Alas, sir, how fell you besides° your five wits?[1]   *out of*

    MALVOLIO. [*Within*] Fool, there was never man so notoriously[2] abused. I am as well in my wits, fool, as thou art.

85   CLOWN. But as well? Then you are mad indeed, if you be no better in your wits than a fool.

    MALVOLIO. [*Within*] They have here propertied me:[3] keep me in darkness, send ministers to me, asses, and do all they can to face[4] me out of my wits.

90   CLOWN. Advise you[5] what you say, the minister is here. [*Speaking as Sir Topaz*] Malvolio, Malvolio, thy wits the heavens restore. Endeavor thyself[6] to sleep, and leave thy vain bibble babble.[7]

    MALVOLIO. [*Within*] Sir Topaz!

    CLOWN. [*As Sir Topaz*] Maintain no words with him, good fellow.

95   [*Speaking as himself*] Who I, sir? Not I, sir! God buy you,[8] good Sir Topaz. [*As Sir Topaz*] Marry, amen. [*As himself*] I will, sir, I will.[9]

    MALVOLIO. [*Within*] Fool! Fool! Fool, I say![10]

    CLOWN. Alas, sir, be patient. What say you, sir? I am shent[11] for speaking to you.

100   MALVOLIO. [*Within*] Good fool, help me to some light, and some paper; I tell thee I am as well in my wits as any man in Illyria.

    CLOWN. Well-a-day that° you were, sir.   *alas, I wish that*

---

1 Mind (sometimes identified as common wit, imagination, fantasy, estimation, and memory).
2 Scandalously.
3 Treated me like a chattel (or perhaps like a stage "prop").
4 Brazenly bully.
5 Be careful.
6 Exert yourself in attempting (i.e., strain to relax).
7 Senseless babbling.
8 God be with you (modern "goodbye").
9 The short phrases may indicate pauses, as if Sir Topaz is whispering further instructions.
10 Probably an increasingly frantic stage whisper, since Malvolio will try to avoid being heard by Sir Topaz.
11 Rebuked.

MALVOLIO. [*Within*] By this hand,[1] I am! Good fool, some ink, paper,
and light; and convey what I will set down to my lady. It shall
advantage thee more than ever the bearing of letter did.   105
CLOWN. I will help you to't. But tell me true, are you not mad indeed,
or do you but counterfeit?
MALVOLIO. [*Within*] Believe me, I am not, I tell thee true.
CLOWN. Nay, I'll ne'er believe a madman till I see his brains! I will
fetch you light, and paper, and ink.   110
MALVOLIO. [*Within*] Fool, I'll requite it in the highest degree. I
prithee, be gone!
CLOWN. [*Singing*]
   I am gone, sir, and anon,[2] sir,
   I'll be with you again,
   In a trice,° like to the old Vice,[3]   *moment*   115
   Your need to sustain;
   Who with dagger of lath,[4] in his rage and his wrath,
   Cries "Ah, ha!"° to the devil,   *i.e., in defiance*
   Like a mad lad, "Pare thy nails,[5] dad![6]
   Adieu, goodman devil."[7]   120
                                               Exit.

1   A conventional oath (which Malvolio used at 2.3.110, TLN 818–19), so there is
no need for his hand to be seen, although in modern productions it often is.
2   "I am gone" picks up Malvolio's last word; "anon" means "straight away."
Internal rhyme continues through the song.
3   In morality plays from a generation earlier, the popular Vice character would
drive the plot forward with broad farce and slapstick, in league with the devil but
impudent.
4   Wood (a stage prop).
5   I.e., have your wings clipped, your power reduced.
6   The Vice character is occasionally the devil's son, but here it may simply be
impudence: "old man."
7   "Goodman" is a respectful form of address, but absurd to the devil.

[4.3]

Enter Sebastian.

SEBASTIAN. [*To the audience*] This is the air, that is the glorious sun,
  [*Indicating the pearl*] This pearl she gave me, I do feel't, and see't,
  And though 'tis wonder that enwraps me thus,
  Yet 'tis not madness. Where's Antonio then?
5 I could not find him at the Elephant,
  Yet there he was,° and there I found this credit,[1]   *had been*
  That he did range the town to seek me out.
  His counsel now might do me golden service,
  For though my soul disputes well (with my sense)[2]
10 That[3] this may be some error, but no madness,
  Yet doth this accident and flood of fortune
  So far exceed all instance,° all discourse,[4]   *example, precedent*
  That I am ready to distrust mine eyes,
  And wrangle with my reason that persuades me
15 To any other trust but that I am mad,
  Or else the lady's mad.[5] Yet if 'twere so,
  She could not sway[6] her house, command her followers,
  Take and give back affairs and their dispatch,[7]
  With such a smooth, discreet, and stable bearing
20 As I perceive she does. There's something in't
  That is deceivable.°   *deceptive*

Enter Olivia, and Priest.[8]
              But here the lady comes.
OLIVIA. Blame not this haste of mine. If you mean well,

---

1 Report (usage unique to Shakespeare).
2 In accord with the evidence of my senses.
3 Reasons convincingly ... that (not "argues with").
4 Reasoning.
5 I.e., argue against my reason, which produces good evidence in favor of any
conclusion except that I am mad or Olivia is.
6 Rule, manage.
7 I.e., "take" in hand business matters ("affairs") and settle them quickly ("give
back their dispatch").
8 In some productions (e.g., the Nunn film) his appearance shows that he is the
real Sir Topaz on whom the Clown has modeled himself.

Now go with me, and with this holy man,
Into the chantry by;¹ there before him,
And underneath that consecrated roof,   25
Plight me the full assurance of your faith,²
That my most jealous³ and too doubtful soul
May live at peace.⁴ He shall conceal it,
Whiles° you are willing it shall come to note⁵   *until*
What time° we will our celebration⁶ keep   *i.e., at what time* 30
According to my birth.° What do you say?   *rank*
SEBASTIAN. I'll follow this good man, and go with you,
And having sworn truth, ever will be true.
OLIVIA. Then lead the way, good father, and heavens so shine
That they may fairly note° this act of mine.   *look on with favor* 35
                                                       Exeunt.

[5.1]

Enter Clown [with a letter] and Fabian.
FABIAN. Now as thou lov'st me, let me see his letter.⁷
CLOWN. Good Master Fabian, grant me another request.
FABIAN. Anything.
CLOWN. Do not desire to see this letter.
FABIAN. This is to give a dog, and in recompense desire my dog   5
    again.⁸

---

1 Nearby chapel (endowed for a priest to sing daily mass for the souls of the
founders or others).
2 I.e., enter with me into a full contract of betrothal (as binding as the marriage
service later).
3 (1) Fearful, (2) mistrustful.
4 A pause is possibly intended here, as the line has only four feet. If so, what follows is urgent reassurance.
5 Become known.
6 I.e., wedding.
7 I.e., Malvolio's to Olivia.
8 Fabian may well have directed this repartee to the audience in early productions, reminding them of Queen Elizabeth's promise to grant a courtier anything
he wished if he would give her his favorite dog. His wish was to have his dog back
again.

Enter Orsino, Viola [as Cesario], Curio, and Lords.[1]

ORSINO. Belong you to the Lady Olivia, friends?

CLOWN. Ay, sir, we are some of her trappings.[2]

ORSINO. I know thee well. How dost thou, my good fellow?

10 CLOWN. Truly, sir, the better for my foes, and the worse for my friends.

ORSINO. Just the contrary; the better for thy friends.

CLOWN. No, sir, the worse.

ORSINO. How can that be?

15 CLOWN. Marry, sir, they praise me, and make[3] an ass of me. Now, my foes tell me plainly I am an ass, so that by my foes, sir, I profit in the knowledge of myself, and by my friends I am abused.[4] So that, conclusions to be as kisses, if your four[5] negatives make your two affirmatives,[6] why then, the worse for my friends and

20 the better for my foes.

ORSINO. Why, this is excellent.[7]

CLOWN. By my troth, sir, no; though it please you to be one of my friends.[8]

ORSINO. Thou shalt not be the worse[9] for me; there's gold.[10]

[Orsino gives him a gold coin.]

25 CLOWN. But that it would be double-dealing,[11] sir, I would you could make it another.

ORSINO. O you give me ill counsel.

---

1 Orsino and others may be booted; see extended note, p. 84.

2 Embellishments (literally, decorated horse-cloths).

3 And thus make.

4 Ill-used, deceived.

5 Unstressed, simply meaning "that you know of" (as with "your two" following).

6 In grammar, a double negative is an affirmative.

7 Orsino's willingness to jest with the Clown marks a distinct departure from his melancholy at their previous encounter in 2.4.

8 An invitation for praise (and, perhaps, a tip).

9 (1) "Abused" (as the Clown said of his friends), (2) poorer.

10 A half-crown was the smallest English gold coin, so the Clown is getting at least five times as much as the silver sixpence given him by Sir Toby (2.3.28, TLN 731), ten times as much if he is given a gold crown (five shillings).

11 (1) Duplicity, (2) giving twice.

CLOWN. Put your grace in your pocket,[1] sir, for this once, and let your flesh and blood obey it.[2]

ORSINO. Well, I will be so much a sinner[3] to be a double-dealer; 30
there's another. [*Orsino gives him another gold coin.*]

CLOWN. *Primo, secundo, tertio*[4] is a good play;[5] and the old saying is, "the third pays for all";[6] the triplex,[7] sir, is a good tripping measure;[8] or the bells of Saint Bennet,[9] sir, may put you in mind: one, two, three. 35

ORSINO. You can fool no more money out of me at this throw.[10] If you will let your lady know I am here to speak with her, and bring her along with you, it may awake my bounty further.

CLOWN. Marry, sir, lullaby[11] to your bounty till I come again. I go, sir, but I would not have you to think that my desire of having is 40
the sin of covetousness—but as you say, sir, let your bounty take a nap; I will awake it anon.

Exit.

Enter Antonio and Officers [guarding him].

VIOLA. Here comes the man, sir, that did rescue me.

ORSINO. That face of his I do remember well;
Yet when I saw it last, it was besmeared 45
As black as Vulcan[12] in the smoke of war.
A baubling[13] vessel was he captain of,

---

1 I.e., (1) put your virtue where it cannot see (to criticize), (2) put your hand in your pocket (for more money), my lord Duke ("your grace").
2 I.e., let your normal human instincts (unwatched by virtuous "grace") obey my "ill counsel."
3 (Because evading divine "grace").
4 First, second, third (Latin). Possibly a children's game, or a reference to a winning three at dice (cf. "tray-trip," p. 138, note 2).
5 Game, or a throw at dice.
6 Proverbial; cf. modern "third time lucky."
7 Triple time in music.
8 Quick time (in music).
9 St. Benedict. There is no way of knowing which of the several churches named for this saint in London Shakespeare was thinking of for its distinctive chime of bells. The Clown may sing the final words in the pitch of the supposed tune.
10 I.e., throw of the dice (continuing gambling references).
11 Soothing repose.
12 Blacksmith of the Roman gods.
13 Paltry (like a child's bauble).

For shallow draught and bulk, unprizable;[1]
With which such scatheful° grapple did he make   *destructive*
50   With the most noble bottom° of our fleet,   *ship*
That very envy, and the tongue of loss,[2]
Cried fame and honor on him. What's the matter?[3]
FIRST OFFICER. Orsino,[4] this is that Antonio
That took the Phoenix,[5] and her fraught from Candy,[6]
55   And this is he that did the Tiger board
When your young nephew Titus lost his leg.
Here in the streets, desperate of shame and state,[7]
In private brabble[8] did we apprehend him.
VIOLA. He did me kindness, sir, drew on my side,[9]
60   But in conclusion put strange speech upon me;[10]
I know not what 'twas, but distraction.[11]
ORSINO. Notable pirate, thou saltwater thief,
What foolish boldness brought thee to their mercies
Whom thou, in terms so bloody and so dear,°   *grievous*
Hast made thine enemies?
65 ANTONIO.   Orsino, noble sir,[12]
Be pleased that I shake off these names you give me.
Antonio never yet was thief, or pirate,
Though I confess, on base and ground[13] enough,
Orsino's enemy. A witchcraft drew me hither:
70   That most ingrateful boy there by your side
From the rude sea's enraged and foamy mouth

---

1 I.e., so small as not to be worth capturing as a "prize."
2 Even Ill-will and the voice of Loss. The emotions of his enemies are personified as proclaiming his honor.
3 Business, allegation.
4 The lack of an honorific before his name is surprising; but see note 12.
5 Like "Tiger" in the next line, the name of a ship.
6 Cargo from Crete.
7 Reckless of (his) reputation and (his) position.
8 Brawling in a personal quarrel.
9 Drew his sword in my defense.
10 Spoke to me strangely.
11 Madness. The meter requires four syllables.
12 Despite the accusations, and Sebastian's apparent betrayal, Antonio's response is both courteous and proud.
13 Foundation. The two words are synonyms.

Did I redeem. A wrack° past hope he was.   *shipwrecked survivor*
His life[1] I gave him, and did thereto add
My love without retention° or restraint,   *reservation*
All his in dedication. For his sake   75
Did I expose myself, pure° for his love,   *purely, only*
Into the danger of this adverse° town;   *hostile*
Drew to defend him, when he was beset;
Where being apprehended, his false cunning,
Not meaning to partake with me in danger,   80
Taught him to face me out of his acquaintance,[2]
And grew a twenty years' removèd thing[3]
While one would wink; denied me mine own purse,
Which I had recommended° to his use   *committed*
Not half an hour before.
VIOLA.   How can this be?   85
ORSINO. When came he to this town?
ANTONIO. Today, my lord; and for three months before,
No int'rim,[4] not a minute's vacancy,
Both day and night did we keep company.

Enter Olivia and Attendants.

ORSINO. Here comes the countess, now heaven walks on earth.   90
[*To Antonio*] But for thee, fellow—fellow, thy words are
    madness.
Three months this youth hath tended upon me;
But more of that anon. [*To Officers*] Take him aside.
OLIVIA. What would my lord, but that[5] he may not have,
Wherein Olivia may seem serviceable?   95
[*To Viola*] Cesario, you do not keep promise with me.
               [*Viola and Orsino speak at the same time.*]
VIOLA. Madam—
ORSINO. Gracious Olivia—
OLIVIA. What do you say, Cesario? [*Silencing Orsino*] Good my lord.

---

1   As Sebastian has already expressed at 2.1.32, TLN 645.
2   Brazenly deny knowing me.
3   I.e., like someone not met for twenty years.
4   Interim (the Folio elision "*intrim*" serves the meter).
5   Except that which (i.e., her love).

100 VIOLA. My lord would speak, my duty hushes me.
    OLIVIA. If it be aught to the old tune, my lord,
      It is as fat and fulsome[1] to mine ear
      As howling after music.
    ORSINO. Still so cruel?
    OLIVIA.   Still so constant, lord.
105 ORSINO. What, to perverseness? You uncivil° lady,   *barbarous*
      To whose ingrate° and unauspicious° altars   *ungrateful; unpropitious*
      My soul the faithful'st off'rings have breathed out
      That e'er devotion tendered! What shall I do?
    OLIVIA. Even what it please my lord, that shall become him.
110 ORSINO. Why should I not, had I the heart to do it,
      Like to th'Egyptian thief at point of death,
      Kill what I love?[2]—a savage jealousy,
      That sometime savors nobly.° But hear me this: *has a noble quality*
      Since you to non-regardance° cast my faith,   *disregard*
115   And that I partly know the instrument
      That screws[3] me from my true place in your favor,
      Live you the marble-breasted[4] tyrant still.
      But [*seizing Viola*] this your minion,[5] whom I know you love,
      And whom, by heaven, I swear I tender° dearly,   *hold, regard*
120   Him will I tear out of that cruel eye
      Where he sits crownèd[6] in his master's spite.[7]
      Come, boy, with me; my thoughts are ripe in mischief.[8]
      I'll sacrifice the lamb that I do love,
      To spite a raven's heart within a dove.[9]
                       [*He moves to exit with Viola.*]

---

1 Gross and repugnant.
2 Orsino's threat to Olivia is based on the story of a bandit who tried to kill a captive with whom he had fallen in love, in order that she not be enjoyed by his victorious enemies.
3 Forces (as with a threaded instrument such as a vice—or thumbscrews).
4 Cf. "heart of stone" (3.4.178, TLN 1718).
5 Darling, favorite (pejorative; and, ironically in view of Orsino's attachment to "Cesario," often of boys loved by men).
6 Cf. "one self king" (1.1.38, TLN 45).
7 To the vexation of his master.
8 Ready to do harm.
9 I.e., the heart of a black (and predatory) bird within the outward appearance of a beautiful, often white (and loving, at least in poetry) bird.

VIOLA. And I most jocund, apt,° and willingly,   *cheerful, ready*   125
    To do you rest,° a thousand deaths would die.   *make you feel easy*
OLIVIA. Where goes Cesario?
VIOLA.   After him I love
    More than I love these eyes, more than my life,
    More, by all mores,[1] than e'er I shall love wife.
    If I do feign, you witnesses above°   *i.e., in the heavens*   130
    Punish my life, for tainting of° my love.   *sullying, betraying*
OLIVIA. Ay me, detested! How am I beguiled!°   *robbed, cheated*
VIOLA. Who does beguile you? Who does do you wrong?
OLIVIA. Hast thou forgot thyself? Is it so long?
    Call forth the holy father.   [*Exit an Attendant.*]
ORSINO. [*To Cesario*]
                Come, away.   135
OLIVIA. Whither, my lord? Cesario, husband, stay![2]
ORSINO. Husband?
OLIVIA.   Ay, husband. Can he that deny?
ORSINO. Her husband, sirrah?
VIOLA.   No, my lord, not I.
OLIVIA. Alas, it is the baseness of thy fear
    That makes thee strangle thy propriety.[3]   140
    Fear not, Cesario, take thy fortunes up,
    Be that thou know'st thou art, and then thou art
    As great as that thou fear'st.°   *him whom you fear (i.e., Orsino)*

Enter Priest.

    O welcome, father!
    Father, I charge thee by thy reverence   145
    Here to unfold (though lately we intended
    To keep in darkness what occasion[4] now
    Reveals before 'tis ripe) what thou dost know
    Hath newly passed between this youth and me.
PRIEST. A contract of eternal bond of love,   150

---

1 All possible comparisons.
2 Olivia refers to the binding contract of betrothal (see p. 183, note 2); the Priest
also refers to it at l. 150 below.
3 Suppress your proper identity (as my husband to be).
4 The turn of events. Cf. 1.2.44 (TLN 94).

Confirmed by mutual joinder° of your hands,   *joining*
Attested by the holy close of lips,
Strengthened by interchangement of your rings,
And all the ceremony of this compact¹
155   Sealed in my function, by my testimony;
Since when, my watch² hath told me, toward my grave
I have travelled but two hours.
ORSINO. [*To Viola*] O thou dissembling cub!³ What wilt thou be
When time hath sowed a grizzle° on thy case?⁴   *gray hair*
160   Or will not else thy craft so quickly grow
That thine own trip⁵ shall be thine overthrow?
Farewell, and take her, but direct thy feet
Where thou and I henceforth may never meet.
VIOLA. My lord, I do protest—
OLIVIA.   O, do not swear,
165   Hold little faith,⁶ though thou hast too much fear.

Enter Sir Andrew⁷ [with his head bloody].
SIR ANDREW. For the love of god, a surgeon!⁸ Send one presently⁹
to Sir Toby.
OLIVIA. What's the matter?
SIR ANDREW. He's broke my head across, and has given Sir Toby a
170   bloody coxcomb¹⁰ too. For the love of god, your help! I had rather
than forty pound I were at home.
OLIVIA. Who has done this, Sir Andrew?

---

1   Covenant, contract: accented on the second syllable.
2   Displaying his (valuable) watch confirms the slight sense of pomposity in the
Priest's speech.
3   Deceitful fox-cub.
4   Skin (here, of the fox "cub").
5   Wrestling move to "overthrow" an opponent.
6   Keep at least a little faith.
7   Evidently Sir Andrew and Sir Toby have met Sebastian again, as we surmise
from the blood and their ensuing comments. The encounter in 4.1 did not produce
these injuries.
8   A practitioner who treats wounds and fractures, seldom at this time educated
to the university level of a physician, and often combining the practice with bar-
bering and pulling teeth.
9   Immediately.
10   Head (based on the fool's cap; see extended note, p. 114).

SIR ANDREW. The count's gentleman, one Cesario. We took him for
a coward, but he's the very devil incardinate.[1]
ORSINO. My gentleman Cesario?   175
SIR ANDREW. [Seeing Viola] 'Od's lifelings,[2] here he is! [To her] You
broke my head for nothing; and that that I did, I was set on to
do't by Sir Toby.
VIOLA. Why do you speak to me? I never hurt you.
You drew your sword upon me without cause,   180
But I bespake you fair, and hurt you not.

Enter Sir Toby [limping, his head bloody,] and [supported by] Clown.
SIR ANDREW. If a bloody coxcomb be a hurt, you have hurt me; I
think you set nothing by[3] a bloody coxcomb. Here comes Sir
Toby halting;[4] you shall hear more. But if he had not been in
drink, he would have tickled[5] you othergates[6] than he did.   185
ORSINO. How now, gentleman? How is't with you?
SIR TOBY. That's all one, he's hurt me, and there's th'end on't. [To
Clown] Sot, didst see Dick Surgeon, sot?
CLOWN. Oh, he's drunk, Sir Toby, an hour agone; his eyes were set[7]
at eight i'th'morning.   190
SIR TOBY. Then he's a rogue, and a passy-measures pavan.[8] I hate
a drunken rogue.
OLIVIA. Away with him! Who hath made this havoc with them?
SIR ANDREW. I'll help you, Sir Toby, because we'll be dressed[9]
together.   195
SIR TOBY. Will you help? An ass-head, and a coxcomb, and a knave?
A thin-faced knave, a gull!
OLIVIA. Get him to bed, and let his hurt be looked to.
[Exeunt Sir Toby and Sir Andrew led off by Clown and Fabian.]

---

1 Sir Andrew's error for "incarnate" ("in the flesh").
2 By god's little lives (a mild oath).
3 Think nothing of.
4 Limping.
5 I.e., beaten.
6 In a different manner (i.e., more effectively).
7 Fixed, immoveable.
8 A variety of pavan, a slow dance; from the Italian *passamezzo pavana*.
9 I.e., have our wounds dressed.

Enter Sebastian. [Everyone else observes the identically dressed Sebastian and Viola.]

SEBASTIAN. I am sorry, madam, I have hurt your kinsman;

200　　But had it been the brother of my blood,°　　　　*my own brother*

　　　I must have done no less with wit and safety.[1]

1　Sensible thought and in self-protection.

5.1.207:　A NATURAL PERSPECTIVE (TLN 2381)

Orsino's "natural perspective, that is, and is not!" cannot be what we normally think of as realistic perspective in drawing. Rather, "perspective" (accented on the first syllable) is either an optical instrument that deceives the eye when looked through, or the trick perspective of "double pictures." Both were fashionable in the Tudor and Stuart period. Orsino's exclamation "One face, one voice, one habit, and two persons!" suggests a perspective glass, revealing "miraculous sights and conceits made and contained in glass.... for you may have glasses so made ... where one image shall seem to be a hundred" (Reginald Scot, *The Discovery of Witchcraft* [1584], Book 13, Chap. 19 [p. 316]).

Alternatively, Orsino may mean graphic distortion of pictures. Two techniques were used: (1) anamorphic drawing, such as that in Holbein's famous painting of "The Ambassadors," in which an ambiguous grey element in the foreground can be seen, if viewed sideways from a particular angle, as a skull, or in which an apparently grotesque picture is revealed, if viewed from an acute angle, as a realistic portrait (as in the anamorphic portrait of Edward VI by William Scrots); or (2) a drawing which appears one thing, but if turned upside down is revealed as something quite different, such as the sixteenth-century anti-Catholic "Perverted Church" images below that satirize the Council of Trent (a famous and strongly anti-Protestant council of the Catholic counter-reformation). One way up they appear to be the Pope and a cardinal; turned upside down ("perverted") the faces have become the devil and a jester. (The Holbein and Scrots perspectives are available at TLN 2381 on the ISE website <http://internetshakespeare.uvic.ca>.) See Inga-Stina Ekeblad, "Webster's

You throw a strange regard[1] upon me, and by that
I do perceive it hath offended you.
Pardon me, sweet one, even for the vows
We made each other but so late ago.   205

---

1   Distant (cold) look. He thinks Olivia is angry, but she, like everyone else, is in
"wonder" (cf. line 215 below).

Realism, or, 'A Cunning Piece Wrought Perspective,'" in Brian Morris,
ed. *John Webster*, Mermaid Critical Commentaries (London: Benn, 1970):
159–78 (esp. 160–64), and Arthur H.R. Fairchild, *Shakespeare and the Arts
of Design* (Columbia: U of Missouri P, 1937; repr. New York: Benjamin
Blom, 1972): 125–30.

ABOVE: Two "perspective" silver medals about 1580, copied from originals of about 1545,
satirizing the Council of Trent. From the Wikimedia Commons, <http://www.com-
mons.wikimedia.org>.

ORSINO. One face, one voice, one habit,[1] and two persons:
A natural perspective, that is, and is not!
SEBASTIAN. Antonio! Oh, my dear Antonio,
How have the hours racked and tortured me
210 Since I have lost thee!
ANTONIO. Sebastian, are you?
SEBASTIAN.   Fear'st thou that,[2] Antonio?
ANTONIO. How have you made division of yourself?
An apple cleft in two is not more twin
Than these two creatures. Which is Sebastian?
215 OLIVIA. Most wonderful.°   *full of wonder*
SEBASTIAN. [*Seeing Viola*] Do I stand there? I never had a brother;
Nor can there be that deity in my nature
Of here and everywhere.[3] I had a sister,
Whom the blind[4] waves and surges have devoured.
220 Of charity,[5] what kin are you to me?
What countryman? What name? What parentage?
VIOLA. Of Messaline. Sebastian was my father.
Such a Sebastian was my brother too;
So went he suited° to his watery tomb.   *i.e., dressed like you*
225 If spirits° can assume both form and suit,   *ghosts*
You come to fright us.
SEBASTIAN.   A spirit I am indeed,
But am in that dimension° grossly[6] clad   *bodily form*
Which from the womb I did participate.[7]
Were you a woman, as the rest goes even,°   *agrees, fits together*
230 I should my tears let fall upon your cheek,
And say, "Thrice welcome, drownèd Viola."[8]
VIOLA. My father had a mole upon his brow.
SEBASTIAN. And so had mine.
VIOLA. And died that day when Viola from her birth

---

1 Costume. See 3.4.345–49, TLN 1900–04.
2 Do you doubt that.
3 To be in two places at once is a divine attribute.
4 I.e., unfeeling, merciless (not seeing Viola's beauty and virtue).
5 Out of your generosity (tell me).
6 Materially, corporeally.
7 Have in common with others.
8 The first mention of her name.

Had numbered thirteen years. 235

SEBASTIAN. Oh, that record[1] is lively in my soul.

He finishèd indeed his mortal act

That day that made my sister thirteen years.

VIOLA. If nothing lets° to make us happy both,   *hinders*

But this my masculine usurped attire, 240

Do not embrace me, till each circumstance

Of place, time, fortune, do cohere and jump°   *accord and agree*

That I am Viola;[2] which to confirm,

I'll bring you to a captain in this town,

Where lie my maiden weeds,° by whose gentle help   *clothes* 245

I was preserved to serve this noble count.

All the occurrence of my fortune since

Hath been between this lady and this lord.

SEBASTIAN. [*To Olivia*] So comes it, lady, you have been mistook.[3]

But nature to her bias drew in that. 250

You would have been contracted to a maid;

Nor are you therein, by my life, deceived:

You are betrothed both to a maid and man.[4]

ORSINO. [*To Olivia*] Be not amazed, right noble is his blood.

If this be so—as yet the glass seems true—[5] 255

I shall have share in this most happy wrack.[6]

[*To Viola*] Boy,[7] thou hast said to me a thousand times

Thou never shouldst love woman like to me.°   *as much as (you love) me*

VIOLA. And all those sayings will I overswear,[8]

And all those swearings keep as true in soul 260

As doth that orbèd continent the fire°   *as the sun keeps its fire*

That severs day from night.°   *i.e., the sun. Cf. Genesis 1:14*

ORSINO.   Give me thy hand,

And let me see thee in thy woman's weeds.

---

1 Recollection. Stressed here on the second syllable.
2 At this emotional high point, few Sebastians obey Viola's injunction not to embrace her.
3 Mistaken.
4 (1) Man who is a virgin, (2) woman and man.
5 I.e., the "perspective" glass is still showing truth rather than illusion.
6 Fortunate wreck (or wreckage thrown ashore).
7 Orsino's joke is both emotionally charged and wryly self-critical.
8 Swear over (and over) again.

NATURE TO HER BIAS
DREW (TLN 2426)

Shakespeare delighted in metaphors deriving from the curved, indirect, path of the weighted ("biased") ball used in bowls. Although the ball initially goes in the direction it is bowled, the bias gradually asserts itself and the ball curves away from the line in which it was first heading, and towards the intended target. (The "bias" is both the off-center lead weight in the ball, and the curved path it follows as a result. Modern lawn bowling no longer uses a weight, but the ball is shaped to perform in the same way.) The application of the metaphor to Olivia's mistaken betrothal to Sebastian is clear: Nature, both human and the personification of the natural order, has ensured that Olivia has curved away from Viola and "kissed" (to use another bowls word, for a ball succeeding in resting against the "jack") the appropriately heterosexual male, Sebastian.

The most famous game of bowls in history: Sir Francis Drake in 1588 insisting on finishing his game despite the approach of the Spanish Armada. John Seymour Lucas, "The Armada in Sight," collection of the Art Gallery of New South Wales. From the Wikimedia Commons, <http://www.commons.wikimedia.org>.

VIOLA. The captain that did bring me first on shore
    Hath my maid's garments; he upon some action   265
    Is now in durance,[1] at Malvolio's suit,
    A gentleman and follower of my lady's.
OLIVIA. He shall enlarge° him. Fetch Malvolio hither—[2]   *free*
    And yet, alas, now I remember me,
    They say, poor gentleman, he's much distract.°   *distraught, mad* 270

Enter Clown with a letter, and Fabian.
    A most extracting frenzy of mine own[3]
    From my remembrance clearly banished his.
    [*To Clown*] How does he,[4] sirrah?
CLOWN. Truly, madam, he holds Beelzebub at the stave's end[5] as well
    as a man in his case may do. He's here writ a letter to you. I should 275
    have given't you today morning, but as a madman's epistles are
    no gospels,[6] so it skills not[7] much when they are delivered.[8]
OLIVIA. Open't, and read it.
CLOWN. Look then to be well edified, when the fool delivers[9] the
    madman. [*Reading madly*] "By the lord, madam—"   280
OLIVIA. How now, art thou mad?
CLOWN. No, madam, I do but read madness. An your ladyship will
    have it as it ought to be, you must allow *vox*.[10]
OLIVIA. Prithee, read i'thy right wits.

---

1 On some legal charge is now imprisoned.
2 This instruction will be to one of her attendants, who presumably has no
idea where Malvolio is. Olivia's next line may preempt the exit; Fabian is sent at
line 299, TLN 2481.
3 I.e., a madness which drew everything else out of my mind.
4 The Clown's convenient entry, Olivia's assumption that he knows about
Malvolio, and his sense of who Olivia's question refers to, are required by the plot,
and will not be questioned in performance.
5 Keeps the devil at a distance (proverbial, from quarterstaff fighting).
6 (1) Letters are not divine truth, (2) New Testament Epistles are not New
Testament Gospels.
7 Does not matter.
8 (1) Given to the addressee, (2) read aloud (in church, like the "gospels").
9 (1) Reads aloud, (2) speaks on behalf of.
10 Voice (appropriate to the rhetorical context; Latin).

285   CLOWN. So I do, madonna. But to read his right wits[1] is to read thus.
      Therefore perpend,° my princess, and give ear.   *weigh carefully*
      OLIVIA. [*To Fabian*] Read it you, sirrah.
      FABIAN. (*Reads.*)
         "By the lord, madam, you wrong me, and the world shall
      know it. Though you have put me into darkness, and given your
290   drunken cousin rule over me, yet have I the benefit of my senses
      as well as your ladyship. I have your own letter, that induced me
      to the semblance I put on; with the which I doubt not but to do
      myself much right, or you much shame. Think of me as you please.
      I leave my duty a little unthought of, and speak out of my injury.
295   The madly-used Malvolio."
      OLIVIA. Did he write this?
      CLOWN. Ay, madam.
      ORSINO. This savors not much of distraction.
      OLIVIA. See him delivered,° Fabian, bring him hither.   *released*
                                      [*Exit Fabian.*]
300   [*To Orsino*] My lord, so please you, these things further thought
        on,
      To think me as well a sister as a wife,[2]
      One day shall crown th'alliance on't,[3] so please you,
      Here at my house, and at my proper° cost.   *own*
      ORSINO. Madam, I am most apt t'embrace your offer.
305   [*To Viola*] Your master quits[4] you; and for your service done
        him,
      So much against the mettle° of your sex,   *nature, disposition*
      So far beneath your soft and tender breeding,
      And since you called me master for so long,
      Here is my hand; you shall from this time be
      Your master's mistress.
310   OLIVIA.   A sister, you are she!

Enter [*Fabian and*] *Malvolio* [*with Maria's letter*].

---

1 His real mental state (madness).
2 Be as pleased with me as a sister-in-law as you would have as a wife.
3 I.e., the relationship created by the double marriage.
4 Releases from service, acquits.

ORSINO. Is this the madman?

OLIVIA.   Ay, my lord, this same.

[*To Malvolio*] How now, Malvolio?

MALVOLIO. Madam, you have done me wrong,
Notorious[1] wrong.

OLIVIA.   Have I, Malvolio? No.

MALVOLIO. Lady, you have. Pray you peruse that letter.[2]   315
[*Giving her the letter*] You must not now deny it is your hand.
Write from it° if you can, in hand, or phrase,[3]   *differently*
Or say 'tis not your seal, not your invention.°   *composition*
You can say none of this. Well, grant it then,
And tell me, in the modesty of honor,   320
Why you have given me such clear lights[4] of favor,
Bade me come smiling and cross-gartered to you,
To put on yellow stockings, and to frown
Upon Sir Toby, and the lighter[5] people;
And acting this in an obedient hope,   325
Why have you suffered me to be imprisoned,
Kept in a dark house, visited by the priest,
And made the most notorious geck and gull°   *fool and dupe*
That e'er invention played on? Tell me, why?

OLIVIA. Alas, Malvolio, this is not my writing,   330
Though I confess much like the character;
But out of question, 'tis Maria's hand.
And now I do bethink me, it was she
First told me thou wast mad; then cam'st[6] in smiling,
And in such forms which here were presupposed   335
Upon[7] thee in the letter. Prithee, be content.
This practice hath most shrewdly passed[8] upon thee;
But when we know the grounds and authors of it,

---

1 Cf. 4.2.83 (TLN 2072) and line 328 below (TLN 2513).
2 Malvolio is given blank verse for the first time in the play, perhaps to allow him
increased dignity.
3 Handwriting or phrasing.
4 Unmistakable signs.
5 Frivolous (i.e., the "servants," 2.5.134–35, TLN 1155).
6 Then (you) came.
7 Previously suggested to.
8 This trick has been cunningly played.

Thou shalt be both the plaintiff and the judge
Of thine own cause.

340 FABIAN.   Good madam, hear me speak,[1]
And let no quarrel, nor no brawl to come,
Taint the condition of this present hour,
Which I have wondered[2] at. In hope it shall not,
Most freely I confess myself and Toby
345 Set this device against Malvolio here,
Upon some stubborn and uncourteous parts
We had conceived against him.[3] Maria writ
The letter, at Sir Toby's great importance,°   *importunity*
In recompense whereof he hath married her.
350 How with a sportful malice it was followed°   *pursued, carried out*
May rather pluck on° laughter than revenge,   *induce*
If that the injuries be justly weighed
That have on both sides passed.

OLIVIA. [*To Malvolio*] Alas, poor fool, how have they baffled[4] thee!
355 CLOWN. [*To Malvolio*] Why, "Some are born great, some achieve greatness, and some have greatness thrown upon them." I was one, sir, in this interlude,[5] one Sir Topaz, sir; but that's all one. "By the lord, fool, I am not mad!" But do you remember: "Madam, why laugh you at such a barren rascal? An you smile
360 not, he's gagged." And thus the whirligig of time[6] brings in his revenges.

MALVOLIO. I'll be revenged on the whole pack of you!
[*Exit.*]

OLIVIA. He hath been most notoriously abused.

ORSINO. Pursue him, and entreat him to a peace. [*Exit Fabian.*][7]
365 He hath not told us of the captain yet.

---

1 Fabian completes Olivia's verse line, which may indicate a quick cue (before things get worse).

2 Marveled. Cf. line 215 above (TLN 2390): a sense of wonder is a vital element in the resolution of the play.

3 As a consequence of willful incivility we saw and resented in him.

4 (1) Confounded, (2) displayed to the world as disgraced. As 2.5.145, TLN 1165.

5 Play, entertainment.

6 Either (1) time's spinning top (which is whipped to keep it turning), or (2) a merry-go-round.

7 Folio gives no exit; Fabian, who has played the peacemaker, seems the obvious choice.

When that is known, and golden[1] time convents,[2]
A solemn combination shall be made
Of our dear[3] souls. [*To Olivia*] Meantime, sweet sister,
We will not part[4] from hence. [*To Viola*] Cesario, come—
For so you shall be while you are a man;   370
But when in other habits you are seen,
Orsino's mistress, and his fancy's queen.

                             Exeunt [*all except Clown*].

CLOWN. (*Sings*)[5]
  When that I was and a[6] little tiny boy,
    With hey, ho, the wind and the rain,
  A foolish thing[7] was but a toy,[8]   375
    For the rain it raineth every day.

  But when I came to man's estate,
    With hey, ho, the wind and the rain,
 'Gainst knaves and thieves men shut their gate,[9]
    For the rain it raineth every day.   380

  But when I came, alas, to wive,
    With hey, ho, the wind and the rain,
  By swaggering° could I never thrive,   *blustering, bullying*
    For the rain it raineth every day.

---

1 I.e., favorable and precious, recalling the idyllic "golden age" of an ideal world.
2 Convenes, calls (us) together. Stress is on the second syllable.
3 (1) Loving, (2) precious.
4 Orsino, by using the emphatic "will" rather than "shall," underlines the harmony of the two couples and households in his promise to remain at Olivia's house.
5 The song is a form of epilogue, acknowledging and bidding farewell to the audience (cf. Puck in A *Midsummer Night's Dream* and Rosalind in *As You Like It*). It is generally agreed to be a thematic comment on the world of *Twelfth Night*; see Introduction, p. 23.
6 Either emphatic, or an extra word to fit the music.
7 (1) Bad behavior, (2) penis.
8 (1) Trifle, (2) useless "thing" (like the Clown's bauble, which may itself be used as a mock phallus).
9 I.e., (once I was an adult) men locked their doors against knaves and thieves (like me).

385 But when I came unto my beds,
       With hey, ho, the wind and the rain,
     With tosspots still 'had drunken heads,[1]
       For the rain it raineth every day.

     A great while ago the world begun,
390   With hey, ho, the wind and the rain,
     But that's all one, our play is done,
       And we'll strive to please you every day.[2]

                                                          [*Exit.*]

---

1 Either (1) when I came to whichever place served me as a bed, like the other drunks ("tosspots") I had ("'had") hangovers all the time ("still"), or (2) when I grew old, I was always drunk.
2 Epilogues traditionally announce the end of the play by seeking audience approval, and often encourage future attendance.

APPENDIX A: SOURCES

[Shakespeare drew on a number of sources to make *Twelfth Night*, as usual changing names and locations and altering the emotional impact of the story. Bullough (1958) surveys a wide range of materials Shakespeare might have been aware of. Here we print sections from the two most important.

First, it is clear that Shakespeare used the tale "Of Apollonius and Silla," from a collection entitled *Barnabe Riche His Farewell to Militarie Profession*, first published in 1581 and reprinted in 1594. Riche derived his version from the Italian of Bandello via the French of Belleforest.

Silla (*Viola*) is the daughter of Pontus, Governor of Cyprus. She falls in love with Apollonius (*Orsino*), a nobleman from Constantinople (modern-day Istanbul). She follows him to Constantinople, disguised as her brother, Silvio (*Sebastian*). Apollonius employs her as a page and sends her to woo Julina (*Olivia*), a noblewoman. Julina falls in love with Silvio and offers herself to him. She makes love to Silla's brother Silvio, and becomes pregnant. Silvio travels to Greece, while Silla is imprisoned because Apollonius thinks she has betrayed him. Nine months later, Julina's pregnancy is evident to all. Silvio returns to Constantinople, happily admits to being the father, and marries Julina. Silla takes off her male disguise, showing she could not be the father, and so Apollonius happily makes her his wife.

Secondly we print key sections from the play *Gl'Ingannati* (*The Deceived*), first performed in Siena in 1531. The text was not available in English in Shakespeare's lifetime, but it is possible he knew of the play or had seen a performance. This version of the story is set in 1527, after the sacking and pillaging of Rome by the troops of Charles V. Virginio has lost his son and his fortune. He leaves his daughter Lelia in a convent. She is in love with Flaminio, but is set down to marry an old man, Gherardo. She pursues her love by disguising herself as a boy called Fabio. She becomes a page for Flaminio, and on his behalf woos Isabella. In turn Isabella falls in love with Fabio. She seduces Fabio and thinks she sleeps with him. In fact she has slept with Lelia's twin brother, Fabrizio. Finally Lelia marries Flaminio, and Fabrizio marries Isabella. The characters find happiness through the many deceptions the play's title suggests (literally meaning "those who are deceived").]

1. FROM BARNABE RICHE,
"OF APOLLONIUS AND SILLA" (1581)[1]

The Argument of the Second History[2]

Apollonius Duke, having spent a year's service in the wars against the Turk, returning homeward with his company by sea, was driven by force of weather to the Isle of Cyprus, where he was well received by Pontus, governor of the same Isle; with whom Silla, daughter to Pontus, fell so strangely in love, that after Apollonius was departed to Constantinople, Silla, with one man, followed; and coming to Constantinople, she served Apollonius in the habit of a man, and after many pretty accidents falling out, she was known to Apollonius, who, in requital of her love, married her.

There is no child that is born into this wretched world but before it doth suck the mother's milk it taketh first a sup of the cup of error, which maketh us, when we come to riper years, not only to enter into actions of injury, but many times to stray from that is right and reason; but in all other things, wherein we show ourselves to be most drunken with this poisoned cup, it is in our actions of love; for the lover is so estranged from that is right, and wandereth so wide from the bounds of reason, that he is not able to deem white from black, good from bad, virtue from vice; but only led by the appetite of his own affections, and grounding them on the foolishness of his own fancies, will so settle his liking on such a one as either by desert or unworthiness will merit rather to be loathed than loved.

If a question might be asked, what is the ground indeed of reasonable love, whereby the knot is knit of true and perfect friendship, I think those that be wise would answer: desert. That is, where the party beloved doth requite us with the like, for otherwise, if the bare show of comeliness of personage might be sufficient to confirm us in our love, those that be accustomed to go to fairs and markets might sometimes fall in love with twenty in a day. Desert must then be, of force, the ground of reasonable love; for to love them that hate us, to

---

1   Text from EEBO.
2   The argument is an outline of the plot and its main themes. "History" means any story or fiction.

follow them that fly from us; to fawn on them that frown on us; to curry favour with them that disdain us; to be glad to please them that care not how they offend us: who will not confess this to be an erroneous love, neither grounded upon wit or reason? Wherefore, right courteous gentlewomen, if it please you with patience to peruse this history following, you shall see Dame Error so play her part with a leash of lovers, a male and two females, as shall work a wonder to your wise judgment, in noting the effect of their amorous devices and conclusions of their actions. The first neglecting the love of a noble Dame, young, beautiful, and fair, who only for his good will played the part of a serving man, contented to abide any manner of pain only to behold him. He again setting his love of a dame, that despising him (being a noble duke) gave herself to a serving man (as she had thought). But it otherwise fell out, as the substance of this tale shall better describe. And because I have been something tedious in my first discourse,[1] offending your patient ears with the hearing of a circumstance overlong, from henceforth that which I mind to write shall be done with such celerity as the matter that I pretend to pen may in any wise permit me; and thus followeth the history.

During the time that the famous city of Constantinople remained in the hands of the Christians, amongst many other noblemen that kept their abiding in that flourishing city, there was one whose name was Apollonius, a worthy Duke, who being but a very young man and even then new come to his possessions, which were very great, levied a mighty band of men at his own proper charges, with whom he served against the Turk during the space of one whole year, in which time, although it were very short, this young Duke so behaved himself, as well by prowess and valiance showed with his own hands, as otherwise by his wisdom and liberality used towards his soldiers, that all the world was filled with the fame of this noble Duke. When he had thus spent one year's service he caused his trumpet to sound a retreat, and gathering his company together and embarking themselves, he set sail, holding his course towards Constantinople; but, being upon the sea, by the extremity of a tempest which suddenly fell, his fleet was

---

1   The first tale in Riche's collection is "Sappho, Duke of Mantona."

severed, some one way, and some another; but he himself recovered the Isle of Cyprus, where he was worthily received by Pontus, Duke and governor of the same isle, with whom he lodged while his ships were new repairing.

This Pontus that was Lord and Governor of this famous isle was an ancient Duke, and had two children, a son and a daughter; his son was named Silvio, of whom hereafter we shall have further occasion to speak, but at this instant he was in the parts of Africa, serving in the wars. The daughter her name was Silla, whose beauty was so peerless that she had the sovereignty amongst all other dames, as well for her beauty as for the nobleness of her birth. This Silla, having heard of the worthiness of Apollonius, this young Duke, who besides his beauty and good graces had a certain natural allurement, that being now in his company in her father's court, she was so strangely attached with the love of Apollonius that there was nothing might content her but his presence and sweet sight; and although she saw no manner of hope to attain to that she most desired, knowing Apollonius to be but a guest, and ready to take the benefit of the next wind and to depart into a strange country, whereby she was bereaved of all possibility ever to see him again, and therefore strived with herself to leave her fondness, but all in vain; it would not be, but, like the fowl which is once limed,[1] the more she striveth, the faster she tieth herself.

So Silla was now constrained perforce her will to yield to love, wherefore from time to time she used so great familiarity with him as her honor might well permit; and fed him with such amorous baits as the modesty of a maid could reasonably afford; which when she perceived did take but small effect, feeling herself outraged with the extremity of her passion, by the only countenance that she bestowed upon Apollonius, it might have been well perceived that the very eyes pleaded unto him for pity and remorse. But Apollonius, coming but lately from out the field from the chasing of his enemies, and his fury not yet thoroughly dissolved nor purged from his stomach, gave no regard to those amorous enticements, which, by reason of his youth, he had not been acquainted withal. But his mind ran more to hear his pilots bring news of a merry wind to serve his turn to Constantinople, which in the end came very prosperously; and giving Duke Pontus hearty thanks for his

---

1 As birds were ensnared with sticky birdlime.

great entertainment, taking his leave of himself and the lady Silla his daughter, departed with his company, and with a happy gale arrived at his desired port. Gentlewomen, according to my promise I will here, for brevity's sake, omit to make repetition of the long and dolorous discourse recorded by Silla for this sudden departure of her Apollonius, knowing you to be as tenderly hearted as Silla herself, whereby you may the better conjecture the fury of her fever.

But Silla, the further that she saw herself bereaved of all hope ever any more to see her beloved Apollonius, so much the more contagious were her passions, and made the greater speed to execute that she had premeditated in her mind, which was this: amongst many servants that did attend upon her, there was one whose name was Pedro, who had a long time waited upon her in her chamber, whereby she was well assured of his fidelity and trust. To that Pedro therefore she bewrayed[1] first the fervency of her love borne to Apollonius, conjuring him in the name of the Goddess of Love herself, and binding him by the duty that a servant ought to have, that tendereth his mistress's safety and good liking, and desiring him with tears trickling down her cheeks that he would give his consent to aid, and assist her in that she had determined, which was for that she was fully resolved to go to Constantinople, where she might again take the view of her beloved Apollonius, that he, according to the trust she had reposed in him, would not refuse to give his consent, secretly to convey her from out her father's court, according as she would give him direction, and also to make himself partaker of her journey, and to wait upon her till she had seen the end of her determination.

Pedro, perceiving with what vehemency his lady and mistress had made request unto him, albeit he saw many perils and doubts depending in her pretence, notwithstanding gave his consent to be at her disposition, promising her to further her with his best advice, and to be ready to obey whatsoever she would please to command him. The match being thus agreed upon, and all things prepared in a readiness for their departure, it happened there was a galley of Constantinople ready to depart, which Pedro understanding, came to the captain, desiring him to have passage for himself, and for a poor maid that was his sister, which were bound to Constantinople upon certain urgent affairs; to

---

1   Revealed.

which request the captain granted, willing him to prepare aboard with all speed, because the wind served him presently to depart.

Pedro now coming to his mistress and telling her how he had handled the matter with the captain, she liking very well of the device, disguising herself into very simple attire, stole away from out her father's court and came with Pedro, whom now she called brother, aboard the galley, where all things being in readiness and the wind serving very well, they launched forth with their oars and set sail. When they were at the sea, the captain of the galley, taking the view of Silla, perceiving her singular beauty he was better pleased in beholding of her face than in taking the height either of the sun or star; and thinking her by the homeliness of her apparel to be but some simple maiden, calling her into his cabin, he began to break with her after the sea fashion, desiring her to use his own cabin for her better ease, and during the time that she remained at the sea she should not want a bed; and then, whispering softly in her ear, he said that for want of a bedfellow he himself would supply that room. Silla, not being acquainted with any such talk, blushed for shame but made him no answer at all.

My captain, feeling such bickering within himself, the like whereof he had never endured upon the sea, was like to be taken prisoner aboard his own ship, and forced to yield himself captive without any cannon shot; wherefore, to salve all sores, and thinking it the readiest way to speed, he began to break with Silla in the way of marriage, telling her how happy a voyage she had made, to fall into the liking of such a one as himself was, who was able to keep and maintain her like a gentlewoman, and for her sake would likewise take her brother into his fellowship, whom he would by some means prefer in such sort that both of them should have good cause to think themselves thrice happy, she to light of such a husband, and he to light of such a brother. But Silla, nothing pleased with these preferments, desired him to cease his talk, for that she did think herself indeed to be too unworthy such a one as he was, neither was she minded yet to marry, and therefore desired him to fix his fancy upon some that were better worthy than herself was, and that could better like of his courtesy than she could do. The captain, seeing himself thus refused, being in a great chafe, he said as followeth: "Then, seeing you make so little account of my courtesy proffered to one that is so far unworthy of it, from henceforth I will use the office of my authority; you shall know that I am the captain of this ship and have power to command and dispose of things at my pleasure; and seeing you have so scornfully rejected me to be your loyal husband, I will now take you by force and use you at my will, and so long as it shall please me will keep you for mine own store; there shall be no man able to defend you, nor yet to persuade me from that I have determined."

Silla, with these words being struck into a great fear, did think it now too late to rue her rash attempt, determined rather to die with her own hands than to suffer herself to be abused in such sort; therefore she most humbly desired the captain so much as he could to save her credit, and seeing that she must needs be at his will and disposition, that for the present he would depart and suffer her till night, when in the dark he might take his pleasure without any manner of suspicion to the residue of his company. The captain, thinking now the goal to be more than half won, was contented so far to satisfy her request, and departed out, leaving her alone in his cabin.

Silla, being alone by herself, drew out her knife, ready to strike herself to the heart, and, falling upon her knees, desired God to receive her soul as an acceptable sacrifice for her follies, which she had so willfully committed, craving pardon for her sins; and so forth continuing a long and pitiful reconciliation to God, in the midst whereof there suddenly fell a wonderful storm, the terror whereof was such that there was no man but did think the seas would presently have swallowed them; the billows so suddenly arose with the rage of the wind that they were all glad to fall to heaving out of water, for otherwise their feeble galley had never been able to have brooked the seas. This storm continued all that day and the next night, and they being driven to put romer[1] before the wind to keep the galley ahead the billow, were driven upon the main shore, where the galley brake all to pieces. There was every man providing to save his own life; some gat upon hatches, boards, and casks, and were driven with the waves to and fro; but the greatest number were drowned, amongst the which Pedro was one; but Silla herself being in the cabin, as you have heard, took hold of a chest that was the captain's, the which by the only providence of God brought her safe to the shore; the which when she had recovered, not knowing what was become of Pedro her man, she deemed that both he and all the rest had been drowned, for that she saw nobody upon the shore but herself; wherefore when she

---

1   This word is unknown, and may be a misprint or error.

had a while made great lamentations, complaining her mishaps, she began in the end to comfort herself with the hope that she had to see her Apollonius, and found such means that she brake open the chest that brought her to land, wherein she found good store of coin and sundry suits of apparel that were the captain's. And now, to prevent a number of injuries that might be proffered to a woman that was left in her case, she determined to leave her own apparel and to sort herself into some of those suits, that, being taken for a man, she might pass through the country in the better safety; and as she changed her apparel, she thought it likewise convenient to change her name; wherefore, not readily happening of any other, she called herself Silvio, by the name of her own brother, whom you have heard spoken of before.

In this manner she traveled to Constantinople, where she inquired out the palace of the Duke Apollonius; and thinking herself now to be both fit and able to play the serving man, she presented herself to the Duke, craving his service. The Duke, very willing to give succor unto strangers, perceiving him to be a proper smug young man, gave him entertainment. Silla thought herself now more than satisfied for all the casualties that had happened unto her in her journey, that she might at her pleasure take but the view of the Duke Apollonius, and above the rest of his servants was very diligent and attendant upon him; the which the Duke perceiving, began likewise to grow into good liking with the diligence of his man, and therefore made him one of his chamber. Who but Silvio then was most near about him in helping of him to make him ready in a morning, in the setting of his ruffs, in the keeping of his chamber? Silvio pleased his master so well that above all the rest of his servants about him he had the greatest credit, and the Duke put him most in trust.

At this very instant there was remaining in the city a noble Dame, a widow, whose husband was but lately deceased, one of the noblest men that were in the parts of Greece, who left his lady and wife large possessions and great livings. This lady's name was called Julina, who besides the abundance of her wealth and the greatness of her revenues had likewise the sovereignty of all the dames of Constantinople for her beauty. To this lady Julina Apollonius became an earnest suitor; and according to the manner of wooers, besides fair words, sorrowful sighs, and piteous countenances, there must be sending of loving letters, chains, bracelets, brooches, rings, tablets, gems, jewels, and presents,

I know not what. So my Duke, who, in the time that he remained in the Isle of Cyprus had no skill at all in the art of love, although it were more than half proffered unto him, was now become a scholar in Love's school, and had already learned his first lesson, that is, to speak pitifully, to look ruthfully, to promise largely, to serve diligently, and to please carefully. Now he was learning his second lesson, that is, to reward liberally, to give bountifully, to present willingly, and to write lovingly. Thus Apollonius was so busied in his new study that I warrant you there was no man that could challenge him for playing the truant, he followed his profession with so good a will; and who must be the messenger to carry the tokens and love letters to the lady Julina but Silvio his man; in him the Duke reposed his only confidence, to go between him and his lady.

Now, gentlewomen, do you think there could have been a greater torment devised wherewith to afflict the heart of Silla than herself to be made the instrument to work her own mishap, and to play the attorney in a cause that made so much against herself? But Silla, altogether desirous to please her master, cared nothing at all to offend herself, followed his business with so good a will as if it had been in her own preferment.

Julina, now having many times taken the gaze of this young youth Silvio, perceiving him to be of such excellent perfect grace, was so entangled with the often sight of this sweet temptation, that she fell into as great a liking with the man as the master was with herself; and on a time, Silvio being sent from his master with a message to the lady Julina, as he began very earnestly to solicit in his master's behalf, Julina, interrupting him in his tale, said: "Silvio, it is enough that you have said for your master; from henceforth either speak for yourself or say nothing at all." Silla, abashed to hear these words, began in her mind to accuse the blindness of love, that Julina, neglecting the good will of so noble a duke, would prefer her love unto such a one as nature itself had denied to recompense her liking.

And now, for a time leaving matters depending as you have heard, it fell out that the right Silvio indeed (whom you have heard spoken of before, the brother of Silla), was come to his father's court into the Isle of Cyprus; where, understanding that his sister was departed in manner as you have heard, conjectured that the very occasion did proceed of some liking had between Pedro her man (that was missing with her) and herself; but Silvio, who loved his sister as dearly as his own life, and the rather for that she was his natural sister, both by father and mother, so the one of them was so like the other in countenance and favor that there was no man able to discern the one from the other by their faces, saving by their apparel, the one being a man, the other a woman. Silvio therefore vowed to his father not only to seek out his sister Silla but also to revenge the villain which he conceived in Pedro, for the carrying away of his sister; and thus departing, having traveled through many cities and towns without hearing any manner of news of those he went to seek for, at the last he arrived at Constantinople; where, as he was walking in an evening for his own recreation, on a pleasant green yard without the walls of the city, he fortuned to meet with the lady Julina, who likewise had been abroad to take the air; and as she suddenly cast her eyes upon Silvio, thinking him to be her old acquaintance, by reason they were so like one another, as you have heard before, said unto him: "Sir Silvio, if your haste be not the greater, I pray you let me have a little talk with you, seeing I have so luckily met you in this place."

Silvio, wondering to hear himself so rightly named, being but a stranger, not of above two days' continuance in the city, very courteously came towards her, desirous to hear what she would say. Julina, commanding her train something to stand back, said as followeth: "Seeing my good will and friendly love hath been the only cause to make me so prodigal to offer that I see is so lightly rejected, it maketh me to think that men be of this condition, rather to desire those things which they cannot come by than to esteem or value of that which both largely and liberally is offered unto them; but if the liberality of my proffer hath made to seem less the value of the thing that I meant to present, it is but in your own conceit, considering how many noblemen there hath been here before, and be yet at this present, which hath both served, sued, and most humbly entreated to attain to that which to you of myself I have freely offered, and I perceive is despised, or at the least very lightly regarded."

Silvio, wondering at these words, but more amazed that she could so rightly call him by his name, could not tell what to make of her speeches, assuring himself that she was deceived and did mistake him, did think notwithstanding it had been a point of great simplicity if he should forsake that which fortune had so favorably proffered unto him, perceiving by her train that she was some lady of great honor, and viewing the perfection of her beauty and the excellency of her grace and countenance, did think it impossible that she should be despised, and therefore answered thus: "Madam, if before this time I have seemed to forget myself in neglecting your courtesy, which so liberally you have meant unto me, please it you to pardon what is past, and from this day forwards Silvio remaineth ready pressed to make such reasonable amends as his ability may any ways permit, or as it shall please you to command."

Julina, the gladdest woman that might be to hear this joyful news, said: "Then, my Silvio, see you fail not tomorrow at night to sup with me at my own house, where I will discourse farther with you what amends you shall make me." To which request Silvio gave his glad consent, and thus they departed very well pleased. And as Julina did think the time very long till she had reaped the fruit of her desire, so Silvio, he wished for harvest before corn could grow, thinking the time as long till he saw how matters would fall out; but not knowing what lady she might be, he presently (before Julina was out of sight) demanded of one that was walking by what she was and how she was called; who satisfied Silvio in every point, and also in what part of the town her house did stand, whereby he might inquire it out. Silvio, thus departing to his lodging, passed the night with very unquiet sleeps, and the next morning his mind ran so much of his supper that he never cared, neither for his breakfast nor dinner; and the day to his seeming passed away so slowly that he had thought the stately steeds had been tired that draw the chariot of the sun, or else some other Joshua had commanded them again to stand, and wished that Phaeton had been there with a whip.[1] Julina, on the other side, she had thought the clock-setter had played the knave, the day came no faster forwards; but six o'clock being once struck, recovered comfort to both parties; and Silvio, hastening himself to the palace of Julina, where by her he was friendly welcomed, and a sumptuous supper being made ready, furnished with sundry sorts of delicate dishes, they sat them down, passing the suppertime with amorous looks, loving countenances, and secret glances conveyed from the one to the other, which did better satisfy them than the feeding of their dainty dishes.

Suppertime being thus spent, Julina did think it very unfitly if she should turn Silvio to go seek his lodging in an evening, desired him

---

1 In the Bible, Joshua made the sun stand still (Joshua 10:13); in Greek mythology, Phaeton, son of Apollo, tried to drive the chariot of the Sun, but a thunderbolt from Zeus overturned the chariot and Phaeton fell to earth.

therefore that he would take a bed in her house for that night; and, bringing him up into a fair chamber that was very richly furnished, she found such means that when all the rest of her household servants were abed and quiet, she came herself to bear Silvio company, where concluding upon conditions that were in question between them, they passed the night with such joy and contentation[1] as might in that convenient time be wished for; but only that Julina, feeding too much of some one dish above the rest, received a surfeit, whereof she could not be cured in forty weeks after, a natural inclination in all women which are subject to longing and want the reason to use a moderation in their diet. But the morning approaching, Julina took her leave and conveyed herself into her own chamber; and when it was fair daylight, Silvio, making himself ready, departed likewise about his affairs in the town, debating with himself how things had happened, being well assured that Julina had mistaken him; and, therefore, for fear of further evils, determined to come no more there, but took his journey towards other places in the parts of Greece, to see if he could learn any tidings of his sister Silla.

The Duke Apollonius, having made a long suit, and never a whit the nearer of his purpose, came to Julina to crave her direct answer, either to accept of him and of such conditions as he proffered unto her, or else to give him his last farewell. Julina, as you have heard, had taken an earnest penny of another, whom she had thought had been Silvio, the Duke's man, was at a controversy in herself, what she might do: one while she thought, seeing her occasion served so fit, to crave the Duke's good will for the marrying of his man; then again, she could not tell what displeasure the Duke would conceive, in that she should seem to prefer his man before himself, did think it best therefore to conceal the matter till she might speak with Silvio, to use his opinion how these matters should be handled; and hereupon resolving herself, desiring the Duke to pardon her speeches, said as followeth: "Sir Duke, for that from this time forwards I am no longer of myself, having given my full power and authority over to another, whose wife I now remain by faithful vow and promise; and albeit I know the world will wonder when they shall understand the fondness of my choice, yet I trust you yourself will nothing dislike with me, sith I have meant no other thing than the satisfying of mine own contentation and liking."

---

1 Satisfaction.

The Duke, hearing these words, answered: "Madam, I must then content myself, although against my will, having the law in your own hands, to like of whom you list and to make choice where it pleaseth you."

Julina, giving the Duke great thanks, that would content himself with such patience, desired him likewise to give his free consent and good will to the party whom she had chosen to be her husband.

"Nay, surely, Madam," quoth the Duke, "I will never give my consent that any other man shall enjoy you than myself; I have made too great account of you than so lightly to pass you away with my good will: but seeing it lieth not in me to let you, having (as you say) made your own choice, so from henceforwards I leave you to your own liking, always willing you well, and thus will take my leave."

The Duke departed towards his own house, very sorrowful that Julina had thus served him; but in the mean space that the Duke had remained in the house of Julina, some of his servants fell into talk and conference with the servants of Julina; where, debating between them of the likelihood of the marriage between the Duke and the lady, one of the servants of Julina said that he never saw his lady and Distress use so good countenance to the Duke himself as she had done to Silvio, his man, and began to report with what familiarity and courtesy she had received him, feasted him, and lodged him, and that in his opinion, Silvio was like to speed before the Duke or any other that were suitors.

This tale was quickly brought to the Duke himself, who, making better inquiry into the matter, found it to be true that was reported; and better considering of the words which Julina had used towards himself was very well assured that it could be no other than his own man that had thrust his nose so far out of joint; wherefore, without any further respect, caused him to be thrust into a dungeon, where he was kept prisoner, in a very pitiful plight.

Poor Silvio, having got intelligence by some of his fellows what was the cause that the Duke, his master, did bear such displeasure unto him, devised all the means he could, as well by mediation by his fellows, as otherwise by petitions and supplications to the Duke that he would suspend his judgement till perfect proof were had in the matter, and then if any manner of thing did fall out against him, whereby the Duke had cause to take any grief, he would confess himself worthy not only of imprisonment but also of most vile and shameful death. With these petitions he daily plied the Duke, but all in vain, for the Duke thought he had made so good proof that he was thoroughly confirmed in his opinion against his man.

But the lady Julina, wondering what made Silvio that he was so slack in his visitation, and why he absented himself so long from her presence, began to think that all was not well; but in the end, perceiving no decoction[1] of her former surfeit, received as you have heard, and finding in herself an unwonted swelling in her belly, assuring herself to be with child, fearing to become quite bankrupt of her honor, did think it more than time to seek out a father, and made such secret search and diligent inquiry that she learned the truth how Silvio was kept in prison by the Duke, his master; and minding to find a present remedy as well for the love she bare to Silvio as for the maintenance of her credit and estimation, she speedily hasted to the palace of the Duke, to whom she said as followeth: "Sir Duke, it may be that you will think my coming to your house in this sort doth something pass the limits of modesty, the which I protest before God, proceedeth of this desire that the world should know how justly I seek means to maintain my honor; but to the end I seem not tedious with prolixity of words, not to use other than direct circumstances, know, sir, that the love I bear to my only beloved Silvio, whom I do esteem more than all the jewels in the world, whose personage I regard more than my own life, is the only cause of my attempted journey, beseeching you that all the whole displeasure, which I understand you have conceived against him, may be imputed unto my charge, and that it would please you lovingly to deal with him whom of myself I have chosen, rather for the satisfaction of mine honest liking than for the vain pre-eminences or honorable dignities looked after by ambitious minds."

The Duke, having heard this discourse, caused Silvio presently to be sent for and to be brought before him, to whom he said: "Had it not been sufficient for thee, when I had reposed myself in thy fidelity and the trustiness of thy service, that thou shouldst so traitorously deal with me, but since that time hast not spared still to abuse me with so many forgeries and perjured protestations, not only hateful unto me, whose simplicity thou thinkest to be such that by the plot of thy pleasant tongue thou wouldst make me believe a manifest untruth; but most

---

1   Reduction.

abominable be thy doings in the presence and sight of God, that hast not spared to blaspheme His holy name, by calling Him to be a witness to maintain thy leasings, and so detestably wouldst thou forswear thyself in a matter that is so openly known."

Poor Silvio, whose innocence was such that he might lawfully swear, seeing Julina to be there in place, answered thus: "Most noble Duke, well understanding your conceived grief, most humbly I beseech you patiently to hear my excuse, not minding thereby to aggravate or heap up your wrath and displeasure, protesting before God that there is nothing in the world which I regard so much or do esteem so dear as your good grace and favor; but desirous that your Grace should know my innocency, and to clear myself of such impositions wherewith I know I am wrongfully accused, which as I understand should be in the practising of the lady Julina, who standeth here in place, whose acquittance for my better discharge now I most humbly crave, protesting before the almighty God that neither in thought, word, nor deed I have not otherwise used myself than according to the bond and duty of a servant, that is both willing and desirous to further his master's suits, which if I have otherwise said than that is true, you, Madam Julina, who can very well decide the depths of all this doubt, I most humbly beseech you to certify a truth, if I have in anything mis-said or have otherwise spoken than is right and just."

Julina, having heard this discourse which Silvio had made, perceiving that he stood in great awe of the Duke's displeasure, answered thus: "Think not, my Silvio, that my coming hither is to accuse you of any misdemeanor towards your master, so I do not deny but in all such embassages wherein towards me you have been employed, you have used the office of a faithful and trusty messenger; neither am ashamed to confess that the first day that mine eyes did behold the singular behavior, the notable courtesy, and other innumerable gifts wherewith my Silvio is endued, but that beyond all measure my heart was so inflamed, that impossible it was for me to quench the fervent love or extinguish the least part of my conceived torment before I had bewrayed the same unto him, and of my own motion craved his promised faith and loyalty of marriage; and now is the time to manifest the same unto the world, which hath been done before God and between ourselves; knowing that it is not needful to keep secret that which is neither evil done nor hurtful to any person, therefore (as I said before) Silvio is my husband by plighted faith, whom I hope to obtain without offense or displeasure of anyone, trusting that there is no man that will so far forget himself as to restrain that which God hath left at liberty for every wight, or that will seek by cruelty to force ladies to marry otherwise than according to their own liking. Fear not then, my Silvio, to keep your faith and promise which you have made unto me; and as for the rest, I doubt not things will so fall out as you shall have no manner of cause to complain."

Silvio, amazed to hear these words, for that Julina by her speech seemed to confirm that which he most of all desired to be quit of, said: "Who would have thought that a lady of so great honor and reputation would herself be the ambassador of a thing so prejudicial and uncomely for her estate! What plighted promises be these which be spoken of altogether ignorant unto me, which if it be otherwise than I have said, you sacred gods consume me straight with flashing flames of fire. But what words might I use to give credit to the truth and innocency of my cause? Ah, Madam Julina, I desire no other testimony than your own honesty and virtue, thinking that you will not so much blemish the brightness of your honor, knowing that a woman is, or should be, the image of courtesy, continency, and shamefastness, from the which so soon as she stoopeth and leaveth the office of her duty and modesty, besides the degradation of her honor, she thrusteth herself into the pit of perpetual infamy. And as I cannot think you would so far forget yourself, by the refusal of a noble duke, to dim the light of your renown and glory, which hitherto you have maintained amongst the best and noblest ladies, by such a one as I know myself to be, too far unworthy your degree and calling; so most humbly I beseech you to confess a truth, whereto tendeth those vows and promises you speak of, which speeches be so obscure unto me as I know not for my life how I might understand them."

Julina, something nipped with these speeches, said: "And what is the matter that now you make so little account of your Julina, that being my husband indeed, have the face to deny me, to whom thou art contracted by so many solemn oaths? What! Art thou ashamed to have me to thy wife? How much oughtest thou rather to be ashamed to break thy promised faith and to have despised the holy and dreadful name of God, but that time constraineth me to lay open that which shame rather willeth I should dissemble and keep secret. Behold me then here, Silvio, whom thou hast gotten with child; who, if thou be of such honesty, as I trust for all this I shall find, then the thing is done without prejudice or any hurt to my conscience, considering that by the professed faith thou didst account me for thy wife, and I received thee for my spouse and loyal husband, swearing by the almighty God that no other than you have made the conquest and triumph of my chastity, whereof I crave no other witness than yourself and mine own conscience."

I pray you, gentlewomen, was not this a foul oversight of Julina, that would so precisely swear so great an oath, that she was gotten with child by one that was altogether unfurnished with implements for such a turn. For God's love take heed, and let this be an example to you when you be with child, how you swear who is the father before you have had good proof and knowledge of the party; for men be so subtle and full of sleight that God knoweth a woman may quickly be deceived.

But now to return to our Silvio, who, hearing an oath sworn so divinely that he had gotten a woman with child, was like to believe that it had been true in very deed; but remembering his own impediment, thought it impossible that he should commit such an act, and therefore, half in a chafe, he said, "What law is able to restrain the foolish indiscretion of a woman that yieldeth herself to her own desires; what shame is able to bridle or withdraw her from her mind and madness, or with what snaffle[1] is it possible to hold her back from the execution of her filthiness? But what abomination is this, that a lady of such a house should so forget the greatness of her estate, the alliance whereof she is descended, the nobility of her deceased husband, and maketh no conscience to shame and slander herself with such a one as I am, being so far unfit and unseemly for her degree; but how horrible it is to hear the name of God so defaced that we make no more account, but for the maintenance of our mischiefs we fear no whit at all to forswear His holy name, as though He were not in all His dealings most righteous, true, and just and will not only lay open our leasings[2] to the world but will likewise punish the same with sharp and bitter scourges."

Julina, not able to endure him to proceed any further in his sermon, was already surprised with a vehement grief, began bitterly to cry out, uttering these speeches following: "Alas, is it possible that the sovereign justice of God can abide a mischief so great and cursed? Why may I not now suffer death rather than the infamy which I see to wander before mine eyes? O happy and more than right happy had I been if inconstant fortune had not devised this treason wherein I am surprised

---

1 Bridle bit.
2 Lies.

and caught! Am I thus become to be entangled with snares, and in the hands of him, who, enjoying the spoils of my honor, will openly deprive me of my fame by making me a common fable to all posterity in time to come? Ah, traitor and discourteous wretch, is this the recompense of the honest and firm amity which I have borne thee? Wherein have I deserved this discourtesy? By loving thee more than thou art able to deserve? Is it I, arrant thief, is it I upon whom thou thinkest to work thy mischiefs? Dost think me no better worth, but that thou mayest prodigally waste my honor at thy pleasure? Didst thou dare to adventure upon me, having thy conscience wounded with so deadly a treason? Ah, unhappy, and above all other most unhappy, that have so charily[1] preserved mine honor, and now am made a prey to satisfy a young man's lust that hath coveted nothing but the spoil of my chastity and good name." Herewithal the tears so gushed down her cheeks that she was not able to open her mouth to use any further speech.

The Duke, who stood by all this while and heard this whole discourse, was wonderfully moved with compassion towards Julina, knowing that from her infancy she had ever so honorably used herself that there was no man able to detect her of any misdemeanor otherwise than beseemed a lady of her estate; wherefore, being fully resolved that Silvio, his man, had committed this villainy against her, in a great fury drawing his rapier, he said into Silvio: "How canst thou, arrant thief, show thyself so cruel and careless to such as do thee honor? Hast thou so little regard of such a noble lady, as humbleth herself to such a villain as thou art, who, without any respect either of her renown or noble estate, canst be content to seek the wrack and utter ruin of her honor? But frame thyself to make such satisfaction as she requireth, although I know, unworthy wretch, that thou art not able to make her the least part of amends, or I swear by God that thou shalt not escape the death which I will minister to thee with mine own hands, and therefore advise thee well what thou doest." Silvio, having heard this sharp sentence, fell down on his knees before the Duke, craving for mercy, desiring that he might be suffered to speak with the lady Julina apart, promising to satisfy her according to her own contentation.

"Well," quoth the Duke, "I take thy word; and therewithal I advise thee that thou perform thy promise, or otherwise I protest before God

---

1 Cautiously.

I will make thee such an example to the world that all traitors shall tremble for fear, how they do seek the dishonoring of ladies."

But now Julina had conceived so great grief against Silvio that there was much ado to persuade her to talk with him; but remembering her own case, desirous to hear what excuse he could make, in the end she agreed; and being brought into a place severally by themselves, Silvio began with a piteous voice to say as followeth: "I know not, madam, of whom I might make complaint, whether of you or of myself, or rather of fortune, which hath conducted and brought us both into so great adversity. I see that you receive great wrong, and I am condemned against all right, you in peril to abide the bruit of spiteful tongues, and I in danger to lose the thing that I most desire; and although I could allege many reasons to prove my sayings true, yet I refer myself to the experience and bounty of your mind." And herewithal loosing his garments down to his stomach, showed Julina his breasts and pretty teats, surmounting far the whiteness of snow itself, saying: "Lo, madam, behold here the party whom you have challenged to be the father of your child; see, I am a woman, the daughter of a noble duke, who only for the love of him, whom you so lightly have shaken off, have forsaken my father, abandoned my country, and, in manner as you see, am become a serving man, satisfying myself but with the only sight of my Apollonius. And now, madam, if my passion were not vehement and my torments without comparison, I would wish that my feigned griefs might be laughed to scorn and my dissembled pains to be rewarded with flouts. But my love being pure, my travail continual, and my griefs endless, I trust, madam, you will not only excuse me of crime, but also pity my distress, the which I protest I would still have kept secret, if my fortune would so have permitted." Julina did now think herself to be in a worse case than ever she was before, for now she knew not whom to challenge to be the father of her child; wherefore, when she had told the Duke the very certainty of the discourse which Silvio had made unto her, she departed to her own house with such grief and sorrow that she purposed never to come out of her own doors again alive, to be a wonder and mocking stock to the world. But the Duke, more amazed to hear this strange discourse of Silvio, came unto him; whom when he had viewed with better consideration, perceived indeed that it was Silla, the daughter of Duke Pontus; and embracing her in his arms he said: "O the branch of all virtue and the flower of courtesy itself, pardon me, I beseech you, of all such discourtesies as I have ignorantly committed towards you: desiring you that without farther memory of ancient griefs, you will accept of me, who is more joyful and better contented with your presence, than if the whole world were at my commandment. Where hath there ever been found such liberality in a lover, which, having been trained up and nourished amongst the delicacies and banquets of the court, accompanied with trains of many fair and noble ladies living in pleasure, and in the midst of delights, would so prodigally adventure yourself, neither fearing mishaps nor misliking to take such pains, as I know you have not been accustomed unto? O liberality never heard of before! O fact that can never be sufficiently rewarded! O true love most pure and unfeigned!" Herewithal sending for the most artificial workmen,[1] he provided for her sundry suits of sumptuous apparel, and the marriage day appointed, which was celebrated with great triumph through the whole city of Constantinople, everyone praising the nobleness of the Duke, but so many as did behold the excellent beauty of Silla gave her the praise above all the rest of the ladies in the troop.

The matter seemed so wonderful and strange that the bruit was spread throughout all the parts of Greece, in so much that it came to the hearing of Silvio, who, as you have heard, remained in those parts to inquire of his sister; he being the gladdest man in the world, hasted to Constantinople where, coming to his sister, he was joyfully received, and most lovingly welcomed, and entertained of the Duke, his brother-in-law. After he had remained there two or three days, the Duke revealed unto Silvio the whole discourse how it happened between his sister and the Lady Julina, and how his sister was challenged, for getting a woman with child. Silvio, blushing with these words, was stricken with great remorse to make Julina amends, understanding her to be a noble Lady, and was left defamed to the world through his default; he therefore bewrayed the whole circumstance to the Duke, whereof the Duke being very joyful, immediately repaired with Silvio to the house of Julina, whom she found in her chamber, in great lamentation and mourning. To whom the Duke said, "take courage Madam for behold here a gentleman, that will not stick, both to father your child and to take you for his wife, no inferior person, but the son and heir of a noble Duke, worthy of your estate and dignity."

---

1 Skilled in making elaborate outfits.

Julina seeing Silvio in place, did know very well that he was the father of her child, and was so ravished with joy, that she knew not whether she were awake, or in some dream. Silvio embracing her in his arms, craving forgiveness of all that past: concluded with her the marriage day, which was presently accomplished with great joy, and contentation to all parties. And thus Silvio having attained a noble wife, and Silla his sister her desired husband, they passed the residue of their days with such delight, as those that have accomplished the perfection of their felicities.

FINIS.

2. FROM GL'INGANNATI—THE DECEIVED (1531)[1]

I.3

[A Street, with the house of Flaminio. [Enter] Lelia, [and] Clementia.]

LELIA (*in male apparel*). It is great boldness in me that, knowing the licentious customs of these wild youths of Modena, I should venture abroad alone at this early hour. What would become of me, if any one of them should suspect my sex? But the cause is my love for the cruel and ungrateful Flaminio. Oh, what a fate is mine! I love one who hates me. I serve one who does not know me; and, for more bitter grief, I aid him in his love for another, without any other hope than that of satiating my eyes with his sight. Thus far all has gone well; but now, what can I do? My father is returned. Flaminio is come to live in the town. I can scarcely hope to continue here without being discovered; and if it should be so, my reputation will be blighted for ever, and I shall become a byword in the city. Therefore I have come forth at this hour to consult my nurse, whom, from the window I have seen coming this way. But I will first see if she knows me in this dress.... one morning early I left the convent in this attire, and went to Flaminio's palazzo. There I waited until Flaminio came out; and Flaminio be praised, he no sooner saw me, than he asked me most courteously, what I wanted and whence I came.

---

1   Playtext reprinted from Furness.

CLEMENTIA. Is it possible that you did not fall dead with shame?

LELIA. Far from it indeed. Love bore me up. I answered frankly, that I was from Rome, and that, being poor, I was seeking service. He examined me several times from head to foot so earnestly, that I was almost afraid he would know me. He then said that if I pleased to stay with him, he would receive me willingly and treat me well; and I answered that I would gladly do so.

CLEMENTIA. And what good do you expect from this mad proceeding?

LELIA. The good of seeing him, hearing him, talking with him, learning his secrets, seeing his companions, and being sure that if he is not mine, he is another's.

CLEMENTIA. In what way do you serve him?

LELIA. As his page in all honesty. And this fortnight I have served him, I have become so much in his favour, that I almost think appearing in my true dress would revive his love.

CLEMENTIA. What will people say when this shall be known?

LELIA. Who will know it, if you do not tell it? Now what I want you to do is this: that, as my father returned yesterday, and may perhaps send for me, you would prevent his doing so for four or five days, and at the end of this time I will return. You may say that I am gone to Roverino with Sister Amabile.

CLEMENTIA. And why all this?

LELIA. Flaminio, as I have already told you, is enamoured of Isabella Foiani; and he often send me to her with letters and messages. She, taking me for a young man, has fallen madly in love with me, and makes me the most passionate advances. I pretend that I will not love her, unless she can so manage as to bring Flaminio's pursuit of her to an end; and I hope that in three or four days he will be brought to give her up. (342-44)

II.1

[*The Street, with the house of Flaminio. Enter Lelia (as Fabio) and Flaminio.*]

...

FLAMINIO. And does it appear to you, Fabio, that she says these things from her heart, or, rather, that she has taken some offense with me? For at one time she showed me favour, and I cannot believe she wishes me ill, while she accepts my letters and messages. I am disposed to follow her till death. Do you not think that I am in the right, Fabio?

LELIA. No signor.

FLAMINIO. Why?

LELIA. Because, if I were in one place, I should expect her to receive my service as a grace and an honor. To a young man like you, noble, virtuous, elegant, handsome, can ladies worthy of you, be wanting? Do as I would do, signor; leave her; and attach yourself to someone who will love you as you deserve. Such will be easily found, and perhaps as handsome as she is. Have you never found one in this country who loved you?

FLAMINIO. Indeed I have, and especially one, who is named Lelia, and to whom, I have often thought I see a striking likeness in you; the most beautiful, the most accomplished, the best mannered young girl in this town; who would think herself happy, if I would show her even a little favour; rich and well received at court. We were lovers nearly a year, and she showed me a thousand favors; but she went to Mirandola, and my fate made me enamored of Isabella, who has been as cruel to me as Lelia was gracious....

LELIA. If you first loved this poor girl, and if she loved and still loves you, why have you abandoned her to follow another? Ah, Signor Flaminio! You do a great wrong, a greater than I know if God can pardon.

FLAMINIO. You are a child, Fabio. You do not know the force of love. I cannot help myself. I must love and adore Isabella. I cannot, may not, will not think of any but her. Therefore, go to her again; speak with her; and try to draw dexterously from her, what is the cause that she will not see me.

LELIA. You will lose your time.

FLAMINIO. It pleases me so to lose it.

LELIA. You will accomplish nothing.

FLAMINIO. Patience.

LELIA. Pray let her go.

FLAMINIO. I cannot. Go, as I bid you.

LELIA. I will go, but—

FLAMINIO. Return with answer immediately. Meanwhile I will go in.

LELIA. When time serves, I will not fail.

FLAMINIO. Do this, and it will be well for you. (345-46)

[The Street with the hotels, and with the house of Gherardo.]

...

LELIA. Remember what you have promised me.

ISABELLA. And do you remember to return to me. One word more.

LELIA. What more?

ISABELLA. Listen.

LELIA. I attend.

ISABELLA. No one is here?

LELIA. Not a living soul.

ISABELLA. Come nearer. I wish—

LELIA. What do you wish?

ISABELLA. I wish that you return after dinner, when my father will be out.

LELIA. I will; but if my master passes this way, close the window, and retire.

ISABELLA. If I do not, may you never love me.

LELIA. Adieu. Now return into the house.

ISABELLA. I would have a favor from you.

LELIA. What?

ISABELLA. Come a little within.

LELIA. We shall be seen.

SCATIZZA. [*aside*] She has kissed him.

CRIVELLO. [*aside*] I had rather lost a hundred crowns than not to have seen this kiss. What will my master do when he knows it.

SCATIZZA. [*aside*] Oh, the devil! You won't tell him?

ISABELLA. Pardon me. Your too great beauty, and the too great love I bear you, have impelled me to this. You will think it hardly becoming the modesty of a maid, but God knows, I could not resist....

v.2

...

FLAMINIO. I think, Clementia, this is certainly the will of heaven, which has had pity on this virtuous girl no less than on me; therefore, Lelia, I desire no other wife than you, and I vow to you most solemnly, that if I do not have you, I will never have any other.

LELIA. Flaminio, you are my lord. I have revealed my heart in my actions.

FLAMINIO. Indeed, you have, and revealed it bravely. And forgive me if I have caused you distress; I am most repentant and acknowledge my error.

LELIA. Your pleasure, Flaminio, has been always mine. I should have found my own happiness in promoting yours.

FLAMINIO. Clementia, I dread some accident. If she is content, I'll lose no time, but marry her instantly.

LELIA. Most content....

ISABELLA. I most certainly thought that you, Fabrizio, were the page of a gentleman of this city. He resembles you so much, that he must surely be your brother.

FABRIZIO. I have been mistaken for another man, more than once today.

ISABELLA. Here is your nurse, Clementia.

CLEMENTIA. This must be he who is so like Lelia. Oh, my dear child, Fabrizio, how is it with you?

FABRIZIO. All well, my dear nurse. And how is it with Lelia?

CLEMENTIA. Well, well; but come in. I have much to say to you all.

Enter Virginio.

VIRGINIO. I am so overjoyed in recovering my son that I am contented with everything.

CLEMENTIA. It was ordained of Heaven that she should not be married to that withered old stick, Gherardo. But let us go into the hotel and complete our preparations.

They enter the hotel.

STRAGUALCIA. Spectators, do not expect that any of these characters will reappear. If you will come to supper with us, I will expect you at *The Madman*; but bring money; entertainment is not *gratis*, there. If you will not come (and you seem to say 'No!') show us that you have been satisfied here, and applaud; and you, *Intronati*,[1] make known your gleeful delight.

Thus ends The Ingannati of The Intronati.

---

1   The play was first produced by *L'Intronati*, the humanist "Academy of the Thunderstruck."

APPENDIX B: RENAISSANCE SHIPWRECKS

[Renaissance audiences knew well the realities of shipwreck and the effects of piracy. They were also familiar with many stories in which shipwreck is a core driver of the plot. Shakespeare uses a shipwreck in several plays (such as *The Tempest* and *Pericles*) to change the fates of his characters. Though Renaissance theaters would not show any remains of the wrecked ship itself, it was common for characters to enter "*all wet as newly shipwrecked and escaped the fury of the Seas*" (Dessen and Thomson, "wet"), as Viola and the sailors are often now seen at their entry in 1.2.

Below are two famous fictional depictions of wrecked ships that Shakespeare had almost certainly read. First, Heliodorus' ancient Greek novel *An Aethiopian History* opens with a ship at the mouth of the Nile that has been completely ransacked by pirates in a fierce battle. Beside the ship can be seen a beautiful woman on the rocks, looking like a goddess, and to whom Viola might be compared. Heliodorus was available to Shakespeare in translation, and Orsino alludes directly to the story when he compares himself to "... th'Egyptian thief at point of death" (5.1.111, TLN 2323; see also Houlahan). Secondly, Sir Philip Sidney's long romance *The Countess of Pembroke's Arcadia* was among the most popular of the prose stories cherished by English readers in Shakespeare's lifetime; in fact, Shakespeare drew the subplot of *King Lear* from this book. Near the beginning, Sidney vividly describes a ship devastated in battle. Beside the ship we see a beautiful young man with long hair "stirred up and down with the wind"; his androgynous appeal is similar to Viola's, which most characters in Illyria are attracted to whether she is dressed as herself or in her male disguise.]

1. FROM HELIODORUS, *AN AETHIOPIAN HISTORY*,[1]
TRANS. THOMAS UNDERDOWNE (1587)

As soon as the day appeared, and the Sun began to shine on the tops of the hills, men whose custom was to live by rapine and violence ran to the top of a hill that stretched towards the mouth of Nylus [Nile], called Heracleot, where standing awhile they viewed the sea

---

1   London: Chapman and Dodd, 1924.

underneath them, and when they had looked a good season afar off into the same, and could see nothing that might put them in hope of prey, they cast their eyes somewhat near the shoar, where a ship, tied with cables to the mainland, lay at road, without sailors, and full fraughted, which thing, they who were afar off might easily conjecture, for the burden caused the ship to draw water within the boards of the deck. But on the shore every place was full of men, some quite dead, some half dead, some whose bodies yet panted, and plainly declared that there had been a battle fought of late. But there could be seen no signs or tokens of any just quarrel, but there seemed to be an ill and unlucky banquet, and those that remained, obtained such end. For the tables were furnished with delicate dishes, some whereof lay in the hands of those that were slain, being instead of weapons to some of them in the battle, so suddenly begun. Others covered such as crop[1] under them to hide themselves, as they thought. Besides, the cups were over-thrown, and fell out of the hands, either of them that drank, or those, who had instead of stones used them. For that sudden mischief wrought new devices, and taught them instead of weapons to use their pots. Of those who lay there, one was wounded with an axe, another was hurt with the shells of fishes, whereof on the shore there was great plenty, another was all to crushed[2] with a lever, many burnt with fire, and the rest by diverse other means, but most of all were slain with arrows. To be brief, God showed a wonderful sight in so short time, brewing blood with wine, joining battle with banqueting, mingling indifferently slaughters with drinkings, and killing with quaffings, providing such a sight for the thieves of Egypt to gaze at. For they when they had given these things the looking on a good while from the hill, could not understand what that sight meant, for as much as they saw some slain there, but the conquerors could they see nowhere, a manifest victory but no spoils taken away, a ship without mariners only, but as concerning other things untouched, as if she had been kept with a guard of many men, and lay at road in a false harbour. But for all that they knew not what that thing meant, yet they had respect to their lucre and gain.

---

1 Crept.
2 Completely crushed.

When therefore they had determined that themselves were the victors, they drew near unto the same: and not being now far from the ship, and those that were slain, they saw a sight more perplexed then the rest a great deal. A maid endued with excellent beauty, which also might be supposed a goddess, sate upon a rock, who seemed not a little to be grieved with that present mischance, but for all that of excellent courage: she had a garland of laurel on her head, a quiver on her back, and in her left hand a bow, leaning upon her thigh with her other hand, and looking downward, without moving of her head, beholding a certain young man a good way off, the which was sore wounded, and seemed to lift up himself, as if he had been wakened out of a dead sleep, almost of death itself: yet was he in this case of singular beauty, and for all that his cheeks were besprinkled with blood, his whiteness did appear so much the more.

2. FROM SIR PHILIP SIDNEY, *THE COUNTESS OF PEMBROKE'S ARCADIA* (1593)

They steered therefore as near thither-ward as they could; but when they came so near as their eyes were full masters of the object, they saw a sight full of piteous strangeness: a ship, or rather the carcass of the ship, or rather some few bones of the carcase hulling[1] there, part broken, part burned, part drowned—death having used more than one dart to that destruction. About it floated great store of very rich things and many chests which might promise no less. And amidst the precious things were a number of dead bodies, which likewise did not only testify both elements' violence, but that the chief violence was grown of human inhumanity; for their bodies were full of grisly wounds, and their blood had (as it were) filled the wrinkles of the sea's visage, which it seemed the sea would not wash away that it might witness it is not always his fault when we condemn his cruelty. In sum, a defeat where the conquered kept both field and spoil; a shipwreck without storm or ill-footing,[2] and a waste of fire in the midst of water.

But a little way off they saw the mast, whose proud height now lay along, like a widow having lost her mate of whom she held her honour.

---

1 Drifting.
2 Running on the rocks.

But upon the mast they saw a young man—at least if he were a man—bearing show of about eighteen years of age, who sat as on horseback, having nothing upon him but his shirt which, being wrought with blue silk and gold, had a kind of resemblance to the sea on which the sun (then near his western home) did shoot some of his beams. His hair (which the young men of Greece used to wear very long) was stirred up and down with the wind, which seemed to have a sport to play with it as the sea had to kiss his feet; himself full of admirable beauty, set forth by the strangeness both of his seat and gesture. For holding his head up full of unmoved majesty, he held a sword aloft with his fair arm, which often he waved about his crown as though he would threaten the world in that extremity.

APPENDIX C: TWINS AND AFFINITY

[Shakespeare was himself the father of twins: "February 2 Hamnet and Judith sonne & daughter to William Shakspere" (Stratford-upon Avon parish register 1585). And he wrote two plays in which identical twins are the main characters. Both of them, as Manningham noted in 1602 (see Introduction, p. 38), are based on Plautus' play *The Menaechmi*, in which twin boys are separated and, many years later, spend a day being mistaken for each other. Shakespeare probably read Plautus when he was learning Latin at school, but could also have read William Warner's translation of 1595, excerpted below. Messenio, the traveling Menaechmus' slave, describes their travels through the Mediterranean, probably giving Shakespeare the idea of locating *Twelfth Night* in Illyria. Eventually the confusion is sorted out and the lost brothers united.

Shakespeare's *The Comedy of Errors* (1594) doubles Plautus by providing identical twin servants as well as the twin masters; one set of master and servant lives in Syracuse, the other in Ephesus. When the Syracusan twins arrive in Ephesus, both pairs—masters and servants—are easily confused with each other. The play ends with not only the twin masters reunited, but also the servant twins, a moment audiences always enjoy.

In *Twelfth Night* the separation of the twins Viola and Sebastian and their final rediscovery of each other are more desperate and more moving than in either *Errors* or Plautus. The play takes up the theme of what it means to be twinned with someone in a wider sense, a concept that links to larger Renaissance ideas of the deep importance of solidarity in friendship. These underpin the reunion of Viola and Sebastian, and also the intense bond we see between Sebastian and Antonio. This bond is explored by George Puttenham in terms of rhetoric, in his influential *Art of English Poesy* (1589); in terms of apt conduct by Richard Brathwaite, in his behavior guide for *The English Gentleman* (1633); and in terms of the twinning of philosophy and friendship by the French essayist Montaigne (English version 1603). Shakespeare uses Montaigne in *The Tempest* and in *Hamlet*, and may have read "On Friendship" in manuscript; the full essay is available on the ISE website (<http://internetshakespeare.uvic.ca>).]

1. FROM PLAUTUS, *MENAECHMI*,
TRANS. WILLIAM WARNER (1595)[1]

THE ARGUMENT

Two twin-born sons a Sicil[ian] merchant had,
Menaechmus one, and *Sosicles* the other.
The first his father lost, a little lad,
The grandsire named the latter like his brother.[2]
This (grown a man) long travel took to seek
His brother, and to Epidamnum came,
Where th'other dwelt enriched, and him so like,
That citizens there take him for the same:
Father, wife, neighbours, each mistaking either,
Much pleasant error, ere they meet together.

2.1

Enter Menaechmus Sosicles, Messenio his servant, and some Sailors.

MENAECHMUS. Surely, Messenio, I think sea-farers never take so comfortable a joy in anything, as when they have been long tossed and turmoiled in the wide seas, they hap at last to ken[3] land.

MESSENIO. I'll be sworn, I should not be gladder to see a whole country of mine own, than I have been at such a sight. But I pray, wherefore are we now come to Epidamnum? Must we needs go to see every town we hear of?

MENAECHMUS. Till I find my brother, all towns are alike to me—I must try in all places.

MESSENIO. Why then, let's even as long as we live seek your brother. Six years now have we roamed about thus, Istria, Hispania, Massilia, Illyria, all the upper sea, all high Greece, all haven towns in Italy: I think if we had sought a needle all this time, we must needs have found it, had it been above ground. It cannot be that he is alive, and to seek a dead man thus among the living, what folly is it?....

---

1 Text from EEBO.
2 Both the brothers are known as Menaechmus.
3 Know.

... Enter Menaechmus the Citizen [to Menaechmus the Traveller and Messenio].

MENAECHMUS (CITIZEN). Forsworn queans,[1] swear till your hearts ache, and your eyes fall out, you shall never make me believe that I carried hence either cloak or chain.

MESSENIO. O heavens, master, what do I see?

MENAECHMUS (TRAVELLER). What?

MESSENIO. Your ghost.

MENAECHMUS (TRAVELLER). What ghost?

MESSENIO. Your image, as like you as can be possible.

MENAECHMUS (TRAVELLER). Surely not much unlike me, as I think.

MENAECHMUS (CITIZEN). O my good friend and helper, well met. Thanks for thy late good help.

MESSENIO. Sir, may I crave to know your name?

MENAECHMUS (CITIZEN). I were to blame if I should not tell thee any thing. My name is Menaechmus.

MENAECHMUS (TRAVELLER). Nay my friend, that is my name.

MENAECHMUS (CITIZEN). I am of Syracuse in Sicilia.

MENAECHMUS (TRAVELLER). So am I.

MESSENIO. Are you a Syracusan?

MENAECHMUS (CITIZEN). I am....

MESSENIO. What a jest is this? Are you Menaechmus?

MENAECHMUS (CITIZEN). Even Menaechmus the son of Moscus.

MENAECHMUS (TRAVELLER). My father's son? ...

MESSENIO. O immortal gods, let it fall out as I hope. And for my life, these are the two twins, all things agree to jump together. I will speak to my master. Menaechmus?

BOTH. What wilt thou?

MESSENIO. I call you not both, but which of you came with me from the ship?

MENAECHMUS (CITIZEN). Not I.

MENAECHMUS (TRAVELLER). I did.

MESSENIO. Then I call you. Come hither.

MENAECHMUS (TRAVELLER). What's the matter?

---

1 Prostitutes.

MESSENIO. This same is either some notable cozening juggler, or else it is your brother whom we seek. I never saw one man so like another. Water to water, nor milk to milk, is not liker than he is to you.

MENAECHMUS (TRAVELLER). Indeed I think thou sayest true. Find it that he is my brother, and I here promise thee thy freedom.

MESSENIO. Well, let me about it. Hear ye sir, you say your name is Menaechmus?

MENAECHMUS (CITIZEN). I do.

MESSENIO. So is this man's. You are of Syracuse.

MENAECHMUS (CITIZEN). True.

MESSENIO. So is he. Moscus was your father?

MENAECHMUS (CITIZEN). He was.

MESSENIO. So was he his. What will you say, if I did find that ye are brethren and twins?

MENAECHMUS (CITIZEN). I would think it happy news.

MESSENIO. Nay, stay, masters both, I mean to have the honor of this exploit. Answer me. Your name is Menaechmus?

MENAECHMUS (CITIZEN). Yea.

MESSENIO. And yours?

MENAECHMUS (TRAVELLER). And mine.

MESSENIO. You are of Syracuse?

MENAECHMUS (CITIZEN). I am.

MENAECHMUS (TRAVELLER). And I.

MESSENIO. Well, this goeth right thus far. What is the farthest thing that you remember there?

MENAECHMUS (CITIZEN). How I went with my father to Tarentum, to a great mart,[1] and there in the press I was stolen from him.

MENAECHMUS (TRAVELLER). O Jupiter!

MESSENIO. Peace, what exclaiming is this? How old were ye then?

MENAECHMUS (CITIZEN). About seven year old, for even then I shed teeth, and since that time, I never heard of any of my kindred.

MESSENIO. Had ye never a brother?

MENAECHMUS (CITIZEN). Yes, as I remember. I heard them say we were two twins.

MENAECHMUS (TRAVELLER). O Fortune!

---

1 Market.

MESSENIO. Tush, can ye not be quiet? Were you both of one name?

MENAECHMUS (CITIZEN). Nay, as I think, they called my brother Sosicles.

MENAECHMUS (TRAVELLER). It is he, what need farther proof? O brother, brother, let me embrace thee.

MENAECHMUS (CITIZEN). Sir, if this be true, I am wonderfully glad. But how is it that ye are called Menaechmus?

MENAECHMUS (TRAVELLER). When it was told us that you and our father were both dead, our grandfather, in memory of my father's name, changed mine to Menaechmus.

MENAECHMUS (CITIZEN). 'Tis very like he would do so indeed. But let me ask ye one question more: what was our mother's name?

MENAECHMUS (TRAVELLER). Theusimarche.

MENAECHMUS (CITIZEN). Brother, the most welcome man to me that the world holdeth.

MENAECHMUS (TRAVELLER). I joy, and ten thousand joys the more, having taken so long travail[1] and huge pains to seek you.

MESSENIO. See now, how all this matter comes about. Thus it was, that the gentlewoman had ye in to dinner, thinking it had been he.

MENAECHMUS (CITIZEN). True it is, I swilled a dinner to be provided for me here this morning, and I also brought hither closely a cloak of my wife's, and gave it to this woman.

MENAECHMUS (TRAVELLER). Is not this the same, brother?

MENAECHMUS (CITIZEN). How came you by this?

MENAECHMUS (TRAVELLER). This woman met me, had me in to dinner, entertained me most kindly, and gave me this cloak, and this chain.

MENAECHMUS (CITIZEN). Indeed she took ye for me; and I believe I have been as strangely handled by occasion of your coming.

MESSENIO. You shall have time enough to laugh at all these matters hereafter. Do ye remember, master, what you promised me?

MENAECHMUS (CITIZEN). Brother, I will entreat you to perform your promise to Messenio. He is worthy of it.

MENAECHMUS (TRAVELLER). I am content.

MESSENIO. *Io triumphe!*

---

1 Work, labor (from the French *travail*).

MENAECHMUS (TRAVELLER). Brother, will ye now go with me to Syracuse?

MENAECHMUS (CITIZEN). So soon as I can sell away such goods as I possess here in Epidamnum, I will go with you.

MENAECHMUS (TRAVELLER). Thanks my good brother!

MENAECHMUS (CITIZEN). Messenio, play thou the crier for me, and make a proclamation.

MESSENIO. A fit office. Come on. O yes. What day shall your sale be?

MENAECHMUS (CITIZEN). This day se'n-night.[1]

MESSENIO. All men, women, and children, in Epidamnum or elsewhere, that will repair to Menaechmus' house this day se'n-night, shall there find all manner of things to sell: servants, household stuff, house, ground, and all—so they bring ready money. Will ye sell your wife too, sir?

MENAECHMUS (CITIZEN). Yea, but I think nobody will bid money for her.

MESSENIO. Thus, gentlemen, we take our leaves; and if we have pleased, we require a *plaudite*.[2]

FINIS.

2. FROM WILLIAM SHAKESPEARE, *THE COMEDY OF ERRORS* (C. 1593)

DROMIO OF SYRACUSE. There is a fat friend at your master's house
That kitchened me for you today at dinner:
She now shall be my sister, not my wife.

DROMIO OF EPHESUS. Methinks you are my glass, and not my brother
I see by you, I am a sweet-faced youth.
Will you walk in to see their gossiping?

DROMIO OF SYRACUSE. Not I, sir, you are my elder.

DROMIO OF EPHESUS. That's a question. How shall we try it?

DROMIO OF SYRACUSE. We'll draw cuts for the senior. Till then, lead thou first.

---

1 In a week.
2 Applause.

DROMIO OF EPHESUS. Nay, then, thus:
We came into the world like brother and brother,
And now let's go hand in hand, not one before another.
(5.1.415-27, TLN 1907-19)

3. FROM GEORGE PUTTENHAM, "HENDIADYS, OR THE FIGURE OF TWINS" (1589)[1]

Ye have yet another manner of speech when ye will seem to make two of one, not thereunto constrained, which therefore we call the figure of Twins, the Greek's *Hendiadys*, thus:

> *Not you coy dame your lours nor your looks.*

For "*your louring looks.*" And as one of our ordinary rhymers said,

> *Of fortune nor her frowning face,*
> *I am nothing aghast.*

Instead of "*fortunes frowning face.*" One praising the Neapolitans for good men at arms, said by the figure of Twins thus:

> *A proud people and wise and valiant,*
> *Fiercely fighting with horses and with barbs:*
> *By whose prowess the Roman Prince did daunt*
> *Wild Africans and the lawless Al-Arabs,*
> *The Nubians marching with their armed carts,*
> *And slaying afar with venom, and with darts.*

Where ye see this figure of Twins twice used, once when he said *horses* and *barbs* for "barbed horses": again when he sayeth "with *venom* and with *darts*" for "venomous darts."

---

1   In *The Arte of English Poesie*, text from EEBO.

4. FROM MICHEL DE MONTAIGNE, "OF FRIENDSHIP," TRANS. JOHN FLORIO (1603)[1]

In the amity I speak of they intermix and confound themselves one in the other, with so universal a commixture that they wear out, and can no more find the seam that hath conjoined them together. If a man urge me to tell wherefore I loved him, I feel it cannot be expressed, but by answering: "because it was he, because it was myself." ... We sought one another, before we had heard of one another; which wrought a greater violence in us than the reason of reports may well bear; I think by some secret ordinance of the heavens we embraced one another by our names. And at our first meeting, which was by chance at a great feast and solemn meeting of a whole township, we found ourselves so surprised, so known, so acquainted, and so combinedly bound together, that from thenceforward nothing was so near unto us as one unto another.

5. FROM RICHARD BRATHWAITE, *THE ENGLISH GENTLEMAN* (2ND ED., 1633): "A DRAFT OF THE FRONTISPIECE"[2]

ACQUAINTANCE is in two bodies individually incorporated, an[d] no less selfly than sociably united. Two twins cannot be more naturally near than these be affectionately dear, which they express in hugging one another, and showing the consenting consort of their mind, by the mutual interchoice of their motto: *Certus amor morum est* ["Steadfast love is the rule"].

---

1 *Essays of Montaigne*, ed. Percival Chubb. London: W. Scott, 1903.
2 Text from EEBO.

Robert Vaughan, "Acquaintance," frontispiece to Richard Brathwaite, *The English Gentleman* (1630). From the collection of the Folger Shakespeare Library; photograph by David McInnis.

APPENDIX D: GENDER AND DISGUISE

[*Twelfth Night* is the last of four Shakespeare comedies that use a cross-dressing heroine to explore the nature of love and desire. Viola, like Rosalind in *As You Like It*, puts on male clothing and finds that people are tricked into finding her manliness attractive. In the Renaissance theater the trick is complicated, as audiences would see a young male actor, dressed as a female (Viola), who then dresses as a man (Cesario), who, while still in male clothes, is betrothed to the man she loves, Orsino.

The debate on the true nature of desire goes as far back as Plato in Athens in fourth century BCE. *The Symposium* presents an imaginary dinner party where these ideas are debated. Aristophanes' fable, presented here in Benjamin Jowett's famous translation, suggests that humans were cut in two by the God Zeus, and that each human then needs to find their other matching half, or else they will be incomplete. Aristophanes also allows for men to be drawn either to woman or man in "pursuit of the whole ... called love."

Shakespeare explores the range of desire in his *Sonnets*, first published as a collection in 1609, in which the young man addressed has androgynous appeal, which he shows also in his heroines Viola and Rosalind. John Lyly's elegant comedy *Galatea* (first published in 1592) shows a complex version of cross-gender desire, in which two young women, both disguised as young men, are attracted to each other. Both Lyly and Shakespeare treat this scenario of cross-gender desire as a game, but, as Levine (1994) describes, some Renaissance commentators were appalled by this. Stephen Gosson's influential Puritan tract, *Plays Confuted in Five Actions* (1582), denounces the dangers of crossdressing in the theater as a breach against the "natural" order of things, according to which men and woman should wear clothes that showed their "real" gender. The anonymous *Hic-Mulier* (1620), published 38 years after Gosson, shows the intensification of this debate. It describes in riveting detail the elaborate clothing prescribed for men and women, and also shows the chaos of a world where men dressed as women and women as men.]

1. FROM PLATO, *THE SYMPOSIUM* (C. 380 BCE)[1]

Aristophanes[2] professed to open another vein of discourse; he had a mind to praise Love in another way, unlike that either of Pausanias or Eryximachus.[3] Mankind, he said, judging by their neglect of him, have never, as I think, at all understood the power of Love. For if they had understood him they would surely have built noble temples and altars, and offered solemn sacrifices in his honor; but this is not done, and most certainly ought to be done: since of all the gods he is the best friend of men, the helper and the healer of the ills which are the great impediment to the happiness of the race. I will try to describe his power to you, and you shall teach the rest of the world what I am teaching you. In the first place, let me treat of the nature of man and what has happened to it; for the original human nature was not like the present, but different. The sexes were not two as they are now, but originally three in number; there was man, woman, and the union of the two, having a name corresponding to this double nature, which had once a real existence, but is now lost, and the word "Androgynous" is only preserved as a term of reproach. In the second place, the primeval man was round, his back and sides forming a circle; and he had four hands and four feet, one head with two faces, looking opposite ways, set on a round neck and precisely alike; also four ears, two privy members, and the remainder to correspond. He could walk upright as men now do, backwards or forwards as he pleased, and he could also roll over and over at a great pace, turning on his four hands and four feet, eight in all, like tumblers going over and over with their legs in the air; this was when he wanted to run fast.

Now the sexes were three, and such as I have described them; because the sun, moon, and earth are three; and the man was originally the child of the sun, the woman of the earth, and the man-woman of the moon, which is made up of sun and earth, and they were all round and moved round and round like their parents. Terrible was their might and strength, and the thoughts of their hearts were great, and they made

---

1   Trans. Benjamin Jowett. Text from Project Gutenberg <http://www.gutenberg. org/catalog/world/readfile?fk_files=3274562>.
2   Famous classical Greek comic playwright (c. 446–c. 386 BCE).
3   Two other guests at the dinner party. Eryximachus was a doctor whose views are mocked by Plato.

an attack upon the gods; of them is told the tale of Otys and Ephialtes[1] who, as Homer says, dared to scale heaven, and would have laid hands upon the gods. Doubt reigned in the celestial councils. Should they kill them and annihilate the race with thunderbolts, as they had done the giants, then there would be an end of the sacrifices and worship which men offered to them; but, on the other hand, the gods could not suffer their insolence to be unrestrained. At last, after a good deal of reflection, Zeus discovered a way. He said: "Methinks I have a plan which will humble their pride and improve their manners; men shall continue to exist, but I will cut them in two and then they will be diminished in strength and increased in numbers; this will have the advantage of making them more profitable to us. They shall walk upright on two legs, and if they continue insolent and will not be quiet, I will split them again and they shall hop about on a single leg."

He spoke and cut men in two, like a sorb-apple which is halved for pickling, or as you might divide an egg with a hair; and as he cut them one after another, he bade Apollo give the face and the half of the neck a turn in order that the man might contemplate the section of himself: he would thus learn a lesson of humility. Apollo was also bidden to heal their wounds and compose their forms. So he gave a turn to the face and pulled the skin from the sides all over that which in our language is called the belly, like the purses which draw in, and he made one mouth at the center, which he fastened in a knot (the same which is called the navel); he also moulded the breast and took out most of the wrinkles, much as a shoemaker might smooth leather upon a last; he left a few, however, in the region of the belly and navel, as a memorial of the primeval state. After the division the two parts of man, each desiring his other half, came together, and throwing their arms about one another, entwined in mutual embraces, longing to grow into one, they were on the point of dying from hunger and self-neglect, because they did not like to do anything apart; and when one of the halves died and the other survived, the survivor sought another mate, man or woman as we call them,—being the sections of entire men or women,—and clung to that. They were being destroyed, when Zeus in pity of them invented a new plan: he turned the parts of generation round to the front, for this had

---

1 Brother giants who challenged the gods by piling Mounts Ossa and Pelion onto Olympus to get to heaven.

not been always their position, and they sowed the seed no longer as hitherto like grasshoppers in the ground, but in one another; and after the transposition the male generated in the female in order that by the mutual embraces of man and woman they might breed, and the race might continue; or if man came to man they might be satisfied, and rest, and go their ways to the business of life: so ancient is the desire of one another which is implanted in us, reuniting our original nature, making one of two, and healing the state of man.

Each of us when separated, having one side only, like a flat fish, is but the indenture of a man, and he is always looking for his other half. Men who are a section of that double nature which was once called Androgynous are lovers of women; adulterers are generally of this breed, and also adulterous women who lust after men: the women who are a section of the woman do not care for men, but have female attachments; the female companions are of this sort. But they who are a section of the male follow the male, and while they are young, being slices of the original man, they hang about men and embrace them, and they are themselves the best of boys and youths, because they have the most manly nature. Some indeed assert that they are shameless, but this is not true; for they do not act thus from any want of shame, but because they are valiant and manly, and have a manly countenance, and they embrace that which is like them. And these when they grow up become our statesmen, and these only, which is a great proof of the truth of what I am saving. When they reach manhood they are lovers of youth, and are not naturally inclined to marry or beget children,—if at all, they do so only in obedience to the law; but they are satisfied if they may be allowed to live with one another unwedded; and such a nature is prone to love and ready to return love, always embracing that which is akin to him. And when one of them meets with his other half, the actual half of himself, whether he be a lover of youth or a lover of another sort, the pair are lost in an amazement of love and friendship and intimacy, and one will not be out of the other's sight, as I may say, even for a moment: these are the people who pass their whole lives together; yet they could not explain what they desire of one another.

For the intense yearning which each of them has towards the other does not appear to be the desire of lover's intercourse, but of something else which the soul of either evidently desires and cannot tell, and of which she has only a dark and doubtful presentiment. Suppose

Hephaestus,[1] with his instruments, to come to the pair who are lying side by side and to say to them, "What do you people want of one another?" they would be unable to explain. And suppose further, that when he saw their perplexity he said: "Do you desire to be wholly one; always day and night to be in one another's company? for if this is what you desire, I am ready to melt you into one and let you grow together, so that being two you shall become one, and while you live live a common life as if you were a single man, and after your death in the world below still be one departed soul instead of two—I ask whether this is what you lovingly desire, and whether you are satisfied to attain this?"—there is not a man of them who when he heard the proposal would deny or would not acknowledge that this meeting and melting into one another, this becoming one instead of two, was the very expression of his ancient need. And the reason is that human nature was originally one and we were a whole, and the desire and pursuit of the whole is called love.

2. FROM JOHN LYLY, *GALATEA* (1592)

[Galatea and Phillida are young women disguised as young men by their fathers so they can avoid being sacrificed as virgins by Neptune. They meet in 3.2, flirtatiously admiring each other's "womanly" manliness or manly "womanliness." The complete text is available at <http://internetshakespeare.uvic.ca/Library/Texts/Gal/>.]

[*Enter*] *Phillida and Galatea* [*both disguised as young men*].
PHILLIDA. It is pity that Nature framed you not a woman, having a
  face so fair, so lovely a countenance, so modest a behavior.
GALATEA. There is a tree in Tylos[2] whose nuts have shells like fire,
  and, being cracked, the kernel is but water.
PHILLIDA.What a toy is it to tell me of that tree, being nothing to
  the purpose? I say it is pity you are not a woman.
GALATEA. I would not wish to be a woman unless it were because
  thou art a man.
PHILLIDA. Nay, I do not wish to be a woman, for then I should not
  love thee, for I have sworn never to love a woman.

---

1 The god of fire and, in tradition, a blacksmith. He uses fire to craft metal objects.
2 An island in the Persian Gulf.

GALATEA. A strange humor in so pretty a youth, and according to mine, for myself will never love a woman.

PHILLIDA. It were a shame, if a maiden should be a suitor (a thing hated in that sex), that thou shouldst deny to be her servant.

GALATEA. If it be a shame in me, it can be no commendation in you, for yourself is of that mind.

PHILLIDA. Suppose I were a virgin (I blush in supposing myself one), and that under the habit of a boy were the person of a maid: if I should utter my affection with sighs, manifest my sweet love by my salt tears, and prove my loyalty unspotted and my griefs intolerable, would not then that fair face pity this true heart?

GALATEA. Admit that I were as you would have me suppose that you are, and that I should with entreaties, prayers, oaths, bribes, and whatever can be invented in love desire your favor, would you not yield?

PHILLIDA. Tush, you come in with "admit."

GALATEA. And you with "suppose."

PHILLIDA. [*Aside*] What doubtful speeches be these! I fear me he is as I am, a maiden.

GALATEA. [*Aside*] What dread riseth in my mind! I fear the boy to be as I am, a maiden.

PHILLIDA. [*Aside*] Tush, it cannot be. His voice shows the contrary.

GALATEA. [*Aside*] Yet I do not think it, for he would then have blushed.

PHILLIDA. Have you ever a sister?

GALATEA. If I had but one, my brother must needs have two. But I pray, have you ever a one?

PHILLIDA. My father had but one daughter, and therefore I could have no sister.

GALATEA. [*Aside*] Ay me! He is as I am, for his speeches be as mine are.

PHILLIDA. [*Aside*] What shall I do? Either he is subtle or my sex simple.

GALATEA. [*Aside*] I have known divers of Diana's nymphs[1] enamored of him, yet hath he rejected all, either as too proud to disdain, or too childish not to understand, or for that he knoweth himself to be a virgin.

---

1 Female companions of the goddess Diana.

PHILLIDA. I am in a quandary. Diana's nymphs have followed him, and he despised them, either knowing too well the beauty of his own face or that himself is of the same mold. I will once again try him. [*To Galatea*] You promised me in the woods that you would love me before all Diana's nymphs.

GALATEA. Ay, so you would love me before all Diana's nymphs.

PHILLIDA. Can you prefer a fond boy as I am before so fair ladies as they are?

GALATEA. Why should not I as well as you?

PHILLIDA. Come, let us into the grove, and make much one of another, that cannot tell what to think one of another.

Exeunt.

3. WILLIAM SHAKESPEARE, SONNET 20 (1609)

A woman's face with Nature's own hand painted
Hast thou, the master mistress of my passion;
A woman's gentle heart, but not acquainted
With shifting change, as is false women's fashion;
An eye more bright than theirs, less false in rolling,
Gilding the object whereupon it gazeth;
A man in hue, all hues in his controlling,
Which steals men's eyes and women's souls amazeth;
And for a woman wert thou first created,
Till Nature, as she wrought thee, fell a-doting,
And by addition me of thee defeated,
By adding one thing to my purpose nothing.
    But since she pricked thee out for women's pleasure,
    Mine be thy love, and thy love's use their treasure.

4. FROM STEPHEN GOSSON, *PLAYS CONFUTED IN FIVE ACTIONS* (1582)[1]

Whatsoever he be that looketh narrowly into our stage plays, or considereth how, and which way they are represented, shall find more filthiness in them, than players dream of. The law of God very straightly forbids men to put on women's garments. Garments are set down for

---

1 Text from EEBO.

signs distinctive between sex and sex. To take unto us those garments that are manifest signs of another sex is to falsify, forge, and adulterate, contrary to the express rule of the word of God, which forbiddeth it by threatening a curse unto the same.

...

The proof is evident, the consequent is necessary, that in stage plays for a boy to put on the attire, the gesture, the passions of a woman; for a mean person to take upon him the title of a prince with counterfeit port and train, is by outward signs to show themselves otherwise than they are, and so within the compass of a lie, which by Aristotle's judgment is naught of itself and to be fled.

5. FROM *HIC MULIER: OR, THE MAN-WOMAN* (1620)[1]

Since the days of Adam women were never so masculine; masculine in their genders and whole generations, from the mother, to the youngest daughter. Masculine in number, from one to multitudes; masculine in case,[2] even from the head to the foot; masculine in mood from bold speech, to impudent action; and masculine in tense:[3] for (without redress) they were, are, and will be still most masculine, most mankind, and most monstrous. Are all women then turned masculine? No, God forbid; there are a world full of holy thoughts, modest carriage, and severe chastity. To these let me fall on my knees, and say, "You, O you women; you good women; you that are in fullness of perfection; you that are the crowns of nature's work, the complements of men's excellencies, and the seminaries of propagation; you that maintain the world, support mankind and give life to societies; you, that armed with the infinite power of virtue, are castles impregnable, infinite treasures, and invincible armies; that are helpers most trusty, sentinels most careful, signs deceitless, plain way failless, true guides dangerless, balms that instantly cure, and honors that never perish. O do not look to find your names in this declamation, but with all honor and reverence do I speak to you. You are Seneca's[4] graces, women, good

---

1   Text from EEBO.

2   Clothing.

3   A joke from Latin and Greek grammar, where students learn the tense of verbs. Women are speaking and behaving as if they were men.

4   Roman playwright and philosopher (c. 4 BCE-65 CE). In his *Moral Essays*, he discusses the three Graces, daughters of Zeus, who personify charm, grace, and beauty.

women, modest women, true women, ever young, because ever virtuous, ever chaste, ever glorious. When I write of you, I will write with a golden pen, on leaves of golden paper; now I write with a rough quill, and black ink, on iron sheets, the iron deeds of an iron generation."

Come then, you masculine-women, for you are my subject, you that have made admiration an ass, and fooled him with a deformity never before dreamed of, that have made yourselves stranger things then ever Noah's Ark unloaded, or Nile engendered,[1] whom to name, He that named all things[2] might study an age to give you a right attribute, whose like are not found in any antiquary's study, in any seaman's travel, nor in any painter's cunning; you that are stranger than strangeness itself, whom wise men wonder at, boys shout at, and goblins themselves start at. You that are the gilt dirt which embroiders playhouses, the painted statues which adorn caroches, and the perfumed carrion that bad men feed on in brothels: 'tis of you I entreat, and of your monstrous deformity. You that have made your bodies like antic boscage[3] or grotesque-work, not half man/half woman, half fish/half flesh, half beast/half monster, but all odious, all Devil; that have cast off the ornaments of your sexes to put on the garments of Shame; that have laid by the bashfulness of your natures to gather the impudence of harlots, that have buried silence to revive slander; that are all things but that which you should be, and nothing less than friends to virtue and goodness; that have made the foundation of your highest detested work from the lowest despised creatures that Record can give testimony of: the one cut from the commonwealth at the gallows; the other is well known. From the first you got the false armory of yellow starch (for to wear yellow on white or white upon yellow is by the rules of Heraldry baseness, bastardy, and indignity), the folly of imitation, the deceitfulness of flattery, and the grossest baseness of all baseness, to do whatever a greater power will command you. From the other you have taken the monstrousness of your deformity in apparel, exchanging the modest attire of the comely hood, cowl, coif, handsome dress or kerchief, to the cloudy ruffianly broad-brimmed hat and wanton feather; the modest upper parts of a concealing straight gown, to the loose, lascivious civil embracement of a French doublet being all unbuttoned to entice, all of one shape to hide deformity, and extreme short-waisted to give

---

1 The Nile was famous for its fertility.
2 Adam names all the beasts in creation, Genesis 2:20.
3 Wild-looking shrubs and trees.

a most easy way to every luxurious action; the glory of a fair large hair, to the shame of most ruffianly short locks; the side, thick gathered, and close guarding safeguards[1] to the short, weak, thin, loose, and every hand-entertaining short bases;[2] for needles, swords; for prayerbooks, bawdy legs; for modest gestures, giantlike behaviors; and for women's modesty, all mimic and apish incivility. These are your founders, from these you took your copies, and, without amendment, with these you shall come to perdition.

...

Such as are able to buy all at their own charges, they swim in the excess of these vanities and will be manlike not only from the head to the waist, but to the very foot and in every condition: man in body by attire, man in behavior by rude complement, man in nature by aptness to anger, man in action by pursuing revenge, man in wearing weapons, man in using weapons, and, in brief, so much man in all things that they are neither men, nor women, but just good for nothing.

...

Nay, look if this very last edition of disguise, this which is so full of faults, corruptions and false quotations, this bait which the Devil hath laid to catch the souls of wanton women, be not as frequent in the demi-palaces of burghers and citizens as it is either at masque, triumph, tiltyard, or playhouse. Call but to account the tailors that are contained within the circumference of the walls of the City and let but their hells and their hard reckonings be justly summed together, and it will be found they have raised more new foundations of this new disguise and metamorphosed more modest old garments to this new manner of short base and French doublet (only for the use of freemans' wives and their children) in one month than hath been worn in court, suburbs, or country since the unfortunate beginning of the first devilish invention.

Let therefore the powerful Statute of Apparel but lift up his battle-axe and crush the offenders in pieces, so as everyone may be known

---

1   Outer skirt or petticoat worn by a woman to protect her skirt, especially when riding.
2   Knee-length open skirts, more lascivious than the safeguard.

by the true badge of their blood or fortune. And then these chimeras[1] of deformity will be sent back to hell and there burn to cinders in the flames of their own malice.

...

And therefore, to knit up this imperfect declamation, let every female-masculine that by her ill example is guilty of lust or imitation cast off her deformities and clothe herself in the rich garments which the poet bestows upon her....

---

1 Fire-breathing female monsters in Greek myth, part lion, part goat, and part snake. The writer asserts that these women, dressed deceptively as men, will be sent to hell.

APPENDIX E: MANNERS AND CODES

[In the Renaissance, conduct books showing how men, women and servants should behave were as popular as modern self-help books. You could learn how to act and speak as a servant or as a lover, as Castiglione shows in his famous *Book of the Courtier*, which was read throughout Europe. Schalkwyk shows how love and service are inextricable in Shakespeare's comedies.

The comic sub-plot of *Twelfth Night* depicts disorder in the household of the Lady Olivia, which, like great Elizabethan households, is normally run with military precision and prescribed duties for all members of the household at set seasons of the year. As the Steward of the household, Malvolio would be expected to manage the duties that Rose describes in his *Perfect School of Instructions*. Disorder in the house indicates a wider chaos, which we see when Sir Toby, Malvolio's antagonist, attacks Puritanism and promotes Misrule (see Appendices F and G).

Shakespeare's comedies show marriage as the ultimate form of order in society, and *Twelfth Night* concludes with three: Orsino and Viola, Olivia and Sebastian, and Sir Toby and Maria. Swinburne's *Treatise of Spousals* emphasizes how simple and how binding it was to verbally pledge your love: "I swear that henceforth I hold thee for my wife." The Priest confirms that this kind of "contract of eternal bond of love" (5.1.150, TLN 2318]) was formed offstage by Olivia with Sebastian, complete with handfast (the clasping of hands to show a marriage contract has been formed), kiss, and exchange of rings. This is proof that they are already married, and enough also for Orsino to assume that Viola, as Cesario, has breached his loyalty to his master as a loving servant.]

1. FROM BALDASSARE CASTIGLIONE, *THE BOOK OF THE COURTIER*, TRANS. SIR THOMAS HOBY (1561)

I will have our Courtier therefore (beside that he hath and doth daily give men to understand that he is of the prowess which we have said ought to be in him) to turn all his thoughts and force of mind to love, and, as it were, to reverence the prince he served above all other things, and in his will, manners, and fashions to be altogether pliable to please him. (Bk 2, 106)

The very same I say of the exercises of the body. But principally in her fashions, manners, words, gestures, and conversation, methinks, that woman ought to be much unlike the man. For right as it is seemly for him to show a certain manliness full and steady, so doth it well in a woman to have a tenderness, soft and mild, with a kind of womanly sweetness in every gesture of hers, that in going, standing, and speaking whatever she listeth, may always make her appear a woman without any likeness of man. (Bk 3, 189)

The Lady Emilia answered: "he that taketh in hand to love, must also please and apply himself full and wholly to the appetites of the wight[1] beloved, and according to them, frame his own; and make his own desires, servants; and his very soul, like an obedient handmaiden; nor at any time to think upon other, but to change his, if it were possible, into the beloved wight's, and reckon this his chief joy and happiness, for so do they that love truly." (Bk 3, 245)

For those lively spirits that issue out at the eyes, because they are engendered nigh the heart, entering in like case into the eyes they are levelled at, like a shaft to the prick,[2] naturally pierce to the heart, as to their resting place and there are at rest with those other spirits; and with the most subtle and fine nature of blood which they carry with them, infect the blood about the heart, where they are come to, and warm it; and make it like unto themselves, and apt to receive the imprinting of the image which they have carried away with them. Wherefore by little and little, coming and going the way through the eyes to the heart, and bringing back with them the thunder and striking iron of beauty and grace, these messengers kindle with the puffing of desire the fire that so burneth, and never ceaseth consuming, for always they bring some matter of hope to nourish it. (Bk 3, 247)

---

1   Person.
2   Like an arrow to the bullseye; a metaphor from archery with a clearly sexual connotation as well.

2. FROM GILES ROSE,
A PERFECT SCHOOL OF INSTRUCTIONS ... (1682)[1]

Le Maître de Hôtel, or, Steward of a Family.
With a brief instruction of what concerns his charge, his business,
and power in the family; being all very amply explained in this place.

In all great men's houses, and more especially amongst persons of
quality, the very name and charge of a steward is none of the least
in a family, no more than his charge is inconsiderable; for the very
name imports the signification of the thing itself. Without making
you a long preamble to give you a definition or distinction of all the
particulars that properly belong to his place and office, which would
be too tedious to make all the divisions thereof here in this place,
and to set them down in order, I shall only say, in short, that as all
crowned heads, as well as other persons of high and eminent qualities,
are not all equals, but differ the one from the other in many degrees
and circumstances, so likewise all stewards are not equals in function
and power. I speak here in the general, according to the succession.
Therefore everyone is to choose, according to his judgment, as he shall
see it necessary and convenient.

Therefore if anyone hath such a place in a house of quality, it will not
be necessary for me here in this place to give him instructions how, or
to whom, he should address himself, whether to his lord, or lady, or
to their attendants; but I suppose him to have given them both a full
satisfaction of all that belongs to his charge and office; so that I now
judge him to be seated and established in his employ and calling. And
being fully informed of all that belongs to his charge, I judge it but
convenient and necessary, in the first place, that he make a general visit
into all offices very exactly, and into the kitchen in particular, taking an
exact inventory in every office; as namely: of all plate, by weight and
number of pieces; as of all the linen, and other things that are moveable
about the house; and so likewise in the kitchen, he must take notice,
and see what is wanting, and what there is belonging to the mouth, as
well as other things that he shall find necessary. And then, having given
his necessary orders to the master of each office, as well as to the master
cook, he should go himself to the market and buy in all the provisions

---

1   Text from EEBO.

that he shall judge necessary for service. And being returned from the market, he goes to the master of each office, and to the kitchen, there giving such necessary orders for all things as he himself hath received for all that must be for that meal, and whether they should hasten or stay. The hour of meals being come, and all things are now in a readiness, *le Maître Hôtel* takes a clean napkin, folded at length, but narrow, and throws it over his shoulder, remembering that this is the ordinary mark, and a particular sign and demonstration, of his office. And to let men see how credible his charge is, he must not be shame-faced, nor so much as blush—no, not before any noble personage—because his place is rather an honor than a service, for he may do his office with his sword by his side, his cloak upon his shoulders, and his hat on his head; but his napkin must be always upon his shoulder, just in the posture I told you of before.

First course being dished up and ready, he must cause it to be carried to the table in very good order by those that are designed for that employment, himself going before it all the way. And being come into the hall, where the company are to eat, he pulls off his hat, but immediately puts it on again upon this head, and so proceeds to covering the table with dishes and plates, beginning at the upper end and continuing till he comes at the lower end....

The company disposing themselves to wash their hands, he takes the towel by both ends and delivers it to the company neatly, with care and respect, and not rudely. And when the ceremony is ended, and all have wiped their hands, then he takes the towel away again, and carries it to the side-cupboard and there leaves it.

The company being seated, he stays in the hall, either behind his master's chair, or some one of the chiefest persons at the table, till it be time to fetch in the second course; for which occasion, let him be sure to take with him people enough to bring all away in good order at once, both dishes and plates, and himself marching along before it as he did at the first. And be sure to observe the same order in placing of the second course as was observed in the first; and more in particular, be sure to have always an eye to the master and lady, still waiting the sign for setting on and taking away, as they shall give him command till the last, that the banquet and all are taken away with the cover. Then he gives order for the covering of the other tables as he shall think fitting and convenient, for all their whole family in order to their degrees and qualities.

And it is farther to be taken notice of, that all the time of meals he hath the sole power in himself of commanding all the officers of the house, except the gentlemen and the gentlewomen, the chamberlain, or *valet de chambre*, and chambermaids, over whom he hath neither power nor command, but only to give them that which is necessary for them, both of meat, drink, and the like. I said here during meals, that is, if there be not a gentleman, or master of the horse, which usually commands those that wear the livery, in whom that power alone depends, as having the whole charge of them in himself to command them.

Neither doth this charge depend upon a steward only, for buying in and providing all services of meats and other necessaries, day by day or from meal to meal, but for the providing of all things at their due season, and at the times when they may best be had, which ought to be one of his first maxims, or one of the first maxims of his economy; so that the steward is as chief minister, of sur-intendant for all expenses whatsoever. Wherefore I advise him to think of this only thing very carefully, as being the chief of his charge. As for example: in summer to provide himself with wood; charcoals; all sorts of sweet-meats, both wet and dry;[1] as likewise for the pastry, all sorts of fruits to serve in the winter; all sorts of refreshing syrups and pickles; as namely, cucumbers, purslane, samphire,[2] champignons, morels,[3] dry mushrooms, vinegar of all sorts of flowers and tastes, to be kept in store for all the winter, etc.

In autumn buy in wines, more wood and charcoals if need require, and that you are not sufficiently provided with them in the summer; so likewise buy in lard, bacon, and candles, with other things that may be wanting, and are fit to be provided in that season.

And in winter store your ice-houses with ice and snow for the ensuing summer, and provide rosa solis, populin, and angelica,[4] etc.

In the spring make your provision for the approaching campaign, fitting all things to go into the army: as lard, bacon, gammons, both *Mayenne* and *Bayonne*,[5] sausages of *Bologna*, dried tongues, buttocks of beef, fatted and dried after the bones are taken out, cheeses of all sorts, and such like things as these; besides olives, capers, anchovies, pepper

---

1 Sugared fruits and nuts.
2 Both small plants used in salads.
3 Edible, non-toxic wild mushrooms and funguses.
4 Respectively, cordial from the sundew plant; crystal from the bark and leaves of the aspen; bright green crystallized stalks of the angelica plant.
5 Hams from Mayenne and Bayonne.

white and black, and long ginger, cloves, mace, nutmegs, cinnamon, green citron, gum-dragon, musk, amber,[1] sugar, almonds, pistachios; wax-lights, sizes, candles, flambeaus of wax, and the like; not forgetting to fill his cellars with bottles well stored with Spanish and Burgundy wines, with other good delicious liquors such as are above said, when he speaks of the provisions that are to be made in the winter, as namely: blanquette,[2] rosa solis, populin, and angelica; besides rose-vinegar, and pure sweet oil for salads, and the like. All which provisions, being made for the approaching campaign, must be as carefully put up into a chest, and well packed for carriage either by wagon or cart, or else for the more speed to be carried by mules, all which must be done by the care and industry of the *Maître de Hôtel*.

And then his next care must be likewise for good packing and carriage of his plate, table-linen, with all other utensils necessary for the kitchen, as well as for all other offices, which plate and linen must be carefully locked up. And now the necessaries for the kitchen are these: first, a copper oven, three skillets, an iron furnace, a preserving pan, a fish-pan, a stone mortar with a pestle, a nest of six pots one in another, saucepans twelve, small gimmal racks with broaches,[3] small and great larding pins, ladles, skimmers, colanders, a chopping knife, a mincing knife, and many such like things not here inserted. And the butler is likewise to provide bottles, glasses, and knives, and all other necessaries belonging to his office.

And now by the by, it will not be amiss to insert another part of very necessary care; that is to say, in case of necessity, if the carriages cannot come in, by reason of bad ways or over-long journeys, that the master of every office, and master cook, do every one of them take something in a budget[4] made of leather for that purpose, and carry in along behind them for their present uses; as namely plates, spoons, forks, knives, and linen, and some small plates for fruit; all of which are necessary for covering of a table, etc.

And the master cook likewise, with his assistants, may in the like manner put in budgets behind each of them as much plate as will serve

---

1 Respectively, a green-yellow fruit; gum; perfume; resin or oil.
2 A white pear.
3 Storage racks for skewers.
4 Pouch or bag.

for their potages[1] and first service, their servants each laying some things upon their horses. And so they may in case of necessity have goods enough, and provisions too, for a whole meal; which may be done with a great deal of ease if all parties are but willing.

And now by this time we judge them ready to march, and the hour of their departure being come, the master cook and the chief of every office are now mounting on horseback. The master cook is desired not to forget his larding-pricks,[2] nor the master butler his *essuie*.[3] They go away before the rest, either to the dining place or to the lodging. And being come to the inn, they are to take up whatsoever is necessary for the table of their master and the rest of his train, upon as good account and honest conditions as they can agree, disposing of all things according to the orders they have received. The meal being ended, and their plate secured, everyone is to give in his account to the Master *de Hôtel*, who is to satisfy all according to equity and justice. They again continue their journey quietly and merrily; for if the master be well served, and his officers contented, and neither he on the one side nor they on the other suffer loss nor damage, then without all doubt all will go well, and they may return in safety, and, as they say, bring the mould to their doublets again if god be so pleased,[4] and that they may by his goodness have the grace to be thankful, then all will be well, etc.

So much for *le Maître de Hôtel*.

3. FROM HENRY SWINBURNE, *A TREATISE OF SPOUSALS, OR MATRIMONIAL CONTRACTS* (1686)[5]

Of Spousals, some are contracted by *Words*, and some by *Signs* ... as the giving and receiving a Ring ... in corroboration of Matrimony. (10)

By what Form of words Spousals De Praesenti *are contracted.*

... Sixthly, albeit both the parties contracting do not use the very same words, but other words, yet of the same importance, including present

---

1   Thick soups.
2   Pointed wooden utensils, for piercing meat and inserting bacon while roasting.
3   Napkins.
4   Possibly proverbial, but the meaning is obscure.
5   Text from EEBO.

consent. As if one of them say: "I take thee to my Wife," or "I swear that henceforth I hold thee for my wife," and the other answer: "I am content," or "I will have thee for my Husband," here is indissoluble matrimony contracted, as well as if this party had repeated the same words first uttered by that party.

Seventhly, albeit the one party use no words at all, but signify his or her present consent by *signs* only; as if the one party say: "I take thee to my wife, desiring of thou likewise dost accept me to thy husband, to receive this ring"; she, receiving the ring, it is in effect as if she had answered: "I do accept thee for my husband."

Eighthly, albeit neither the one party, nor the other, do utter the words of the contract, but some third person pronouncing the words; as if he say to the man: "dost thou take this woman to thy wife," and he answer: "yea, or I do" or what else; and likewise to the woman: "dost thou take this man to thy husband?," and she answer: "yea," or "I do so" or "what else?," it is of the same efficacy, as if the priests themselves had with their own mouths pronounced all the words of the contract, and said respectively: "I take thee to my wife" and "I take thee to my husband, etc."

Ninthly, albeit the words of the contract, neither of their own natural signification, neither yet by common use and acceptation conclude matrimony.... Yet whereas the parties do thereby intend to contract matrimony, they are inseparable man and wife ... not only before God, but also before man....

Tenthly, albeit there be no witnesses of the contract, yet the parties having verily (though secretly) contracted matrimony, they are very man and wife before God ... neither can either of them with safe conscience marry elsewhere, so long as the other party liveth ... for proof is not of the essence of matrimony ... and if it were, yet their consciences shall be as a thousand witnesses before the tribunal of the immortal God ... though it be otherwise in the judgment of mortal man. (86-87)

APPENDIX F: FOOLS, FESTIVITY, AND MISRULE

[Renaissance courts often had an "all-licensed fool" (*King Lear* 1.4.198, TLN 712), whose task was to amuse by speaking and singing witty truths to his King or Queen. The Clown in *Twelfth Night* and the Fool in *King Lear* are excellent stage examples. Both parts were first played by Robert Armin, one of a series of fools used by Shakespeare's theater companies, for whom roles requiring clowning, making jokes (like a stand-up comedian), and singing where needed (see A Note on the Music and Songs, p. 69, and Wiles). Armin was also a writer and a playwright, using publication to promote himself and his style of fooling (Van Es). Many archives record people actually engaged in forms of carnival-sanctioned misbehavior known as misrule. Below are good examples from the Court (F5 and F8), the Middle Temple (F10), from Oxford (F6) and from Shropshire (F7).

Ritual festivities and licensed periods of misbehavior were an intrinsic part of Renaissance culture, and play a central part in *Twelfth Night*, which is named after the Feast of Epiphany, 6 January (see Introduction, pp. 11–12). For that holiday, a Lord of Misrule (sometimes already in residence) would be appointed to license a set period of drunkenness, hilarity, and bawdiness. Barber shows how crucial these rituals (at Christmas, May Day, and Midsummer) are for understanding Shakespeare's comedies.]

1. FROM ROBERT ARMIN, *FOOL UPON FOOL* (1600)[1]

[In *Fool upon Fool* and *Quips upon Questions*, published just before Shakespeare was composing *Twelfth Night*, Armin describes the kinds of comic routines audiences could expect of him, self-consciously reflecting the role of fool, thinking back to Will Somer, the court fool from the reign of Henry VIII (whom the texts here also call Somers and Summers). This catechism (a religious form of question and answer) between the King (Harry) and Will is very similar to the catechism the Clown puts Olivia through in 1.5.]

---

1   Text from EEBO.

Take heed then and let us lay our heads together, not to be faulty in our labor—I in writing, you in working—lest our title be laid to our charge. But all's one; many nowadays play the fools and want no wit, and therefore 'tis no wonder for me to set down fools natural, when wise men, before they'll be unprofitable, will seem fools artificial. Is it then a profit to be foolish? Yea, so some say, for under show of simplicity some gain love, while the wise with all they can do, can scarce obtain love.

...

A Lean Fool. The true description of lean Leanard of merry Sherwood, who is now living well known of many.

Far differing from the other two I grant,
They fat with flesh, he lean as plagued with want:
Yet given more unto swearing than they two,
As hear and mark what he did do.

Lean like to envy, reasonable tall,
Not gross of body but indifferent small;
In his long coat of frieze,[1] both hot and cold
Would he be ever, of him many told.

A little head, high forehead, one squint eye,
And as he goes he holds his neck awry,
One hand stands crooked and the other right,
Big arms, small waist, his body light.

His knees swelled big, his legs are great,
His foot is long, good stomach to his meat,
Behind well made, in brief all parts
Fitly applied are unto his deserts.

He stoops a little, and he bends his neck,
Ready and willing he is at one's beck,
Drink he will ever, and endure much pain,

---

1   Coarse wool.

Being made of purpose long and lean.

His wheelbarrow, or else he hath no bed,
His broom he makes his pillow for his head,
Thus he sleeps, no glutton at his cheer,
And how he lives and labors you shall hear.

Few takes delight in him or joys,
He is so fraught with envy, not with toys;
Work he will or anything he'll do,
But spoil more in one day, than mend in two.

...

How this merry fool Will Sommers, to make the King merry,
asked him three questions.

Howsoever these three things came in memory, and are for mirth inserted into stage plays, I know not, but that Will Sommers asked them of the king, it is certain there are some will affirm it now living in Greenwich.[1] The King upon a time being extreme melancholy and full of passion, all that Will Sommers could do would not make him merry. "Ah," says he, "this cloud must have a good shower to cleanse it," and with that goes behind the arras. "Harry," says he, "I'll go behind the arras and study these three questions, and come again. See therefore you lay aside this melancholy muse, and study to answer me." "Ay," quoth the King, "they will be wise ones no doubt." At the last out comes William with his wit, as the fool of the play doth with an antic look to please the beholders. "Harry," says he, "what is that the lesser it is the more it is to be feared?" The King mused at it, but to grace the jest the better (for he was in that humor to grace good Will, the excellent Prince of the earth) the king made answer he knew not. Will made answer it was a little little bridge over a deep river; at which he smiled, knowing it was fearful indeed. "What is the next, William" says the King. "Marry, this is next: what is the cleanliest trade in the world." "Marry," says the King, "I think a comfit-maker,[2] for he

---

1 A short trip downstream from London, Greenwich was one of many royal palaces used frequently by Henry VIII (and, subsequently, Elizabeth I).
2 Maker of sugared almonds and fruits.

deals with nothing but pure ware, and is attired clean in white linen, when he sells it." "No, Harry," says Will, "you are wide." "What say you, then?" quoth the King. "Marry," says Will "I say a dirt dauber."[1] "Out on it," says the King, "that is the foulest, for he is dirty up to the elbows." "Ay," says Will, "but then he washes them clean again, and eats his meat cleanly enough." "I promise thee, Will," says the King, "thou hast a pretty foolish wit." "Ay, Harry," says he, "it will serve to make a wiser man than you a fool methinks." At this the King laughed, and demands the third question. "Now tell me," says Will, "if you can, what it is that being born without life, head, nose, lip or eye, and yet runs terribly roaring through the world till it dies?" "This is a wonder," quoth the King, "and no question, and I know it not." "Why," quoth Will, "it is a fart." At this the King laughed heartily, and was exceeding merry, and bids Will ask any reasonable thing and he would grant it. "Thanks, Harry," says he, "now against I want I know where to find, for yet I need nothing, but one day I shall, for every man sees his latter end, but knows not his beginning." The King understood his meaning, and so pleasantly departed for that season, and Will lays him down amongst the spaniels to sleep.

2. FROM ROBERT ARMIN, *QUIPS UPON QUESTIONS* (1600)[2]

He Plays the Fool.

True it is, he plays the fool indeed;
But in the play he plays it as he must:
Yet when the play is ended then his speed
Is better than the pleasure of thy trust:
> For he shall have what thou that time hast spent,
> Playing the fool, thy folly to content.

He plays the wise man then, and not the fool,
That wisely for his living so can do:
So doth the carpenter with his sharp tool,
Cut his own finger oft, yet lives by't too.

---

1   Someone who plasters mud on buildings—an unskilled, low-status job, often satirized.
2   Text from EEBO.

He is a fool to cut his limb say I,
But not so with his tool to live thereby.

Then 'tis his case[1] that makes him seem a fool,
It is indeed, for it is antique made:
Thus men wax wise when they do go to school,
Then for our sport we thank the tailor's trade,
     And him within the case the most of all,
     That seems wise foolish, who a fool you call.

Meet him abroad, and he is wise, methinks,
In courtesy, behavior, talk or going,
Of garment: eke[2] when he with any drinks,
Then are men wise, their money so bestowing,
     To learn by him one time a fool to seem,
     And twenty times for once, in good esteem.

Say I should meet him, and not know his name,
What should I say, "Yonder goes such a fool"?
Ay, fools will say so; but the wise will aim
At better thoughts, whom reason still doth rule.
     Yonder's the merry man, it joys me much
     To see him civil, when his part is such.

3. FROM PHILIP STUBBES, *THE ANATOMY OF ABUSES* (1583)[3]

[Philip Stubbes's account in his *Anatomie of Abuses*, since it was designed as an attack on misrule rituals, is exaggerated but gives a vivid sense of energetic merrymaking.]

First, all the wild-heads of the Parish, conventing together, choose them a grand-captain of all mischief whom they innoble with the title of my Lord of Misrule, and him they crown with great solemnity, and adopt for their king. This king, anointed, chooseth forth twenty, forty, three-score or a hundred lustyguts like to himself to wait upon his

---

1 Costume.
2 Also.
3 Text from EEBO.

lordly majesty, and to guard his noble person. Then every one of these his men he investeth with his liveries of green, yellow or some other light, wanton color. And as though that were not bawdy (gaudy enough I should say), they bedeck themselves with scarfs, ribbons, and laces hanged all over with gold rings, precious stones, and other jewels. This done, they tie about either leg 20 or 40 bells, with rich handkerchiefs in their hands, and sometimes laid across over their shoulders and neck, borrowed for the most part of their pretty Mopsies and loving Besses, for bussing[1] them in the dark. Thus all things set in order, then have they their hobbyhorses, dragons, and other antics, together with their bawdy pipers and thundering drummers to strike up the devil's dance withal. Then march these heathen company towards the church and churchyard, their pipers piping, their drummers thundering, their stumps dancing, their bells jingling, their handkerchiefs swinging about their heads like madmen, their hobbyhorses and other monsters skirmishing amongst the rout. And in this sort they go to the church, I say, and into the church (though the minister be at prayer or preaching), dancing and swinging their handkerchiefs over their head: in the church, like devils incarnate, with such a noise that no man can hear his own voice.

4. FROM THOMAS NASHE, *SUMMER'S LAST WILL AND TESTAMENT* (1600)[2]

[The playwright Thomas Nashe (1567-c. 1601) reflects also on Will Somer's legacy, using Will as the link person in an allegorical story that debates the merits of Summer and Winter, in a form that looks like a play, with scripted dialogue and inset songs. It was performed in a Hall in Croydon in 1592.]

SUMMER. Summon them one by one to answer me.
First *Ver*, the spring, unto whose custody
I have committed more then to the rest:
The choice of all my fragrant meads and flowers,
And what delights soe'enature affords.

---

1 Kissing.
2 Text from EEBO.

VERTUMNUS. I will, my Lord. *Ver*, lusty *Ver*, by the name of lusty *Ver* come into the court, lose a mark in issues.[1]

Enter Ver with his train, overlaid with suits of green moss, representing short grass, singing.

The Song.

Spring, the sweet spring, is the year's pleasant king,
Then blooms each thing, then maids dance in a ring,
Cold doth not sting, the pretty birds do sing:
Cuckoo, jug jug, pu we, to witta woo.

The palm and may make country houses gay,
Lambs frisk and play, the shepherds pipe all day,
And we hear aye, birds tune this merry lay:
Cuckoo, jug jug, pu we, to witta woo.

The fields breathe sweet, the daisies kiss our feet,
Young lovers meet, old wives a-sunning sit,
In every street, these tunes our ears do greet:
Cuckoo, jug jug, pu we, to witta woo.

Spring the sweet spring.

WILL SUMMER. By my troth, they have voices as clear as crystal.
    This is a pretty thing, if it be for nothing but to go a begging with.
SUMMER. Believe me, *Ver*, but thou art pleasant bent,
    This humor should import a harmless mind:
    Know'st thou the reason why I sent for thee?
VER. No faith, nor care not, whether I do or no.
    If you will dance a galliard,[2] so it is. If not,

Falangtado, falangtado,[3]

---

1 A fine for failure to appear in court.
2 See extended note on p. 90.
3 Refrain of a popular song.

To wear the black and yellow,[1]
Falangtado, falangtado,
My mates are gone, I'll follow.

SUMMER. Nay, stay a while. We must confer and talk.
Ver, call to mind I am thy sovereign lord,
And what thou hast, of me thou hast, and hold'st.
Unto no other end I sent for thee
But to demand a reckoning at thy hands,
How well or ill thou hast employed my wealth.
VER. If that be all, we will not disagree.
A clean trencher and a napkin you shall have presently.
WILL SUMMER. The truth is, this fellow hath been a tapster in his days.

Ver goes in, and fetcheth out the hobbyhorse and the morris dance, who dance about.
SUMMER. How now? Is this the reckoning we shall have?
WINTER. My lord, he doth abuse you: brook it not.
AUTUMN. *Summa totalis*, I fear, will prove him but a fool.
VER. About, about, lively. Put your horse to it, rein him harder, jerk him with your wand. Sit fast, sit fast, man. Fool, hold up your ladle there.
WILL SUMMER. O brave hall! O, well said, butcher. Now, for the credit of Worcestershire. The finest set of morris-dancers that is between this and Streatham. Marry, methinks there is one of them danceth like a clothier's horse, with a wool-pack on his back. You, friend with the hobbyhorse, go not too fast, for fear of wearing out my lord's tile-stones with your hobnails.
VER. So, so, so, trot the ring twice over, and away. May it please my lord, this is the grand capital sum, but there are certain parcels behind, as you shall see.
SUMMER. Nay, nay, no more; for this is all too much.
VER. Content yourself, we'll have variety.

---

1   Nashe's lines may have contributed to the comic use of Malvolio's yellow stockings.

Here enter 3 clowns and 3 maids singing this song, dancing.

> Trip and go, heave and ho,
> Up and down, to and fro,
> From the town, to the grove,
> Two and two, let us rove.

> A Maying, a playing,
> Love hath no gainsaying;
> So merrily trip and go.

WILL SUMMER. Beshrew my heart, of a number of ill legs I never
saw worse dancers. How blessed are you, that the wenches of the
parish do not see you!

SUMMER. Presumptuous *Ver*, uncivil-nurtured boy,
Think'st I will be derided thus of thee?
Is this th'account and reckoning that thou mak'st?

VER. Troth, my Lord, to tell you plain, I can give you no other
account: *nam quae habui, perdidi;*[1] what I had, I have spent on
good fellows, in these sports you have seen, which are proper
to the spring, and others of like sort, (as giving wenches green
gowns, making garlands for fencers, and tricking up children
gay) have I bestowed all my flowery treasure, and flower of my
youth....

SUMMER. O monstrous unthrift, who e'er heard the like?
The seas vast throat in so short tract of time,
Devoureth nor consumeth half so much.
How well might'st thou have lived within thy bounds?

VER. What talk you to me, of living within my bounds? I tell you,
none but asses live within their bounds....

WILL SUMMER. Thus we may see the longer we live, the more we
shall learn: I ne'er thought honesty an ass till this day.

---

1 What I had, I have lost (Latin).

5. FROM REVELS OFFICE DOCUMENTS ON THE LORD OF MISRULE (1551)[1]

[The Revels Office Accounts for 1551 show the range of props needed for the Court's extensive Christmas entertainments, with the building of a set, with pillory, gibbet, stocks and a block for beheading (for mock punishments and to satirize the execution of the Duke of Somerset). The Lord of Misrule (George Ferrers) and his accompanying fools were also provided with swords and a "Vice's dagger and a ladle," so that, just as the Clown sings in *Twelfth Night*, he could appear

> In a trice, like to the old Vice, ...
> Who with dagger of lath, in his rage and his wrath,
> Cries "Ah, ha!" to the devil ... (4.2.115–18 TLN 2161–64)]

[Paid to carpenter] John Taylor for making of a pillory—4 shillings. A pair of stocks—16 pence. For a gibbet[2]—20 pence. For a seat—5 shillings. For making of a canopy—16 pence. For the making of an heading ax—12 pence. A heading block—8 pence. And for timber boards and other parcels small and great for the same stocks, pillory, etc.—23 shillings in all, made for the Lord of Misrule ... this Christmas [1551].

[Paid to coppersmith] Jasper for one copper chain double gilded for the Lord of Misrule and another for William Somer [the royal jester] at 20 shillings the piece with the gilding of them ... at Christmas.

[Paid for properties] Nicholas Germayne for one Vice's dagger and a ladle, with a bauble pendant, by him garnished, and delivered to the Lord of Misrule's Fool: price together—3 shillings. And for 4 days work by him done in and about the furniture of one Sclavonian [Slavic] blade falchion, one Bilbao blade,[3] and other weapons for the Lord of Misrule and his Fools at 8 pence the day—2 shillings and 8 pence in December.

---

1   *Documents Relating to the Revels at Court in the Time of King Edward* VI *and Queen Mary* (*The Loseley Manuscripts*). Ed. Albert Feuillerat. Louvain: Uystpruyst, 1914; reprinted Vaduz: Kraus, 1963.
2   Gallows.
3   Sword from Bilbao in Spain, thought to be of very high quality.

6. FROM THE RECORDS OF CORPUS CHRISTI COLLEGE, OXFORD (1566)[1]

[A complaint about the College Warden (the head of the college) behaving like a real-life Sir Toby Belch, staying up late and singing drunkenly (the sound would echo round the quadrangle), both at Christmas and at Candlemas, the Feast of Purification on February 2, the day the play was performed at the Middle Temple in 1602 (see Introduction, p. 11).]

Item: he hath in progress as I have heard minstrels and women in the infamy of our College and dimunition of our goods. Item: he resorteth to bullbaitings and bearbaitings in London and commendeth his man to put it on another score. Item: in Christmas last past he coming drunk from the Town sat in the hall amongst the scholars until 1 of the clock tottering with his legs, tippling with his mouth, and hearing bawdy songs with his ears as, "my Lady hath a pretty thing," and such like; in the end drawing to bed could not be persuaded that it was yet 9 of the clock where indeed it was past 2. And in like sort at Candlemas last he was notoriously drunk.

7. FROM SHROPSHIRE PARISH DOCUMENTS (1556–1635)[2]

[These show the increasing concern of Church authorities for maintaining religious order, clamping down on "unseemly scoff, jests, ribaldry" and "any other profane usages" upon holy days.]

a) From *Articles of Enquiry of Bishop William Overton* (1584)
Whether the minister or churchwardens have suffered any lords of misrule, or summer lords or ladies, or any disguised persons, or morris dancers, or others at Christmas, or any time in summer to come unreverently piping, dancing, or playing in church or churchyard, with unseemly scoffs, jests, ribaldry, or at any other place and time, namely

---

1   *Records of Early English Drama: Oxford*. Vol 1: *The Records*. Ed. John R. Elliott Jr., Alan H. Nelson, Alexandra F. Johnston, and Diana Wyatt. Toronto and London: U of Toronto P/British Library, 2004.
2   *Records of Early English Drama: Shropshire*. Vol. 1: *The Records*. Ed. J. Alan B. Somerset. Toronto: U of Toronto P, 1994.

in time of divine service, or sermons, and what they be that commit such disorders, or accompany, or maintain them?

b) From *Articles of Enquiry of Archbishop Richard Bancroft* (1609)
Item: ... have you or your predecessors, church-wardens, there suffered since the last parson any plays, feasts, banquets, church-ales, drinkings, or any other profane usages to be kept in your church, chapels, or churchyard, or bells to be rung in superstitiously upon holy days or days abrogated by law?

c) From *Articles of Enquiry of Bishop Matthew Wren* (1635)
Have any plays, feasts, banquets, suppers, church-ales, drinkings, temporal courts or leets,[1] lay-juries, musters, exercise of dancing, stoolball,[2] foot-ball, or the like, or any other profane usage been suffered to be kept in your church, chapel, or churchyard? And is the whole consecrate ground kept free from swine, and all other nastiness?

8. FROM SIR JOHN HARINGTON, "ON THE ENTERTAINMENT FOR THE KING OF DENMARK" (1606)[3]

[At Court, the forms of aristocratic indulgence Sir Toby allows himself are evident in Sir John Harington's famous letter describing a feast honoring the King of Denmark, brother-in-law to James I of England. Such visitors would be feasted and entertained as Harington describes, with "shows, sights, and banquetings from morn to eve." A formal occasion degenerates as the inevitable result of drinking for too many hours. Harington was the godson of Elizabeth I, and a keen observer of her court and that of James I, her successor. He was a poet, a translator (of Virgil's *Aeneid* and Ariosto's epic, *Orlando Furioso*), and a satirist. His letter was first published with other private manuscripts in 1769.]

---

1 A special kind of annual or semi-annual court.

2 A country game somewhat resembling cricket (the stool was the wicket), played chiefly by young women or, as an Easter game, between young men and women (*OED*).

3 *Nugae Antiquae: being a miscellaneous collection of original papers in prose and verse written in the reigns of Henry VIII, Queen Mary, Elizabeth, and King James.* 3 vols. London: 1792.

My good Friend,

In compliance with your asking, now shall you accept my poor account of rich doings. I came here a day or two before the Danish King[1] came, and from the day he did come until this hour I have been well nigh overwhelmed with carousal and sports of all kinds. The sports began each day in such manner and such sort as well nigh persuaded me of Mahomet's paradise.[2] We had women, and indeed wine too, of such plenty as would have astonished each sober beholder. Our feasts were magnificent, and the two royal guests did most lovingly embrace each other at table. I think the Dane hath strangely wrought on our good English nobles; for those, whom I never could get to taste good liquor, now follow the fashion and wallow in beastly delights. The ladies abandon their sobriety, and are seen to roll about in intoxication. In good sooth, the parliament did kindly to provide his Majesty so seasonably with money, for there hath been no lack of good living: shows, sights, and banquetings from morn to eve.

One day a great feast was held, and after dinner the representation of Solomon his Temple and the coming of the Queen of Sheba was made, or, as I may better say, was meant to have been made, before their Majesties, by device of the Earl of Salisbury and others. But, alas! As all earthly things do fail to poor mortals in enjoyment, so did prove our presentment hereof. The lady who did play the Queen's part did carry most precious gifts to both their Majesties; but, forgetting the steps arising to the canopy, overset her caskets into his Danish Majesty's lap, and fell at his feet, though I rather think it was in his face. Much was the hurry and confusion. Cloths and napkins were at hand to make all clean. His Majesty then got up and would dance with the Queen of Sheba; but he fell down and humbled himself before her, and was carried to an inner chamber and laid on a bed of state—which was not a little defiled with the presents of the Queen which had been bestowed on his garments: such as wine, cream, jelly, beverage, cakes, spices, and other good matters. The entertainment and show went forward, and most of the presenters went backward or fell down, wine did so occupy their upper chambers. Now did appear, in rich dress, Hope, Faith, and Charity. Hope did assay to speak, but wine rendered her endeavours so feeble that she withdrew, and hoped the King would excuse her brevity:

---

1   Christian IV.
2   The Koran describes a paradise of beautiful gardens, seductive women, and delicious food and drink.

Faith was then all alone, for I am certain she was not joined with good works, and left the court in a staggering condition.

9. FROM "KING JAMES, DECLARATION TO THE BISHOP OF CHESTER, 24 MAY 1618"[1]

[King James allows both for good religious conduct, and a measure of "lawful" recreation, forestalling Puritan attempts to disrupt May games, morris dances, and the drinking of ale. Olivia describes the Clown as an "allowed fool" (1.5.77, TLN 388), which suggests a similar discreet permissiveness.]

Our express pleasure therefore is, that the laws of our kingdom, and canons of our church be as well observed in that county [Lancashire] as in all other places of this our kingdom. And on the other part, that no lawful recreation shall be barred to our good people which shall not tend to the breach of our aforesaid laws and canons of our church: which to express more particularly, our pleasure is that the bishop and all other inferior churchmen and churchwardens shall, for their parts, be careful and diligent both to instruct the ignorant, and convince and reform them that are misled in religion, presenting them that will not conform themselves, but obstinately stand out, to our judges and justices, whom we likewise command to put the law in due execution against them.

Our pleasure therefore is that the bishop of that diocese take the like straight order with all the Puritans and Precisians[2] within the same, either constraining them to conform themselves or to leave the county according to the laws of our kingdom and canons of our church, and so to strike equally on both hands, against the condemners of our authority, and adversaries of our church. And as for our good people's lawful recreation, our pleasure likewise is that, after the end of divine service, our good people be not disturbed, letted, or discouraged from any lawful recreation, such as dancing, either of men or women, archery for men, leaping, vaulting, or any other such harmless recreation, nor from having of May games, Whitsun ales, and morris dances, and the setting up of maypoles, and other sports therewith used, so as the same

---

1 From L. A. Govett, *The King's Book of Sports*. London: Elliot Stock, 1890.
2 Those who held precise views on Christian doctrine; see Appendix G2.

be had in due and convenient time, without impediment or neglect of divine service.

10. FROM SIR BENJAMIN RUDYERD, *LE PRINCE D'AMOUR: OR, THE PRINCE OF LOVE* (1660)[1]

[This description of *The Prince of Love* revels at the Middle Temple in 1597 (not published until 1660) is an excellent example of the chaos the Lord of Misrule might initiate; it also suggests the milieu of the 1602 performance (see Introduction, p. 11).]

Sunday being the first day of the new year, and the second year of the Prince's most happy reign, the hard-hearted Thames had thought to have frozen quite over; but upon better advisement it forbore, yet was it so hard that a sculler in the midst of the ice was like a rat in a glazier's shop.

Upon Monday at night there happened a comedy, and dancing, which was no wonder, and a banquet, which was not looked for.

Wednesday the Prince's excellency was invited to the Lord Mayor's, and expected; but he deferred his coming because of preparation for barriers[2] and a masque to the court.

Thursday was also spent in that business.

Upon Friday, being Twelfth-day,[3] at night there went to the Court 11 knights and 11 esquires, 9 masquers , and 9 torchbearers. Their setting forth was with a peal of ordnance,[4] a noise[5] of trumpets always sounding before them, the herald next, and after two esquires and two knights. The knights for their upper parts in bright armor, their hose of cloth of gold and silver; the esquires in jerkins laced with gold and silver, and their hose as fair; all upon great horses, all richly furnished. Then came the masquers by couples upon velvet footcloths, their short cloaks, doublets, and hose of cloth of gold and silver of nine colors representing nine several passions. To every masquer a torchbearer upon a footcloth carrying his device, besides a hundred torches born

---

1 Text from EEBO.
2 A regulated form of tournament foot-fighting across a single waist-high bar that separated combatants to reduce the risk of injury.
3 The day of Twelfth Night, 6 January.
4 Cannon fire.
5 Consort, small band.

by servants. Never any Prince in this kingdom, or the like made so glorious and so rich a show. When they came to the Court the knights broke every man a lance and two swords; the nine masquers, like passions, issued out of a heart. All was fortunately performed, and received gracious commendation.

Upon Saturday at night there was a solemn barriers by two Knights Challengers against all commoners in honor of the Prince's fair mistress. Cavaliero Saint George and Cavaliero de Bombardo[1] began a quarrel in their combat, which had not so ended but that the Prince's wise care moderated their choler and prevented further danger.

There was a masque that night, and therefore why should it not be set down?

Upon Sunday the Prince was invited to supper to a royal gentleman where he was royally welcomed with great plenty of all things; but the provision of ladies fell short.

Here Milorsius Stradilax,[2] scorning the soberness of the company, fell drunk without a rival. He made a festival oration, and in his new drunkenness repeated his old comparison of pork to the dispraise of noblewomen there present. Coming home he went to sleep upon a stall, where the bellman found him, and delivered him to the Prince's porter to be sent according to the superscription.

---

1 Knights on horseback. St. George is the Patron Saint of England. Bombardo is a satirical name, probably coined from "bombard," a great gun—both fat and noisy.
2 Another satirical invented name: My lord who is strewn (stradi) carelessly (lax) about; hence someone who lolls drunkenly.

[The terms Puritanism and Puritan are extremely complex, covering a wide range of meanings from their first use in England in the 1560s and 1570s (according to *OED*) to the present. The terms are crucial to the play's battle between Sir Toby Belch as a Lord of Misrule (see Appendix F) and Malvolio as "a kind of Puritan" (2.3.124, TLN 833). Shakespeare's depiction of Malvolio is central to Collinson's claim that playwrights were influential in constructing the popular image of the Puritan.

Reform of the Church of England was an ongoing issue in the period leading up to and after the English Civil War of the 1640s and 1650s. What should the English Church look like? How many of the practices of the Catholic Church, if any, was it safe to continue? Protestant reformers, mostly Calvinist, demanded ever more "purity" of Church rituals, unadorned churches, and abandonment of elaborate vestments for ministers (which they condemned as dangerously ornate and Catholic): hence the term Puritan. Underdown (20-22) concisely reviews the range of Puritan beliefs. Puritans were reputed to be overly insistent in their way of arguing, and militant about demanding purity of conduct for all. They were often thought censorious and hypocritical, as Malvolio is shown to be. Puritans also tended to condemn as ungodly nearly all traditional forms of pleasure, as Malvolio is denounced by Sir Toby for being against "cakes and ale" (2.3.104, TLN 811). Macaulay, the great nineteenth-century historian, brilliantly captures this idea of Puritanism, in terms specific to the theater and particularly *Twelfth Night*, when he concludes that "the Puritan hated bearbaiting, not because it gave pain to the bear, but because it gave pleasure to the spectators" (121).

Throughout the period, arguments against and for Puritan beliefs were energetically debated in print. The anonymous play *The Pilgrimage to Parnassus* (1598-1602), gives a lively picture of a "puling puritan," an "artless ass." The writer thinks of "the puritan" the way Maria, Sir Toby and the Clown think of Malvolio. Thomas Nashes's three pamphlets extend the satirical attack on Puritans: these are part of the extensive print response to the seven anti-episcopal Marprelate tracts, published anonymously in 1588 and 1589. In these tracts, the fictional Martin Marprelate pretends to be a son of Martin Luther, the German theologian whose agitation for reform in Roman Catholic practices had led to the Protestant Reformation throughout northern Europe. The term "martinist" here means someone who devotedly follows Luther's doctrines, and therefore attacks the Church of England. Nashe, one of the most energetic Elizabethan writers, probably wrote his satiric anti-Marprelate pamphlets very quickly, which partly explains why they are so rollicking and appealing. He pretends to carry on Marprelate's task, but by actually using extremes of hyperbole he is clearly evoking the kind of Puritan character Malvolio is shaped to be.]

1. FROM *THE PILGRIMAGE TO PARNASSUS* (C. 1598-1602)[1]

AMORETTO. But who comes yonder? Philomusus and Studioso!
  I saw them lately in the company
  Of strict Stupido, that puling puritan,
  A moving piece of clay, a speaking ass,
  A walking image and a senseless stone!
  If they be of his humor I care not, I,
  For such pure honest-seeming company.
PHILOM. Fie, Studioso! What now almost caught
  By Stupido, that plodding puritan,
  That artless ass, and that earth-creeping dolt,
  Who, for he cannot reach unto the arts,
  Makes show as though he would neglect the arts,
  And cared not for the spring of Helicon?[2]

2. FROM THOMAS NASHE, *THE RETURN OF THE RENOWNED CAVALIERO PASQUIL OF ENGLAND* (1589)[3]

[PASQUIL.] At the last, hearing the scholars of the English seminary merry as they returned from their vineyard, and full of fine tauntings when they talked of the sects and opinions sprung up in England, I stole out of Rome by night to make trial myself of the truth of their reports. When I came to England, for the good will I carried to my old occupation I entered at London into Sprignol's

---

1 Ed. W.D. Macray. Oxford: Oxford UP, 1886.
2 Flowing from Mt. Helicon in Greece, and thought sacred to the Muses.
3 Text from EEBO.

shop, where the first news I heard among two or three gentlemen as they were a-trimming[1] was of a Martinist,[2] a Broker, the next door by, which with a face of Religion, having gotten other men's goods into his hands, was but new run away and left his wife to the charity of the Parish. With this tidings I grew very inquisitive to know what Martin was? "A knave" quoth one; "a thief" quoth another; "he teacheth the court a religion to rob the Church." And some of the City that favor him, apt scholars to take such an easy lesson, begin to practise their cunning upon their neighbors. Having gotten this thread by the end, I never left winding till I came to the paper that made the bottom. I frequented the churches of the Pruritane preachers, that leap into the pulpit with a pitchfork to teach men before they have either learning, judgement, or wit enough to teach boys.

MAR[FORIUS]. I pray you sir, why doe you call them Pruritanes?

PAS[QUIL]. *A pruritu*[*s*].[3] They have an itch in their ears that would be clawed with new points of doctrine never dreamed of, and an itch in their fingers that would be anointed with the golden *Aenulatum*[4] of the Church. I know they are commonly called Puritans, and not amiss, that title is one of the marks they bear about them. They have a mark in the head, they are self-conceited, *They take themselves to be pure*, when they are filthy in God's sight. They have a mark in the eye, their looks are haughty. They have a mark in the mouth, a very black tooth, they are *A generation that curse their father*.

* * *

[A3ᵛ] I have ... set down all the upstart religions in this land. The Anabaptists;[5] the Family of Love;[6] the seven capital heresies for

---

1   Having their beards trimmed; evidently Sprignol was a barber.

2   A Puritan, a follower of Martin Luther; see above, p. 280.

3   From the Latin "to itch"; hence the invented word, "Pruritans," Puritans excessively bothered by the "itches" of disputes on small matters of doctrine, and perhaps, hypocritically, of lust.

4   A cure for itching: "The root of the *Enula* [elecampane] boiled ... with fresh butter and the powder of Ginger, maketh an excellent ointment against the itch" (John Gerard, *Herbal* [1597], p. 794).

5   A Puritan sect that insisted on adult rebaptism.

6   Another Puritan sect, which preached that religion consisted in the exercise of love.

which some have been executed of late years in Suffolk; the diversi-
ties of Puritans and *Martinists;* with a number more which you shall
hear of when that book is printed. A lamentable spectacle it will be
to see so many faces in one hood. But God knoweth, before whom
I stand, I desire not to cast it out as a block in the ways of men for
any to stumble at, or to stand at defiance with all religion; but as a
sea-mark to discover the quicksands of new religions.

* * *

[B3ᵛ] How whorishly scriptures are alleged by them I will discover, by
God's help, in another new work which I have in hand, and intitled
it *The May-game of Martinism*. Very deftly set out, with pomps, pag-
eants, motions, masks, scutcheons,[1] emblems, impresas,[2] strange
tricks and devices between the ape and the Owl; the like was never
yet seen in Paris-garden. *Penry* the Welshman is the foregallant[3] of
the Morris, with the treble bells, shot through the wit with a woodcocks bill. I would not, for the fairest horn-beast in all his country,
that the Church of England were a cup of Metheglin[4] and came in
his way when he is over-heated. Every bishopric would prove but a
draught when the mazer is at his nose. *Martin* himself is the Maid
Marian,[5] trimly dressed up in a cast gown, and a kercher[6] of Dame
Lawson's, his face handsomely muffled with a diaper-napkin to cover
his beard, and a great nosegay in his hand of the principalest flowers
I could gather out of all his works. *Wigginton* dances round about
him in a cotton coat, to court him with a leathern pudding and a
wooden ladle. *Paget*[7] marshalleth the way with a couple of great
clubs, one in his foot, another in his head, and he cries to the people
with a loud voice, *"Beware of the man whom God hath marked."*

---

1   Heraldic shields, escutcheons.
2   Emblems or devices with mottoes.
3   Chief performer, lead dancer.
4   Spiced mead.
5   The name often awarded to the maiden appointed queen of the festivities.
6   Kerchief, scarf.
7   Giles Wigginton and Eusebius Pagit were ministers suspected of being authors
of the Martin Marprelate tracts, and were persecuted for their nonconformity. Pagit
had injured his arm as a young man, and referred to it as lameness; enemies apparently believed it to be his leg—hence the reference to a club foot.

It is therefore thought the best way (for experience and time tries all things), and some wise men were before of that judgement, and the wise man himself doth so advise us, and *Martin* the fool himself is of the same opinion, to answer the fools according to their foolishness. For I have here at this time only played with their foolish coxcomb; purposing in my next, to decipher their knavish head also. And when they shall put off their fool's coat, and leave snapping of their wooden dagger, and betake themselves to a soberer kind of reasoning (which will be very hard for such Vices[2] to do), to accept of their glorious glove. Till then, we will return them the cuff instead of the glove[3] and hiss the fools from off the stage, as the readiest means to out-face them—though, besides that they hide their heads, they be most impudent and cannot blush. For what face soever they set on the matter, these jigs and rhymes have nipped the father in the head and killed him clean, seeing that he is overtaken in his own *foolery*. And this hath made the young youths his sons to chafe and fret above measure, especially with the players (their betters in all respects, both in wit and honesty), whom (saving their *liveries*, for indeed they are her Majesty's men, and these not so much as her good subjects) they call *Rogues* for playing their interludes, and Asses for travelling *all day for a penny*; not remembering that both they and their Father, playing the fools without any livery, are rogues indeed, by the laws of this land; and that for nothing, now two years together are the veriest Asses of all the rest.

And yet shalt thou find, good reader, in this jesting with him (but especially in the next), that the fool is bobbed withal in good earnest, and that he is proved a plain *hermaphrodite:* that is, both a foolish knave, and a knavish fool also. And the veriest fool in the world, if he be not as very a knave withal, may soon see to what [a] pass, both religion and the state would shortly come, if *Mad Martin, and his mates' marrings and his sons' shiftings*, might, by such as are of might (which the God of all might forefend), be made account of.

...

---

1 Text from EEBO.
2 For Vice characters see p. 181, note 3; and Appendix F5.
3 Accept the challenge of the glove with a blow, all a lower class opponent deserves.

After that Old *Martin*, having taken a most desperate cause in hand, as the troubling of the State, and overthrow of the Church ... and being therefore, and well worthy, sundry ways very curstly handled—as first *dry beaten*, and thereby his bones broken, then whipped (that made him wince), then wormed and lanced,[1] that he took very grievously, to be made a *May Game* upon the *stage*, and so banged, both with prose and rhyme on every side, as he knew not which way to turn himself— ... Every stage player made a jest of him, and put him clean out of countenance. Yea, his own familiars disdained to acknowledge him, and so had both friends and foes, both good and bad, even the whole realm (save a few of his faction), that cried out shame upon him.

4. FROM THOMAS NASHE, *A COUNTERCUFF GIVEN TO MARTIN JUNIOR* (1589)[2]

Valiant *Martin*, if ever the earth carried any giants, as fabulous antiquity hath avouched, which entered into wars and conspiracies against God, thy father *Marprelate* was a whelp of that race; who, to revive the memory of his ancestors almost forgotten, hath broken into heaven with his blasphemies. If the monster be dead I marvel not, for he was but an error of nature, not long lived; hatched in the heat of the sins of *England*, and sent into these peaceable seas of ours to play like a dolphin before a tempest. The heads this *Hydra*[3] lost in a famous place of late, where every new bug no sooner puts out his horns but is beaten down. The anatomy lately taken of him, the blood and the humors that were taken from him by lancing and worming him at *London* upon the common stage, the main buffets that are given him in every corner of this realm, are evident tokens that being thorough soused in so many showers, he had no other refuge but to run into a hole, and die as he lived, belching.

---

1 Purged, and cut into to drain pus.

2 *A countercuff given to Martin Junior: by the venturous, hardy, and renowned Pasquill of England, Cavaliero. Not of old Martin's making, which newly knighted the saints in heaven, with rise up Sir Peter and Sir Paul; but lately dubbed for his service at home in the defence of his country, and for the clean breaking of his staff upon Martin's face.* London: 1589. Text from EEBO.

3 Monster in Greek myth, a snake with many heads. When one head is cut off, another grows in its place.

APPENDIX H: MUSIC

[Music plays a central role in the pleasure *Twelfth Night* offers its audience (see Introduction, p. 28, and A Note on the Music and Songs, p. 69). Music held philosophical meaning in the Renaissance and was also thought to be capable of physically altering (and calming) humans whose humors were thought to be out of balance.

Marsilio Ficino was an influential Florentine philosopher, a key advocate of the ideas that underpinned the development of Renaissance thought across Europe from the late fifteenth century. Ficino's commentary on Plato's *Symposium*, composed between October 1474 and March 1475, links the eight tones of the Western music scale to the eight crystal spheres that were traditionally thought to surround the earth. When the spheres moved together they would make a celestial sound so pure, according to Cicero, that humans could hardly hear it, and if they could they would be astounded.

In his influential treatise on *The Passions of the Mind* ..., Thomas Wright describes the power of music to excite and disturb but also to calm humans and, at best, to balance the four humors[1] which Elizabethans believed controlled all bodies. In performance, the music and singing would ideally bring the "body" of anyone who heard it "into a good temper."]

1. FROM MARSILIO FICINO, *COMMENTARY ON PLATO'S SYMPOSIUM* (1474)

... musical harmony is born in that swift and orderly revolution of the heavens: eight tones from eight orbits, but out of them all a certain ninth harmony is produced. And so we name the nine sounds of the heavens, from their musical harmony, the muses. Our soul was from the beginning endowed with the principal of this music, for the heavenly harmony is rightly said to be innate in anything whose origin is heavenly. This harmony is then imitated by various instruments and songs. This gift like the rest was given us through the love of the divine providence. (181)

---

1 Of choler, phlegm, melancholy, and blood, believed at the time to influence human behavior. See Paster 2004.

2. FROM CICERO, *ON THE COMMONWEALTH AND ON THE LAWS* (C. 50 BCE)

... what is the sound which fills my ears, so great and so sweet?

This is the sound that is caused by the action and motion of the spheres themselves. Its harmony is based on uneven intervals, but the inequality of the intervals is proportional and based on reason, and by blending high notes with low itself causes balanced music.... the highest sphere of the heavens with the stars in it, which turns very rapidly, moves with a high and agitated sound, and the lowest sphere of the Moon with a very deep one—the ninth, the Earth, is unmoving and always stays in the same place, embracing the center of the universe.... The sound made by the paid revolution of the universe is so great that human ears cannot grasp it, just as you are unable to look directly into the Sun, because your sight and sense are overcome by its rays. (Bk. 6.18)

3. FROM THOMAS WRIGHT, *THE PASSIONS OF THE MIND IN GENERAL* (1604)

How Passions are moved with music and instruments

How music, songs, and sounds stir up passions, we may discover in little sucklings, who with their nurse's songs are brought to rest; the mules without bells will scarcely travel; the car-man with whistling causeth his sturdy jades to walk more merrily. The Arcadian signory[1] considering that, in regard of the situation of their country, the inhabitants for most part were barbarous, savage and wild, to mollify more their minds and to render them more mild, gentle, and humane, judged no means more effectual than to introduce music among them. For in very deed a certain kind of tickling symphony maketh men effeminate and delicate. The Spaniards play their zarabanda[2] upon the gittern,[3] which moveth them (as I hear reported) to dance, and do worse. *Pythagoras*[4] once chanced to fall into the company of drunkards,

---

1   Rulers of Arcadia, a mountainous region of Ancient Greece, by tradition the home of poets and shepherds.

2   Saraband, a decorous Spanish dance.

3   An early form of guitar.

4   Greek mathematician (c. 582-507 BCE), theorist of music and cosmic harmony.

where a musician ruled their lascivious banquet: he presently commanded him to change his harmony and sing a Dorian,[1] and so with
this manner of melody brought them to sobriety, and casting their
garlands from their heads were ashamed of all they had done. Saul
being possessed or at least much vexed with the devil, David played
upon his cithern, and he was comforted and the evil spirit departed[2]....
Or the devil ... molested him with the vehemency of some melancholy
humor, as the falling sickness[3] or some other sort of melancholy madness; and then as this perverse malignant humor causeth fears, sadness, and such like melancholy passions, so music causeth mirth, joy,
and delight, the which abate, expel, and quite destroy their contrary
affections, and withal, rectify the blood and spirits, and consequently
digest melancholy, and bring the body into a good temper. (159-60)

---

1   Form of music associated with Apollo, sober and solemn. Milton records this as
the sound made by "flutes and soft recorders" (*Paradise Lost*, Book 1, l. 551).
2   "And it came to pass, when the evil spirit from God was upon Saul, that David
took an harp, and played with his hand: so Saul was refreshed, and was well, and the
evil spirit departed from him" (1 Samuel 16:23).
3   Epilepsy. In *Julius Caesar*, Casca describes how Caesar "fell down in the market-
place, and foamed at mouth, and was speechless." Brutus replies: "He hath the falling
sickness" (1.2.252-54, TLN 357-58).

Allen, Shirley S. *Samuel Phelps and Sadler's Wells Theatre*. Middletown, CT: Wesleyan UP, 1971.

Anderson, Linda. *A Kind of Wild Justice: Revenge in Shakespeare's Comedies*. Newark: U of Delaware P, 1987.

Arlidge, Anthony. *Shakespeare and the Prince of Love: The Feast of Misrule in the Middle Temple*. London: Giles de la Mare, 2000.

Auden, W.H. *Lectures on Shakespeare*. Ed. Arthur Kirsch. London: Faber and Faber, 2000.

Barber, C.L. *Shakespeare's Festive Comedy: A Study of Dramatic Form and its Relation to Social Custom*. 1959. Cleveland and New York: Meridian, 1963.

Barnet, Sylvan. "Charles Lamb and the Tragic Malvolio." *Philological Quarterly* 33 (1954): 178–88.

Barton, Ann. "*As You Like It* and *Twelfth Night*: Shakespeare's Sense of an Ending." *Shakespearean Comedy*, Stratford upon Avon Studies 14. London: Edward Arnold, 1972. 160–81.

Bate, Jonathan. *Soul of the Age: the Life, Mind and World of William Shakespeare*. London: Viking, 2008.

———, and Eric Rasmussen, eds. *William Shakespeare: Complete Works*. London: Macmillan, 2007.

Belsey, Catherine. "Disrupting Sexual Difference: Meaning and Gender in the Comedies." *Alternative Shakespeares*. Ed. John Drakakis. New Accents. London: Methuen, 1985. 166–91.

Bentley, Gerald Eades. *The Profession of Dramatist in Shakespeare's Time, 1590–1642*. Princeton: Princeton UP, 1972.

Billington, Michael, ed. *Approaches to Twelfth Night*, by Bill Alexander, John Barton, John Caird, Terry Hands. RSC Directors' Shakespeare. London: Nick Hern Books, 1990.

Blake, Ann. "Location, Imagination and Heterotopia in *Twelfth Night*." Procházka 66–80.

Booth, Stephen. *Precious Nonsense: The Gettysburg Address, Ben Jonson's Epitaphs on His Children, and Twelfth Night*. Berkeley: U of California P, 1998.

———. "*Twelfth Night* 1.1: The Audience as Malvolio." *Shakespeare's "Rough Magic": Renaissance Essays in Honor of C.L. Barber*. Ed. Peter

Erickson and Coppélia Kahn. Newark: U of Delaware P; London and Toronto: Associated University P, 1985. 149–68.

Bradbrook, Muriel. *Shakespeare the Craftsman: the Clark Lectures 1968.* Cambridge: Cambridge UP, 1969.

Bradley, A.C. "Feste the Jester." Gollancz 164–69.

Brittin, Norman A. "The *Twelfth Night* of Shakespeare and of Professor Draper." *Shakespeare Quarterly* 7.2 (Spring 1956): 211–16.

Brown, John Russell. *Shakespeare's Plays in Performance.* London: Edward Arnold, 1966.

Bullough, Geoffrey. *Narrative and Dramatic Sources of Shakespeare Volume II: The Comedies, 1597–1603.* London: Routledge and Kegan Paul, 1958.

Callaghan, Dympna. "'And all is semblative a woman's part': Body Politics in *Twelfth Night.*" *Textual Practice* 7.3 (Winter 1993): 428–53.

Carnegie, David. "'*Maluolio within*': Performance Perspectives on the Dark House." *Shakespeare Quarterly* 52.3 (Fall 2001): 393–414.

―――. "'What country, friends, is this?': Australian and New Zealand Productions of *Twelfth Night* in the Twentieth Century." *Multicultural Shakespeare: Translation, Appropriation and Performance* 8.23 (2011): 19–38.

Castiglione, Baldassare. *The Book of the Courtier.* Trans. Sir Thomas Hoby (1561). Everyman's Library. London: Dent, 1966.

Chalk, Darryl. "'To Creep in at Mine Eyes': Theatre and Secret Contagion in *Twelfth Night.*" *Rapt in Secret Studies: Emerging Shakespeares.* Eds. Darryl Chalk and Laurie Johnson. Newcastle upon Tyne: Cambridge Scholars, 2010. 172–93.

Chambers, E.K. *William Shakespeare: A Study of Facts and Problems.* 1930. 2 vols. Oxford: Clarendon, 1951.

Charlton, H.B. *Shakespeare's Comedies: the Culmination.* Manchester: Manchester UP, 1937.

Cicero, *On the Commonwealth and on the Laws.* Ed. James E.G. Zeitel. Cambridge Texts in the History of Political Thought. Cambridge: Cambridge UP, 1999.

Clayton, Tom, Susan Brock, and Vicente Forés, eds. *Shakespeare and the Mediterranean: The Selected Proceedings of the International Shakespeare Association World Congress Valencia, 2001.* Newark: U of Delaware P, 2004.

Coddon, Karin S. "'Slander in an Allow'd Fool': *Twelfth Night*'s Crisis of the Aristocracy." *SEL: Studies in English Literature* 33 (1993): 309–25.

Collinson, Patrick. "The Theatre Constructs Puritanism." *The Theatrical City*. Eds. David L. Smith, Richard Strier, and David Bevington. Cambridge: Cambridge UP, 1995. 157–70.

Cook, Ann Jennalee. "Off the Book: Extra-Textual Effects in Trevor Nunn's *Twelfth Night*." Clayton, Brock and Forés 75–87.

Cressy, David. "Gender Trouble and Cross-Dressing in Early Modern England." *Journal of British Studies* 35.4 (October 1996): 438–65.

Cunnington, Phillis, and Catherine Lucas. *Occupational Costume in England*. London: Adam and Charles Black, 1967.

Dean, David M. *Law-Making and Society in Late Elizabethan England: The Parliament of England, 1584–1601*. Cambridge Studies in Early Modern British History. Cambridge: Cambridge UP, 2002.

Dean, Paul. "'Comfortable Doctrine': *Twelfth Night* and the Trinity." *Review of English Studies* New Series 52.208 (2001): 500–15.

Dessen, Alan C., and Leslie Thomson. *A Dictionary of Stage Directions in English Drama, 1580–1642*. Cambridge: Cambridge UP, 1999.

Dobson, Michael. "Shakespeare Performances in England, 2003." *Shakespeare Survey* 57 (2004): 258–89.

Donnelan, Declan. Dir. *Twelfth Night: Cheek by Jowl*. Programme for Sydney Festival, 2006.

Doughtie, Edward, ed. *Lyrics from English Airs 1596–1622*. Cambridge, MA: Harvard UP, 1970.

Drakakis, John. "Michael Bogdanov in Conversation." *Shakespeare Survey* 60 (2007): 196–214.

Draper, John W. *The Twelfth Night of Shakespeare's Audience*. Stanford: Stanford UP, 1950.

Duffin, Ross W. *Shakespeare's Songbook*. With a companion CD. New York: Norton, 2004.

Dutton, Richard, Alison Findlay, and Richard Wilson. *Region, Religion and Patronage: Lancastrian Shakespeare*. Manchester: Manchester UP, 2003.

Eagleton, Terry. *William Shakespeare*. Rereading Literature. Oxford: Basil Blackwell, 1986.

Edmondson, Paul. *Twelfth Night*. The Shakespeare Handbooks. Basingstoke: Palgrave Macmillan, 2005.

Elam, Keir, ed. *Twelfth Night*. The Arden Shakespeare: Third Series. London: Cengage Learning, 2008.

Empson, William. *Seven Types of Ambiguity*. 1929. London: Chatto and Windus, 1949.

Erne, Lukas. *Textual Performances: The Modern Reproduction of Shakespeare's Drama*. Ed. Lukas Erne and Margaret Jane Kidnie. Cambridge: Cambridge UP, 2004.

Evans, Bertrand. *Shakespeare's Comedies*. Oxford: Clarendon, 1960.

Ficino, Marsilio. *Marsilio Ficino's Commentary on Plato's Symposium*: The Text and a Translation, with an Introduction by Sears Reynolds Jayne, A.M. The University of Missouri Studies. Columbia: U of Missouri P, 1944.

Finkelpearl, Philip J. *John Marston of the Middle Temple: An Elizabethan Dramatist in His Social Setting*. Cambridge, MA: Harvard UP, 1969.

Fischer, Sandra K. *Econolingua: A Glossary of Coins and Economic Language in Renaissance Drama*. Newark: U of Delaware P, 1985.

Fisher, Will. "Staging the Beard: Masculinity in Early Modern English Culture." *Staged Properties in Early Modern English Drama*. Ed. Jonathan Gil Harris and Natasha Korda. Cambridge: Cambridge UP, 2002. 230–57.

Foakes, R.A. "The Owl and the Cuckoo: Voices of Maturity in Shakespeare's Comedies," in *Shakespearian Comedy*. Stratford-Upon-Avon Studies 14. London: Edward Arnold, 1972. 121–42.

Forman, Valerie. "Material Dispossessions and Counterfeit Investments: the Economies of *Twelfth Night*." *Money and the Age of Shakespeare: Essays in New Economic Criticism*. Ed. Linda Woodbridge. London: Palgrave Macmillan, 2003. 112–27.

Freeman, Penelope. "The Pronouns of Propriety and Passion: *you* and *thou* in Shakespeare's Italian Comedies." Clayton, Brock and Forés 168–79.

Furness, Horace Howard, ed. *Twelfth Night or, What You Will: A New Variorum Edition of Shakespeare*. 1901. New York: Dover, 1964.

Gay, Penny. *The Cambridge Introduction to Shakespeare's Comedies*. Cambridge: Cambridge UP, 2008.

Gollancz, Israel. "Bits of Timber: Some Observations on Shakespearian Names—'Shylock'; 'Polonius'; 'Malvolio.'" Gollancz (1916), 170–78.

————, ed. *A Book of Homage to Shakespeare*. Oxford: Humphrey Milford/Oxford UP, 1916.

Gras, Henk K. "Direct Evidence and Audience Response to *Twelfth Night*; The Case of John Manningham of the Middle Temple." *Shakespeare Studies* 21 (1993): 109–54.

Greenblatt, Stephen. *Shakespearean Negotiations*. Berkeley and Los Angeles: U of California P, 1988.

Greif, Karen. "A Star Is Born: Feste on the Modern Stage." *Shakespeare Quarterly* 39.1 (1988): 61–78.

Gurr, Andrew. *The Shakespearean Stage 1574–1642*, 3rd ed. Cambridge: Cambridge UP, 1992.

————, and Mariko Ichikawa. *Staging in Shakespeare's Theatres*. Oxford Shakespeare Topics. Oxford: Oxford UP, 2000.

Hakluyt, Richard. T*he Principal Navigations, Voyages, Traffiques, and Discoveries of the English Nation*. London, 1599.

Halliwell. James O. *The Works of William Shakespeare*. The text Formed From a new Collation of Early Editions: to which are added all the original novels and tales on which the plays are founded; copious archaeological annotations on each play, an essay on the formation of the text; and a life of the poet. The Illustrations and Wood-Engravings by Frederick William Fairholt, Esq. 16 volumes. F.S.A. London: 1853.

Hanna, Sara. "From Illyria to Ellysium: Geographical Fantasy in *Twelfth Night*." Procházka 21–46.

Harrison, G.B. *The Elizabethan Journals: Being a Record of Those Things Most Talked of During the Years 1591–1603*. 1938. London: Routledge and Kegan Paul, 1955.

Hartman, Geoffrey H. "Shakespeare's Poetical Character in *Twelfth Night*." *Shakespeare and the Question of Theory*. Ed. Patricia Parker and Geoffrey Hartman. London: Methuen, 1985. 37–54.

Hawkes, Terry. "Comedy, Orality and Duplicity: *Twelfth Night*." Waller 168–74.

Hay, Natasha. "Love's a Beach." Rev. of Auckland Theatre Company *Twelfth Night*, *New Zealand Listener* 29 July (2006), 9 February 2012. <http://www.listener.co.nz.ezproxy.waikato.ac.nz/culture/theatre/loves-a-beach/>.

Henslowe, Philip. *Henslowe's Diary*. Ed. R.A. Foakes. 2nd ed. Cambridge: Cambridge UP, 2002.

Hinman, Charlton. *The Printing and Proof-Reading of the First Folio of Shakespeare*. 2 vols. Oxford: Clarendon, 1963.

Hirsch, Brett. "Rousing the Night Owl: Malvolio, *Twelfth Night*, and Anti-Puritan Satire." *Notes and Queries* 56.1 (2009): 53–55.

Hollander, John. *The Untuning of the Sky: Ideas of Music in English Poetry 1500–1700*. Princeton: Princeton UP, 1961.

Hotson, Leslie. *The First Night of Twelfth Night*. London: Mercury Books, 1961. R. Hart-Davis, 1954.

Houlahan, Mark. "'Like to th'Egyptian thief': Shakespeare Sampling Heliodorus in *Twelfth Night*." *Rapt in Secret Studies: Emerging Shakespeares*. Eds. Darryl Chalk and Laurie Johnson. Cambridge: Cambridge Scholars, 2010. 305–17.

Howard, Jean. "Shakespeare, Geography, and the Work of Genre on the Early Modern Stage." *Modern Language Quarterly* 64.3 (September 2003): 299–322.

———. *The Stage and Social Struggle in Early Modern England*. London: Routledge, 1994.

Howard-Hill, T.H. "Shakespeare's Earliest Editor, Ralph Crane." *Shakespeare Survey* 44 (1992): 113–31.

Jardine, Lisa. "Twins and Travesties: Gender, Dependency and Sexual Availability in *Twelfth Night*." *Erotic Politics: Desire on the Renaissance Stage*. Ed. Susan Zimmerman. New York: Routledge, 1992. 27–39.

Jonson, Ben. *The Complete Poems*. Ed. George Parfitt. Penguin English Poets. Harmondsworth: Penguin, 1980.

Jorgensen, Caitlin L. "'A Madman's Epistles Are No Gospels': Alienation in *Twelfth Night* and Anti-Martinist Discourse." *Renaissance Papers* (1999): 67–78.

Kermode, Frank. *Pieces of My Mind: Essays and Criticism 1958–2002*. New York: Farrar, Strauss and Giroux, 2002.

———. *Shakespeare's Language*. London: Allen Lane, 2000.

Kerwin, William. *Beyond the Body: the Boundaries of Medicine and English Renaissance Drama*. Amherst: U of Massachusetts P, 2005.

Kiernander, Adrian. "'You'll be the man!': Homophobia and the Present in Performances of *Twelfth Night* and *Romeo and Juliet*." *Presentism, Gender and Sexuality in Shakespeare*. Ed. Evelyn Gajowski. New York: Palgrave Macmillan, 2009. 125–43.

Kott, Jan. *Shakespeare Our Contemporary*. Trans. Boleslaw Taborski. 2nd ed. London: Methuen, 1967.

Krieger, Elliot. "*Twelfth Night:*'The morality of indulgence.'" White 37–71.

Lamb, Charles. *Elia and the Last Essays of Elia*. Ed. Jonathan Bate. Oxford World's Classics. Oxford: Oxford UP, 1987.

Leclercle, Anne. "Country House, Catholicity and the Crypt(ic) in *Twelfth Night*." Dutton, Findlay and Wilson 84–101.

Leech, Clifford. *Twelfth Night and Shakespearean Comedy*. Toronto: U of Toronto P, 1965.

Leggatt, Alexander. *Shakespeare's Comedy of Love*. 1973. London: Methuen, 1974.

Levine, Laura. *Men in Women's Clothing: Anti-theatricality and Effeminization 1579–1642*. Cambridge: Cambridge UP, 1994.

Lewalski, Barbara. "Thematic Patterns in *Twelfth Night*." *Shakespeare Studies* 1 (1965): 168–82.

Lindley, David. *Shakespeare and Music*. The Arden Critical Companions. London: Thomson Learning, 2006.

Little, Arthur. "'A Local Habitation and a Name': Presence, Witnessing and Queer Marriage in Shakespeare's Romantic Comedies." *Presentism, Gender and Sexuality in Shakespeare*. Ed. Evelyn Gajowski. New York: Palgrave MacMillan, 2009. 207–36.

Lothian, J.M., and T.W. Craik, eds. *Twelfth Night*. The Arden Shakespeare: Second Series. London: Methuen, 1975.

Loxton, Harry. Rev. of Unicorn Theatre *Twelfth Night* (2009), 20 February 2012. <http://www.britishtheatreguide.info/reviews/12thnightunicorn-rev.htm>.

Luce, Morton, ed. *The Works of Shakespeare: Twelfth Night or What You Will*. Arden Shakespeare. 1906. London: Methuen, 1937.

——, ed. *Rich's 'Apolonius and Silla,' an Original of Shakespeare's 'Twelfth Night.'* The Shakespeare Classics. London: Chatto and Windus, 1912.

Macaulay, Thomas Babington. *Macaulay's History of England from the Accession of James II*. Vol. 1. Everyman's Library. 1907. London: J.M. Dent and Sons, 1957.

McEachern, Claire, ed. *Twelfth Night*. Barnes and Noble Shakespeare. New York: Barnes and Noble, 2007.

Maguire, Laurie, and Thomas Berger, eds. *Textual Formations and Reformations*. Newark: U of Delaware P, 1998.

Mahood, M.M. *Bit Parts in Shakespeare's Plays*. Cambridge: Cambridge UP, 1992.

Mallin, Eric S. *Inscribing the Time: Shakespeare and the End of Elizabethan England*. Los Angeles: U of California P, 1995.

Mann, David. *The Elizabethan Player: Contemporary Stage Representation*. London and New York: Routledge, 1991.

Manningham, John. *The Diary of John Manningham of the Middle Temple, 1602–1603*. Ed. Robert Parker Sorlien. Hanover, NH: UP of New England, 1976.

Massai, Sonia, ed. *William Shakespeare's Twelfth Night: A Sourcebook*. London: Routledge, 2007.

Menon, Madhavi. *Shakesqueer: A Queer Companion to the Complete Works of Shakespeare*. Durham, NC and London: Duke UP, 2011.

Milward, Peter. "The Religious Dimension of Shakespeare's Illyria." Clayton, Brock and Forés 381–87.

Muir, Kenneth. *The Sources of Shakespeare's Plays*. London: Methuen, 1977.

Mulryne, J.R., and Margaret Shewring, eds. *Theatre of the English and Italian Renaissance*. London: Macmillan, 1991.

Munro, Lucy. "Music and Sound." *The Oxford Handbook of Early Modern Theatre*. Ed. Richard Dutton. Oxford: Oxford UP, 2009. 543–60.

Novy, Marianne. *Love's Argument: Gender Relations in Shakespeare*. Chapel Hill and London: U of North Carolina P, 1984.

Odell, George C.D. *Shakespeare from Betterton to Irving*. 2 vols. With a new introduction by Robert Hamilton Ball. New York: Dover, 1966.

O'Harvey, Richard, ed. *History of the Middle Temple*. Oxford and Portland, OR: Hart, 2011.

Orgel, Stephen. *Impersonations: the Performance of Gender in Shakespeare's England*. Cambridge: Cambridge UP, 1996.

Osborne, Laurie E. *The Trick of Singularity: Twelfth Night and the Performance Editions*. Iowa City: U of Iowa P, 1996.

Palfrey, Simon, and Tiffany Stern. *Shakespeare in Parts*. Oxford: Oxford UP, 2007.

Palmer, D.J. "Art and Nature in *Twelfth Night*." *Critical Quarterly* 9.3 (1967): 201–12.

——, ed. *Shakespeare: Twelfth Night: A Selection of Critical Essays*. London: Macmillan, 1972.

Parker, Patricia. "Barbers and Barbary: Early Modern Cultural Semantics." *Renaissance Drama* NS 33 (2004): 201–45.

——. "Was Illyria as Mysterious and Foreign as We Think?." *The Mysterious and the Foreign in Early Modern England*. Ed. Helen Ostovich, Mary V. Silcox, and Graham Roebuck. Newark: U of Delaware P, 2008: 209–34.

Paster, Gail Kern. *Humoring the Body: Emotions and the Shakespearean Stage*. Chicago: U of Chicago P, 2004.

Pentland, Elizabeth. "Some early modern backgrounds to *Twelfth Night*." Schiffer 149–66.

Pequigney, Joseph. "The Two Antonios and Same-Sex Love in *Twelfth Night* and *The Merchant of Venice*." *English Literary Renaissance* 22 (1992): 201–21.

Plautus. *Menaecmi. A pleasant and fine Conceited Comædie, taken out of the most excellent wittie Poet Plautus*. Whitworth 188–221.

Potter, Lois. *Twelfth Night: Text and Performance*. Basingstoke: Macmillan, 1985.

Procházka, Martin. "Introduction." Procházka (2002), 1–5.

——. "Shakespeare's Illyria, Sicily and Bohemia: Other Spaces, Other Times, or Other Economies." Procházka (2002), 130–50.

——, ed. *Shakespeare's Illyrias: Heterotopias, Identities, Counterhistories*. Special issue of *Litteraria Pragensia* 12.23 (2002).

Rich, Barnabe. *Rich's Farewell to Military Profession 1581*. Ed. Thomas Mabry Cranfill. Austin: U of Texas P, 1959.

Rowe, Nicholas. "Preface to Shakespeare" (1709). David Nichol Smith 27–38.

Ryan, Kiernan. *Shakespeare's Comedies*. London: Palgrave Macmillan, 2009.

Salgádo, Gámini, ed. *Eyewitnesses of Shakespeare: First Hand Accounts of Performances 1590–1890*. London: Sussex UP, 1975.

Schafer, Elizabeth. "Unsettling AustrIllyria: *Twelfth Night*, Exotic Englishness and Empire." *Contemporary Theatre Review* 19.3 (2009): 342–53.

————, ed. *Twelfth Night.* Shakespeare in Production. Cambridge: Cambridge UP, 2009.

Schalkwyk, David. *Shakespeare, Love and Service.* Cambridge: Cambridge UP, 2008.

Scheil, Katherine West. *The Taste of the Town: Shakespearian Comedy and the Early Eighteenth-Century Theater.* Lewisburg, PA: Bucknell UP, 2003.

Schiffer, James, ed. *Twelfth Night: New Critical Essays.* Shakespeare Criticism Volume 34. New York: Routledge, 2011.

Shakespeare, William. *Mr William Shakespeares comedies, histories and tragedies: published according to the true originall copies.* London: 1623.

Shapiro, James. *1599: A Year in the Life of Shakespeare.* London: Faber and Faber, 2005.

Shapiro, Michael. *Gender in Play on the Shakespearean Stage: Boy Heroines and Female Pages.* Ann Arbor: U of Michigan P, 1994.

Sherley, Anthony, Sir. *A True Report of Sir Anthony Shierlies Journey overland to Venice, from thence by sea to Antioch, Aleppo, and Babilon, and soe to Casbine in Persia: his entertainment there by the great Sophie....* London: 1600.

Shore, Robert. "Some like it in black and white." Rev. of Cheek by Jowl *Twelfth Night. TLS*, 30 June 2006: 19.

Sidney, Sir Philip. *The Countess of Pembroke's Arcadia.* Ed. Maurice Evans. Harmondsworth: Penguin, 1977.

Simmons, J.L. "A Source for Shakespeare's Malvolio: The Elizabethan Controversy with the Puritans." *Huntington Library Quarterly* 36.3 (1973): 181–201.

Simpson, Percy. "King Charles the First as Dramatic Critic." *Bodleian Quarterly Record* 8.92 (1936–37): 257–62.

Smith, Bruce. *Ancient Scripts and Modern Experience on the English Stage 1500–1700.* Princeton, NJ: Princeton UP, 1983.

Smith, Bruce R. *The Acoustic World of Early Modern England: Attending to the O-Factor.* Chicago: U of Chicago P, 1999.

Smith, David Nichol, ed. *Shakespeare Criticism: A Selection.* 1916. London: Oxford UP, 1949.

Spurgeon, Caroline. *Shakespeare's Imagery and What It Tells Us.* 1935. Cambridge: Cambridge UP, 1966.

Stanivukovic, Goran. "Illyria Revisited: Shakespeare and the Eastern Adriatic." Clayton, Brock and Forés 401–15.

———. "'What country, friends, is this?': The Geographies of Illyria in Early Modern England." Procházka 5–21.

Stevens, John. "Shakespeare and the Music of the Elizabethan Stage." *Shakespeare in Music*. Ed. Phyllis Hartnoll. London: Macmillan, 1966. 3–48.

Stewart, Alan. *Shakespeare's Letters*. Oxford: Oxford UP, 2009.

Stubbes, Phillip. *The Second Part of the Anatomie of Abuses*. 1583. New York and London: Garland, 1973.

Styan, J.L. *Shakespeare Revolution: Criticism and Performance in the Twentieth Century*. Cambridge: Cambridge UP, 1977.

Taylor, Gary, and John Jowett. *Shakespeare Reshaped, 1606–1623*. Oxford: Oxford UP, 1993.

Taylor, Michael. *Shakespeare Criticism in the Twentieth Century*. Oxford Shakespeare Topics. Oxford: Oxford UP, 2001.

Tennenhouse, Leonard. *Power on Display: the Politics of Shakespeare's Genres*. New York: Methuen, 1986.

Theobald, Lewis. *The Works of Shakespeare*. 7 vols. London: Tonson, 1733.

Thomson, Peter. *Shakespeare's Theatre*. Theatre Production Studies 1. London: Routledge and Kegan Paul, 1983.

Tilley, Maurice. *A Dictionary of the Proverbs in England in the Sixteenth and Seventeenth Centuries*. 1950. Ann Arbor: U of Michigan P, 1966.

Traub, Valerie. *Desire and Anxiety: Circulations of Sexuality in Shakespearean Drama*. London and New York: Routledge, 1992.

———. "The (In)significance of 'Lesbian' Desire in Early Modern England." *Erotic Politics: Desire on the Renaissance Stage*. Ed. Susan Zimmerman. New York: Routledge, 1992. 150–70.

Turner, Robert K. "The Text of *Twelfth Night*." *Shakespeare Quarterly* 26.2 (Spring 1975): 128–39.

Underdown, David. *Fire from Heaven: Life in an English Town in the Seventeenth Century*. 1992. London: Fontana, 1993.

Van Es, Bart. "Pedlar of Print." *TLS* 25 January 2013. <http://www.the-tls.co.uk>.

Vickers, Brian, ed. *Shakespeare: The Critical Heritage*. 5 vols. London: Routledge and Kegan Paul, 1974–81.

Vitkus, Daniel. *Turning Turk: English Theatre and the Multicultural Mediterranean*. London: Palgrave Macmillan, 2003.

Waller, Gary, ed. *Shakespeare's Comedies*. Longman Critical Readers. London and New York: Longman, 1991.

Warren, Roger, and Stanley Wells, eds. *Twelfth Night*. The Oxford Shakespeare. Oxford: Clarendon, 1994.

Wells, Stanley. *Royal Shakespeare: Four Major Productions at Stratford-upon-Avon*. Furman Studies. Manchester: Manchester UP, 1976.

————, Gary Taylor with John Jowett and William Montgomery. *William Shakespeare: A Textual Companion*. Oxford: Clarendon P, 1987.

White, R.S, ed. *Twelfth Night: Contemporary Critical Essays*. London: Macmillan, 1996.

Whitworth, Charles, ed. *The Comedy of Errors*. The Oxford Shakespeare. Oxford: Oxford UP, 2002.

Wiles, David. *Shakespeare's Clown: Actor and Text in the Elizabethan Playhouse*. Cambridge: Cambridge UP, 1987.

Woolf, Virginia. *Passionate Apprentice: the Early Journals 1897–1909*. Ed. Mitchell A. Leaska. San Diego: Harcourt, Brace, Jovanovich, 1990.

————. "Twelfth Night at the Old Vic." *Death of the Moth and Other Essays*. 1942. London: Hogarth P, 1981. 34–37.

Wright, Thomas. *The Passions of the Minde in Generall*. London: 1604.

Wrightson, Keith. "'Sorts of People' in Tudor and Stuart England." *The Middling Sort of People: Culture, Society and Politics in England, 1550–1800*. Ed. Jonathan Barry and Christopher Brooke. London: Macmillan, 1994. 28–51.

Yamada, Akihiro. "The Textual Problems of *Twelfth Night* 1623." *Bulletin of the Liberal Arts Department Meisei University* 26 (July 1962): 57–63.

FILMOGRAPHY

Armfield, Neil, dir. *Twelfth Night*. Australian Film Institute, 1986. VCR.

Branagh, Kenneth, dir. *Twelfth Night*. Directed for television by Paul Kaeno. Thames Television, 1988. DVD.

Dexter, John, dir. *Twelfth Night*. Granada, 1969. VCR.

Frid, Yakov, dir. *Dvenadtsataya noch (Twelfth Night)*. Lenfilm, 1955.

Gorrie, John, dir. *Twelfth Night*. BBC, 1980.

McAnuff, Des, dir. *Twelfth Night*. Directed for film by Barry Avrich. Stratford Festival, Ontario. Entertainment One Films Canada, 2012. DVD.

Muat, Maria, dir. *Twelfth Night*. Shakespeare: the Animated Tales. Screenplay by Leon Garfield. Soyuzmultfilm/Christmas Films with S4C Channel 4 Wales, 1992. VCR.

Nunn, Trevor, dir. *Twelfth Night*. Fine Line, 1995. DVD.

Silent Shakespeare. Music by Laura Rossi. London: BFI, 1999. VCR.

Supple, Tim, dir. *Twelfth Night*. Channel Four, 2003. DVD.

Supple, Tim, dir. *Twelfth Night*. Directed for the screen by Ian Russell. Shakespeare's Globe, 2013. DVD.

From the Publisher

A name never says it all, but the word "Broadview" expresses a good deal of the philosophy behind our company. We are open to a broad range of academic approaches and political viewpoints. We pay attention to the broad impact book publishing and book printing has in the wider world; for some years now we have used 100% recycled paper for most titles. Our publishing program is internationally oriented and broad-ranging. Our individual titles often appeal to a broad readership too; many are of interest as much to general readers as to academics and students.

Founded in 1985, Broadview remains a fully independent company owned by its shareholders—not an imprint or subsidiary of a larger multinational.

For the most accurate information on our books (including information on pricing, editions, and formats) please visit our website at www.broadviewpress.com. Our print books and ebooks are also available for sale on our site.

broadview press
www.broadviewpress.com

The interior of this book is printed on 100% recycled paper.